The Public Relations Writer's Handbook

The Public Relations Writer's Handbook

The Digital Age
Second Edition

Merry Aronson

Don Spetner

Carol Ames

JOSSEY-BASS
A Wiley Imprint
www.josseybass.com

Published by Jossey-Bass.
A Wiley Imprint
989 Market Street, San Francisco, CA 94103-1741   www.josseybass.com

Jossey-Bass books and products are available through most bookstores. To contact Jossey-Bass directly call our Customer Care Department within the U.S. at 800-956-7739, outside the U.S. at 317-572-3986, or fax 317-572-4002.

Jossey-Bass also publishes its books in a variety of electronic formats. Some content that appears in print may not be available in electronic books.

Credits are on page 350.

Library of Congress Cataloging-in-Publication Data

Aronson, Merry.
     The public relations writer's handbook : the ditigal age / Merry Aronson, Don Spetner, Carol Ames.—2nd ed.
          p. cm.
     Includes bibliographical references and index.
     ISBN-13: 978-0-7879-8631-5 (cloth)
1. Public relations.   2. Public relations—Authorship.   3. Publicity.
I. Spetner, Don.   II. Ames, Carol.   III. Title.
     HM263.A7864 2007
     659.2—dc22

                                                  2006101785

Printed in the United States of America
FIRST EDITION

HB Printing   10 9 8 7 6 5 4 3 2 1

Contents

This book is dedicated to my mother and father, Jeanne and Zola Aronson, who gave me, among many other gifts, a profound love and respect for the English language; and to David M. Rubin and Richard Petrow, who asked me to teach and thought I had something to say. God bless 'em.

—M.A.

To Laurie, Jamie, and Michael, for being there every day for me; and to Buddy and Lil, for teaching me the value of hard work, honesty, and focus.

—D.S.

To Philippe, my first great reader; and to Charlotte, who inspires me every day to do my best and to have fun.

—C.A.

About the Authors

Merry Aronson, a journalist, publicist, and television promotion executive, is founder of MerryMedia, Inc., an entertainment marketing firm based in Studio City, California. Previously she worked for twelve years at the NBC Television Network, first as an entertainment publicist and later as a director in advertising and promotion. Her public relations background also includes launching the Fox Broadcasting Company and, for Group W Satellite Communications, The Nashville Network, as well as directing publicity for the American Society of Composers, Authors & Publishers. Her feature articles and theater reviews have appeared in national publications, and she also wrote for *Good Morning America*. She has served as an adjunct professor of journalism at New York University, where she received a B.A., and later taught in the UCLA Extension program.

Don Spetner is senior vice president of global marketing for Korn/Ferry International, the world's largest provider of executive search and talent management solutions. Spetner oversees all marketing, public relations, and corporate communications for the firm's seventy-two offices in forty countries. Prior to joining Korn/Ferry, he served as vice president of corporate communications for SunAmerica Inc., where he was responsible for all corporate advertising, communications, and public relations. He also served as vice president of corporate communications for Nissan North America, overseeing all North American communications for the automotive giant. In his twenty-five-year career

xii   ABOUT THE AUTHORS

in public relations, he has also worked in management roles for three of the largest public relations agencies in the world. He has been named an "Industry All Star" by *Inside PR* and writes and lectures frequently on communications. He graduated with honors with a degree in journalism from New York University.

Carol Ames teaches entertainment studies and public relations on the faculty of California State University, Fullerton. She has more than twenty years of experience as an independent public relations professional, an executive producer of movies for television, and a corporate communications executive for Paramount Pictures. With writing credits that encompass journalism and scholarly articles, as well as speeches, multimedia presentations, event time lines, media kits, newsletters, and financial writing, she also holds a Ph.D. from the State University of New York, Buffalo, and an M.A. and B.A. with honors from the University of Illinois, Champaign-Urbana.

Introduction

Since the first edition of this book was published in 1993, the digital revolution has changed the way we live and do business, with computers, e-mail, cell phones, and the World Wide Web now familiar parts of everyday life.

News, information, and promotional material are available everywhere on twenty-four-hour global television news channels, wireless Internet service, and PDAs. Even some elevators and supermarket checkout lines have streaming video of news, weather, and promotions. Just around the corner are additional methods of information delivery most of us have yet to imagine.

What this means to the public relations professional and those aspiring to join the field is that more job opportunities become available every day that require greater vigilance, acumen, and communication skills. Public relations professionals are essential to the process of originating and disseminating information. They must be prepared to respond immediately and react efficiently to demands placed on them by media requests. They must be able to generate campaigns that influence actions ranging from consumer spending to new legislation. And they must keep up with and learn to use new digital tools as they develop and become part of the mainstream.

One factor that has not changed with the advent of the digital age is good writing, which remains at the core of effective public relations.

A successful professional must have the skill to communicate ideas, information, and emotions. Clear, concise, accurate, and credible, a professional must be able to write in many styles, tones, and voices for many different audiences. The public relations writer often functions as a ghostwriter for others, such as a company's chief executive officer and other members of senior management. Trade publications and Internet newsletters may run well-written news releases under their own reporters' bylines, making few, if any, changes.

Working on a tight deadline as a provider of background information, facts, details, and access to interviews or credible news sources, the public relations professional serves as an invaluable link in the chain between the client or company and media coverage.

This new edition of *The Public Relations Writer's Handbook* shows how to keep up with the best practices of the public relations profession and with the speed made possible and required by the digital age. Meeting these new demands requires, as always, respect for truth, accuracy, and adherence to a rigorous ethical code. While always acting as an advocate for the client or company and always having a specific point of view, the true professional does not exaggerate, equivocate, or misrepresent the facts. Ultimately the success of one's ongoing relationships with members of the media is built on consistent credibility and reliability.

To help public relations writers achieve their professional goals, this book offers a simple, step-by-step approach to creating a wide range of writing, from basic news releases, pitch letters, biographies, and media alerts to more complex and sophisticated speeches, media campaign proposals, crisis responses, and in-house publications. Examples from successful public relations campaigns and hypothetical cases illustrate the fundamentals, as well as some possible flourishes.

For students aspiring to enter the field, this is a how-to book, best followed in sequence. For working professionals who do not have a news writing background or those who have discovered a gap in their writing repertoire, this book is a resource to be opened at whatever chapter might apply to the writing assignment at hand.

We do not claim to have all the solutions to the ever-growing demands of public relations writing. Drawing on our many years of combined experience at world-famous companies and public relations agencies, our work with students, and our conversations with fellow writers, however, we are offering you our secrets to cracking the public relations writing barriers and getting your message heard by as wide a public as possible. We were motivated to write this book because we could find no others on the market that approached the same topics as simply and practically as we have here.

Our experience as working professionals and as leaders of seminars on public relations writing has convinced us of one fact: we can all use a manual that reminds us of the essential steps and offers models for completing complex assignments.

For their help in bringing this revised manual to fruition, we particularly acknowledge our editors, Jessie Mandle, Mark Karmendy, and Beverly Miller, along with Beth Evans for her advice on writing for broadcast; William Bartlett for his insights into, and samples of, great speeches; Rick Reed for his counsel on crisis communications; Kathryn Paulsen for her suggestions for Appendix B; and invaluable support from Karen S. Abrams, Virginia Anagnos, Emily Aronson, Ted R. Aronson, Marty Callner, Stephanie Cohen, September Forsyth, Tom Goodman, Jon Gordon, Maggie Habib, Jeff Herman, Sheena Manek, Bob Meyer, Andrea Nelson, Larry Payne, Charlotte Perebinossoff, Philippe Perebinossoff, Stacy Roth, Heather Rush, and Barbara Tranchito.

This book will not tell you everything you will ever need to know about public relations in the digital age. It is narrowly focused on writing. We disagree with those who feel that writing is strictly an inborn talent that cannot be taught. Good writing is born of many factors, such as clear thinking, avid reading, and—most elusive of all—original, imaginative ideas. It also draws on many basic skills that can be practiced and honed. The writing process can be simplified and demystified, so that skills can be improved and talent developed. Although no book alone can impart all of these qualities to its readers, this one provides each reader and writer with a strong foundation for successful public relations writing.

The Public Relations Writer's Handbook

1

PUBLIC RELATIONS GOES DIGITAL

The digital age has profoundly changed the demands placed on public relations professionals and the ways they do their work. In fact, it is not an exaggeration to say that the digital age has profoundly altered the nature of the public relations profession itself.

With the media now fragmented into thousands of communication channels, high-level public relations advice and planning are more critical than ever before, as companies, product marketers, and organizations all compete to develop, enhance, and project positive public images.

Effective public relations writing forms the core of nimble, innovative marketing made possible by digital technology. Today, businesses and nonprofit organizations use digital communications, as well as traditional PR tools, to reach target audiences, communicate with customers, and expand audiences. E-mail, Web sites, digital newsletters, blogs, viral marketing, search engines, live conference calls, RSS, and podcasting are just some of the tools now available to PR professionals. And almost every communications effort requires writing.

This book provides a road map for writing effective public relations copy for both traditional and innovative public relations initiatives. Each chapter offers clear, step-by-step advice and positive models to use when creating effective copy suitable to specific situations and needs.

Mass communications—broadcast and basic cable television, radio, newspapers, and major magazines—still reach vast audiences, but not as vast as in the recent past and not as reliably. The media that can cover your company's story now include hundreds of niche cable channels, high-definition split-offs of radio stations, thousands of online publications, and millions of blogs. Neither a few well-placed advertisements nor even a comprehensive, multimillion-dollar advertising campaign in broadcast and print can dependably reach the majority of consumers these days. Finding conventional advertising less effective, companies increasingly are turning to public relations for new ideas. In fact, "public relations spending is growing at almost double the rate of advertising," this according to Veronis Suhler Stevenson in New York, a private equity firm that targets media industries (van der Pool, 2006).

Companies are experimenting and diversifying their approaches to reach niche audiences, and they are using public relations to achieve their communications goals. Computers, the Internet, e-mail, broadband, and wireless all increase the ease and decrease the cost of researching, writing, publishing, printing, and, especially, distributing written materials, as well as producing graphics, short videos, audio downloads from the Internet, and multimedia presentations.

Public relations professionals have found themselves on a sharp learning curve as they discover more uses for digital tools. The first challenge of the digital age was learning to save money and eliminate time-intensive, repetitive tasks such as stuffing envelopes with press releases or faxing them to a hundred media outlets one by one by one.

The next challenge of the digital PR revolution is discovering how to go beyond saving time and money to create new methods of communicating effectively with customers, employees, investors, media, and the general public. Creativity and public relations training, combined with people skills and computer savvy, have enabled new ways of communicating a company's image, or a product's benefits, or an organization's community goals. The demands of this stage are to harness the potential of e-mail, interactive communications, handheld devices, the convergence of computers with telephones, television, and digital music players to communicate "personally" with hundreds, thousands, or potentially millions at a time. You may be writing for a company Web site, a blog, a social Web site, a live chat, or the PR war room of a large company facing a public relations crisis. In every case, clear, persuasive written communication, the stock in trade of the public relations writer, is the core skill that can be leveraged by each new technology and technique.

Whether you are writing for newspapers, broadcast outlets, books, or public relations purposes, the basics of good expository writing remain the same and never go out of date:

- Clarity
- Accuracy
- Vividness
- Aptness of details, examples, and quotations
- Correct grammar
- A clear, varied style

The digital age, however, has put new pressure on the media, and therefore on public relations, for speedy responses and on companies for accessibility and forthrightness.

Today, news stories can be posted on the Internet around the clock. The mass media used to have specific deadlines: once a month (monthly magazines), once a week (weekly magazines), once a day (daily newspapers and network evening news), twice a day (local television news), or more frequently for radio and wire services such as the Associated Press that fed updates throughout the day. Having a deadline meant that media outlets and their sources knew the time by which details needed confirmation, so that the story was as complete as possible when printed or aired. Public relations writers and other PR professionals were well aware of the deadlines for the media outlets they covered. They knew how much time they had to write a thoughtful response approved by upper management or to find a ten-minute gap in a top executive's schedule for an interview to present the company's point of view or set the record straight.

Now, many editors are pressuring journalists not just to complete the story for the next deadline, but also to post it immediately on the media company's Web site to beat the competition. More media Web sites now opt for a scoop on a partial story, with updates—and corrections—as new details are gathered, rather than waiting to file a complete, correct story after an in-depth investigation.

Traditionally, there has been a give-and-take between journalists and the public relations or information officers they deal with. PR people interact with journalists as sources, sounding boards, and restraints on the impulse to go to press too soon with too few facts. Many journalists have been saved from the embarrassing need to print a correction when they listened to a trusted PR source who said, "I don't think you have the full story. What's your deadline? I want to e-mail our new product fact sheet, and I think you should talk to one of our executives before you go to press with that rumor." That was then.

Now, companies are given less time to discuss a journalist's question, confirm the relevant facts, decide on a response, and prepare an official, company-approved statement or set up an executive interview. Journalists dial the organization, while simultaneously writing and posting, "The company had no immediate response to our inquiry."

In addition, thousands of rants and rumors are being written and posted on the World Wide Web by anonymous bloggers who have no particular interest in earning a reputation for accuracy or fairness. Not contacted by the blogger, the company learns about a rumor only as it gains traction and readers, and rises to become a page-one result on the major search engines. Some of the ways that companies and public relations professionals can deal with digital communications crises are covered in Chapters Twelve and Thirteen.

Both public relations and traditional journalism are challenged by the digital age. In addition to new deadline pressures, the way stories are structured is changing. To tantalize and tease readers, headlines used to employ sophisticated rhetorical techniques such as puns, word play, alliteration, and literary allusion. Now headlines must meet the demands for literal meaning of digital search engines, which are computer programs that crawl the Web aggregating keywords. Headlines for both Web stories and print stories that are simultaneously posted on the Web are now more literal and direct or have two headlines: a clever headline on the first page to attract a human reader and a literal, descriptive headline on the second page to attract Web crawlers (Lohr, 2006).

People responsible for Web pages that sell advertising, products, or subscriptions are all concerned about "keyword optimization, search engine optimization, search engine marketing, or page one results." All of these terms equate to finding a way for your company's Web site URL to appear on the first page of search results for popular search terms, either by your company's buying a pay-per-click ad or by appearing among the first five to ten listings after becoming one of the most popular choices of recent searchers.

Internet search engines such as Google find and post stories worldwide. The global exposure that stories, press releases, and Web sites can receive through search engines can result in new readers for publications and bloggers and new customers for products and companies.

In addition to competing with other media companies' Web sites, professional journalists now battle for scoops and readers with uncounted numbers of "citizen journalists" and bloggers who are posting stories, rumors, reviews, and their sometimes fevered speculations about what "shoulda, woulda, coulda, mighta" happened. Therefore, public relations professionals need to monitor what is said in the blogosphere and make quick decisions about which misstatements or allegations or rumors require a correction or response to head off a viral rumor that can permanently dam-age the reputation of a brand, a client including a celebrity, or an entire hundred-year-old company.

The 24/7 deadlines, intense competition, and trigger-finger readiness to post an unconfirmed story—a rumor—all put pres-sure on public relations writing, companies, and the client approval process.

Both the media and the public have heightened expecta-tions for accessibility and speedy response. Management and the media expect the public relations representative or official com-pany spokesperson or public relations writer to be reachable at any time by PDA, cell phone, e-mail, or even instant messaging. At the same time, hastily written press announcements, offi-cial statements, Web publications, and video remain retrievable indefinitely by using search engines and electronic archives.

Media fragmentation means, for example, that there are hun-dreds of niche cable channels instead of three or four main broadcast networks; thousands of online forums and blogs in the computer industry versus three or four main trade publications; and millions of Web sites and blogs versus a few thousand local newspapers and local television stations. This fragmentation has decreased companies' reliance on advertising and increased the importance of public relations. A 2005 industry study concluded, "The value of PR as a resource to corporations, government and institutions has increased, based on the need to address compli-cated issues and fragmented targets." At the same time public relations initiatives need to be more nimble and creative because "a decade ago, only one or two different media channels would be used to reach targeted groups. In general, the message would be a full-blown, well-thought out, well-researched explanation." But now "there is a complex, chaotic environment of half-truths, whole truths... the wild, wild West," according to the Public Relations Global Network, an organization of independent PR agencies (Public Relations Global Network, 2005). In the old Wild West, the motto was, "Shoot first and ask questions later."

The new Wild West known as the blogosphere seems to go by the motto, "Post first. Correct later... if ever... whatever." It takes vigilant and nimble public relations and crystal-clear writing to keep ahead of today's fragmented media and an unruly blogosphere that confuses self-righteous opinions with facts.

A Few Words About the Truth

Tell the truth or say nothing. Practice gracefully saying, "We have no comment at this time."

Never lie to the media. Even something regarded as "a little white lie" can damage your reputation with journalists and make you an ineffective spokesperson or writer for your company. For example, don't say, "She's not giving interviews," if the reporter is going to find an interview in his main competitor's paper.

Reasonable people can arrive at different interpretations of the same facts or circumstances. The image of public relations as a profession suffers today, however, because of the minority who have lied to the media or distorted the truth. The consequences of past lies include the disparaging terms and names by which some PR people have come to be known: spin doctors, flacks, hacks, mouthpieces. When you are tempted to lie, remember that in the governmental arena, the profession is called public information officer—not public misinformation officer! Also keep in mind that stockholders of public companies can sue, and the Securities and Exchange Commission can investigate and fine a company if public statements differ from what was known internally at the time.

As a professional, part of your job is to research the facts, know the truth, and advocate within your organization or with your client for being forthright and truthful to the fullest extent possible. If your supervisor or client ever suggests that you lie to a journalist or assumes that certain inconvenient facts will remain hidden while an investigative journalist writes a major magazine article, be prepared to articulate why a lie or attempted cover-up is not productive and probably dangerous and destructive.

A lie compromises your own personal relationships of trust with individual journalists, which damages your future ability to do your job effectively. Journalists talk to one another about the PR people they work with and who is, or is not, reliable and helpful.

A lie also destroys the company or client's relationship with the media in general, as the stories of lies and cover-ups and questions spread. Public relations writers must advocate openness even in crisis situations (see Chapter Thirteen).

A Few Words About Grammar

Write in correct English, even in e-mail and other informal communications because people, especially trained journalists, recognize bad grammar and make negative judgments about people who are too careless, lazy, or uneducated to write correctly. Consider this e-mail (shown exactly as sent) from a college student to his professor: "where at on the page is the information about the show were suspos to write." This student neglected a "Dear Professor" opening and used no capitalization, no punctuation, and no proofreading or use of the computer's grammar and spell-check function. What would you think on receiving this e-mail? Could you stop yourself from having a negative prejudgment or prejudice as you prepared to read this student's paper? As a public relations writer, do you want your e-mailed pitch to a journalist to be the morning's big laugh in the newsroom?

Take time to figure out why your grammar and spell-check programs are underlining possible errors, and make corrections and changes. Proofread. When possible, ask a colleague to check your copy. Then take time to read your e-mail aloud to yourself to catch additional errors and awkwardness. When in doubt, check, double-check, and use references such as a dictionary, thesaurus, or Appendix B in this book. Remember that the quality of your writing represents both you and your organization.

E-Mail Is Not Private; E-Mail Is Forever

You cannot fully delete, recall, erase, or conceal e-mail. E-mail you send or read from a company computer is no more private than a notice you publish in the company newsletter. So despite the lure and the illusion that an e-mail communication is between you and the recipient, don't be tempted to write and e-mail anything you don't want the world (your boss and the media) to learn about.

In addition, companies must retain business records for specified lengths of time, and a wide range of e-mail communications and instant messages sent on the company computer network are business records. Be sure to read and understand your organization's policies about e-mail and other digital communications.

A Few Words About Style

Some people have more facility with language than others. Almost everyone, however, can learn to write in a clear, straightforward, readable style through practice, being open to editing and suggestions from others, and rewriting. These are the keys to improving, no matter how easy or difficult writing initially is for you.

As you work toward clarity and aptness of phrasing, remember a few basics:

- Whenever possible use action verbs (*go, work, decide*).
- Avoid overreliance on "being" verbs (*is, are, was, seemed*).
- Use the active voice of verbs ("She decided the outcome").
- Avoid the passive voice of verbs ("It was decided" or "It was decided by her," which is wordy but at least has the virtue of saying who is responsible).
- Vary the length and structure of sentences. Instead of "Dick ran. Jane ran. Sally ran too," try, "As Dick and Jane ran, Sally toddled after them."

- Since most people have heard English spoken much more than they have read it or written it, most people can benefit by reading their own prose aloud and letting their ear for the language pick out awkward sentences and imprecise or wordy phrasing.
- Have someone else read your writing aloud to you. If the reader stumbles, revise the sentence.

Any good writing is probably 20 percent writing and 80 percent rewriting. In public relations, expect 90 percent rewriting because a number of people will make suggestions and changes during the approval process.

You have to be willing to work toward clarity. Even with the pressure of instant deadlines, you must insist on making and then taking the time to create readable prose that achieves your communications goals. Then proofread, proofread, proofread! Once your writing is sent digitally into cyberspace, an error is forever.

When you become adept at writing newsworthy press releases, informative biographies, fact sheets, media kits, and stories that are specific to a newsletter's target audience, you will find plenty of new challenges ahead: speeches, multimedia presentations, broadcast scripts, event presentations and time lines, as well as Internet communications, editorials, opinion pieces, crisis communications, and official statements. This book provides useful models as you confront each new challenge, including how to write a complete public relations program or proposal and budget.

Whatever digital distribution channel you may be using—perhaps one not even invented at the time this book is published—remember your main responsibilities as a public relations writer:

- Clearly understand your product, client, company, or message.
- Know your target audiences.
- Write clear, engaging prose that effectively communicates your message to your audience.

Chapter Recap

- Use the examples in this handbook as models for each type of public relations writing assignment you encounter.
- Work toward clarity, accuracy, vividness, and aptness of details, examples, and quotations.
- Tell the truth, or issue a graceful, "No comment."
- Use correct grammar.
- Remember that company e-mail is not private.
- Develop a clear, direct style that uses active verbs and varied sentence structures.
- Be ready and willing to accept editorial suggestions and changes during the approval process.
- Rewrite.
- Proofread more than once.
- Remember that in the digital age, an error is forever.

2

NEWS RELEASES, PHOTO CAPTIONS, AND MEDIA KITS

Making Your Story Newsworthy

Many published news and feature stories originate from news releases, the most common form of public relations writing. Also called press releases, news releases announce a client's news or publicize its products or services.

Almost 60 percent of the editorial content of the *New York Times* and the *Washington Post* are generated by public relations efforts, according to a classic study (Sigal, 1973). A more recent study of six major newspapers, including those two prestigious ones, showed that on the environmental beat, an average of 39 percent of sources were from business, which means they were most likely mediated by public relations sources. Within that figure, 48 percent of sources used by science writers and 70 percent of sources used by business writers on the topic of the environment were from business—again, public relations sources (Lacy and Coulson, 2000).

News releases, press conferences, official proceedings, and other nonspontaneous events continue to make major contributions to news coverage in newspapers large and small, with the percentage of nonspontaneous material in smaller newspapers being even higher than in larger ones (Song, 2002). In other words, many journalists are receptive when a story comes to them from business—especially if it is well written and particularly if the reporter or editor has a prior relationship of trust with the public relations practitioner (Curtain, 1997).

The media are inundated by dozens of news releases every day. If your release is to be read and considered for coverage, it must offer a newsworthy story, stated clearly and simply, long on information and short on adjectives. A news release typically introduces a new product, service, or idea; reports new findings from a survey; alerts the media to an upcoming event; announces a staff change; or simply presents new information. Sometimes a release is the basis of an entire story. More often, an idea in it suggests a related story or affects a story an editor or reporter already has in progress.

Inverted-Pyramid News Style

To write a good news release, first you must understand what it is about your subject that is important. Then you must know how to summarize that information at the beginning of the release, quickly back up the lead statement with facts, and save the less important details for last. This is known as the inverted-pyramid style of news writing.

The lead of a news release is all-important and should read like the lead of a news story. All of the essential information summarizing the whole story—and answering journalism's five W's (who, what, when, where, and why)—should be contained in the first paragraph of news-style releases. With the most comprehensive information put in the lead, the reader gets the point of the story even if he or she reads only the first sentence or paragraph. A press release must be a complete story, because some publications, especially trade papers, run a release verbatim. Publications for larger audiences generally have larger staffs and allow their reporters more time for further reporting and rewriting.

Trade Versus Consumer Press

Print journalism comprises two categories: trade and consumer. A trade publication is intended for a specific profession or industry. For example, *Modern Baking* is a trade publication for the food business, *Firehouse Magazine* is a trade publication for firefighters, *Variety* is a trade newspaper for the entertainment industry, and *Women's Wear Daily* is a trade publication for the fashion field.

Consumer press is designed for general readers. Like *Women's Wear Daily*, *Vogue* magazine is devoted primarily to fashion, but it is a consumer magazine. Its market is readers with a general interest in fashion, not fashion professionals. *Newsweek*, *Time*, and *People* are also consumer publications. Local newspapers such as the *St. Louis Post-Dispatch*, the *Chicago Tribune*, and the *Fort Worth-Star Telegram* are all consumer publications.

Most TV and radio programs, including news, magazine, talk, and information shows, are for consumer audiences—people of varied ages and backgrounds, with different hobbies and jobs. Cable television, however, has introduced niche channels targeting specific demographics or audiences with special interests. MTV, for example, is targeted to younger music lovers, while Home & Garden TV and the Food Network appeal to more mature audiences. Corporations may want their business stories to appear on CNBC or Bloomberg, the cable channels that target investors. Daily talk shows such as *The Oprah Winfrey Show* reach a mass audience of consumers, mostly women.

Regardless of the client you represent and the industry you work in, you yourself are also a consumer, a representative of the lay audience. When judging a story for its value to the trade and consumer press, use yourself as a yardstick to measure consumer interest in the story. As a nonindustry member, do you care about it? Does it affect your life or that of your neighbors and friends outside your business? Does the information stand out from the ordinary to you? When you can answer yes to these questions, you may have a release for the consumer press.

Adjusting Your Style: Consumer Versus Trade

A news release to consumer media should be clear enough that a general reader can easily understand it. A trade release can use technical terms that are in common use in a particular profession or trade but that a general audience might not be familiar with.

In public relations, you must constantly analyze your own stories and decide if they are appropriate for the trade press, the consumer press, or both. Rarely, if ever, will you have a story only for the consumer press, but you may often have releases that will interest only the trades.

Before You Write

Ask yourself the following questions before you prepare a release:

- Is this story truly newsworthy, and will it interest the intended audience? Much has been written on the subject of what is news and what should be covered. Some say news is anything people didn't know about yesterday or anything that affects their lives. The late newspaper columnist Walter Winchell used to say that news is anything that protrudes from the ordinary. The debate about judging news value is sure to continue as long as news is reported, but you can begin to measure the news value of your story by asking if it offers any significant information that was not available before and whether anybody will care about this information.

- Does this story answer all the questions it is likely to raise?

- Will this story, if covered, advance my client's objectives?

- Are all the facts and figures in the story accurate? Has every name, date, and piece of information been double-checked with a reliable source?

When the answer is yes to every question on this list, you are ready to write the first draft of a press release. When an answer is no, it is probably not appropriate for you to issue a release yet. There may be times when you will advise your client against putting out a release until the story warrants one. Every time you send a nonstory to a media outlet, you weaken your credibility as a public relations representative, and you also waste your client's time and money.

Research

The first step in preparing a news release, as with all other effective public relations writing, is to research the story. Learn as much as you can about the subject of the release. For example, review any existing client material such as press kits or news releases that could illuminate your topic. If you're writing about a product, study its development, and use the product yourself. If you're writing about a television program, watch it, and learn about its background and production. If you're writing about a survey or a book, read it carefully, and perhaps talk to the surveyor or author. If you're announcing an event, familiarize yourself with all available details—even those you will not include in the release. Some of this research is done by talking to the people involved, informally interviewing them to gather background information, gain insight, and focus perspective. You should also determine who in the company will be your main source of information and who will be quoted. You will probably be getting your information from the quotable source or from a direct report of the quotable source, for example, from a division president if the quotation will be attributed to the chief executive officer. The direct report will make suggestions for what your draft quotation should say. Before release, of course, the quotation must be approved by the person to whom it is attributed.

Your research for writing a news release should also include checking the files to see how similar releases were covered by the media and where they were distributed. This research will alert you to particular journalists or publications that may have ongoing coverage of an issue. It will also keep you from annoying journalists by sending them a story that has already been covered and is therefore not news, unless your release offers substantial new information.

As a public relations writer, you are likely to be privy to all or most of the information and background on the subject you are representing, but some of that information may not be for immediate or even eventual disclosure. You are ethically bound to keep your client's or company's information confidential and not to use it for your own or others' financial gain. For example, trading a stock on the basis of confidential knowledge ahead of a news release is insider trading, a criminal offense. If you are ever uncertain, make sure to ask what information is for release and what is not. If you own stock in a company affected by your confidential knowledge, you may trade your stock only after that information is released to the general public. (See Chapter Nine.)

Conforming to a Standard Style

Unless you are writing a company's first news release ever, you should study the files of similar types of announcements to learn the way the company typically handles such stories. Some larger companies have their own style guides for handling such things as whether titles are capitalized after a person's name. The standard guide for journalists is *The Associated Press Stylebook and Briefing on Media Law* (2004), which is updated frequently to keep pace with changes in language and usage. It is also available as a yearly online subscription that allows personal notations of special terms and usage (http://www.apstylebook.com).

Content

Outline the release before you write it to ensure a clear and logical flow of information, and try to limit the length to one or two pages. Also, be sure to define technical terms used and to attribute announcements to officials. If the story lends itself to humorous interpretation, let the reporter be the one to have fun with it. You should present the story in a straightforward manner.

News releases can be divided into two categories: hard news and soft (or feature) stories. Thousands of subjects are covered in press releases, from free lunches offered at the local YMCA to multibillion-dollar corporate takeovers. Typical hard news releases cover such areas as personnel appointments; new products, companies, and services; events; and survey results. Feature story releases typically cover such areas as trends, human interest items, and ongoing projects.

Let's take a look at some common types of releases and review how they are structured and written.

The Appointment Release

Companies hire, fire, and promote people all the time. News releases on personnel changes are thus frequently required, and they are structured in this way:

1. State the appointee's name and title, and attribute the announcement to an official from the company. Also state the name of the person to whom the appointee will report and when the appointment becomes effective. (If this last fact is not included, it is implied that the appointment is effective immediately.)

2. State the name of the person being replaced (optional; it may be a touchy subject), or, if the position is new, say that the subject of the release "has been appointed to the newly created position of..."

3. State the scope of the appointee's responsibilities in relation to the company or client, and describe the nature of the business. Sometimes a quotation from the appointee's boss is used in this second paragraph; rarely, however, is the quotation used by the press unless it contains newsworthy information about the company's new initiatives and not just boilerplate praise about what a wonderful person the appointee is.

4. State the appointee's professional and educational history, covering the most recent position and accomplishments first and working backward in time. This conforms to the inverted pyramid news style of summarizing the most important information at the top and supporting the lead with, first, the most relevant or important details and, then, details of lesser importance. The inverted pyramid allows the story to be cut to any length; if only the first paragraph is used because of space limitations, the whole story is still conveyed. You may also offer a few personal facts, such as his or her place of residence, place of origin, and, sometimes, marital status. Although such details are rarely covered in a news article, they are helpful for individualizing the appointee and establishing common ground between the appointee and someone who later accesses the release from your company Web site.

5. Include your client's approved company description, also known as boilerplate including trademark™, registered®, and copyright © designations, as well as the company's Web site address.

6. End with the name, telephone number, and e-mail address of the designated media spokesperson.

Notice that an appointment release first focuses on the responsibilities of the appointee and the business the appointee works for. Only after these facts have been established is the appointee's background brought in. Here is an appointment release written in paragraph form. This press release received coverage ranging from short items in major business publications to articles in marketing trade papers to reproduction in full on the oddly spelled Web site www.strategiy.com that bills itself as the "Middle East's Largest Portal for Marketing and Advertising and Media Professionals."

FAIRFIELD, Conn.—(BUSINESS WIRE)—Jan. 24, 2006—GE announced today the appointment of Dan

Henson to Chief Marketing Officer, effective immediately. He succeeds Beth Comstock, who was promoted to President of NBC Universal Digital Media and Marketing Development. Henson will report directly to GE Chairman & CEO Jeff Immelt.

Henson, 44, will focus on customer satisfaction and enhancing the capabilities of GE's 45,000+ sales and marketing professionals. He will be responsible for driving sales and marketing excellence, sales force effectiveness, enterprise accounts, strategic marketing, advertising, branding and communications.

"Dan is an outstanding GE leader committed to helping our customers grow their businesses by tapping the breadth of GE's products, services and expertise," Immelt said. "His broad skills in sales, marketing, quality and operations combined with his global experience will be great assets to our commercial and communication team as well as our customers around the world."

Henson's responsibilities will also include cross-business marketing and sales initiatives including:

- Imagination Breakthroughs—GE's marketing-led innovation pipeline with 90+ projects designed to generate $50–$100 MM of new revenue within three years,
- Ecomagination—GE's cross-business commitment to aggressively bring to market new technologies that will help customers meet pressing environmental challenges, and
- Experienced Commercial Leadership Program—A two-year global training program designed to develop the next generation of GE's sales and marketing leaders. Participants complete four six-month assignments at a GE business and upon graduation, are considered for key commercial leadership roles.

An 18-year GE veteran, Henson most recently served as Chief Commercial Officer for GE Commercial Finance where he led the global expansion of the business' enterprise selling efforts that simplified, from a customer perspective, GE's go-to-market process by providing a single point of contact. Previously, as president and CEO of Vendor Financial Services from 2002 to 2005, he led a $675 million business with more than 9,000 employees. In that period, the business transformed from a successful financer of small and medium equipment to the world's leading supply chain finance company.

Henson has extensive experience outside the U.S. He led teams in London for European Equipment Finance and in Mexico City for Commercial Equipment Finance, and has spent considerable time in Japan, Australia and New Zealand. He also served as the quality leader for GE Capital where he used six sigma methodologies to improve processes for the business and its customers. Henson joined GE in 1987 and was named a Company officer in 1999.

Henson earned a bachelor's degree in marketing from George Washington University in Washington, D.C. He lives in Connecticut with his wife and two children.

GE (NYSE: GE) is Imagination at Work—a diversified technology, media and financial services company focused on solving some of the world's toughest problems. With products and services ranging from aircraft engines, power generation, water processing and security technology to medical imaging, business and consumer financing, media content and advanced materials, GE serves customers in more than 100 countries and employs more than 300,000 people worldwide. For more information, visit the company's Web site at www.ge.com.

Contacts
General Electric CompanyMedia: Jonathan Klein
+1-203-373-2241
jonathan.klein@ge.com

GE also posted the release on its Web site accessible by clicking a tab on its home page labeled "For Journalists" and as part of its "Press Release Archive" that posts all releases in reverse chronological order. This serves as another reminder that in the digital age, public relations writing becomes a readily accessible part of a company's public image and public record and lives on indefinitely.

Before release and posting, be sure each press announcement is carefully researched, accurately written in clear journalistic style, grammatically correct, and approved by the company or client's chain of command.

The Product Release

Communique PR, representing software developer Melodeo, Inc., announced the debut of a new software product that made mobile Podcasting possible for the first time and used this lead, made jointly with its service partner:

SEATTLE—(BUSINESS WIRE)—Feb. 1, 2006—Rogers Wireless, Canada's leading wireless communications service provider, and Melodeo, Inc., a developer of software and services that bring digital media content to mobile phones, have announced the launch of Rogers Podcast Service, North America's first mobile Podcast service.

Rogers Wireless customers now have exclusive access to more than 1,500 Podcasts, covering a range of topics including News and Sports, Comedy and Music. The catalogue of Podcasts is updated throughout the day as new feeds are received, bringing fresh content to subscribers continually. Rogers Podcast Service can be accessed on subscribers' cell phones through the Rogers Wireless navigate mobile portal, within the GET INFO category.

Melodeo's software was a trade news story until it became available to consumers with the agreement with Rogers Wireless. At this point, the Canadian consumer media became interested in the story.

The expansion of product lines is also usually trade news. Here's the lead paragraph from a representative press release prepared by Apple:

> CUPERTINO, California—March 30, 2006—Apple® is now shipping the first Universal version of its Final Cut® Studio video production suite that delivers up to 2.5x the performance when running on a MacBook™ Pro* notebook computer. Final Cut Studio features state-of-the-art tools that complement Final Cut Pro 5 including Soundtrack® Pro, a revolutionary audio editing and sound design application that makes video projects sound as good as they look; Motion 2, the world's first real-time motion graphics application with GPU accelerated 32-bit float rendering; and DVD Studio Pro 4 for professional DVD authoring.

Although this product announcement is of interest primarily to the trade press covering video editing and postproduction, announcements of the numerous extensions of Apple's widely popular iPod digital music player product line frequently are covered in a range of consumer publications with accompanying photographs of the latest version's sleek design.

After their lead paragraphs, product releases elaborate on the attributes of the products and give the reasons for their development.

Lifestyle, Trend, and Survey Releases

A new consumer trend or lifestyle adaptation of a company's product can make an enticing feature-style press release, such as the following one, which is cleverly timed with a holiday hook for the week of Valentine's Day:

> MILPITAS, Calif., Feb. 11/PRNewswire/—Some social commentators say technology isolates people, but the lives of palmOne™ device users tell a different story. Handhelds can rev up romance and bring couples together, according to a survey that ran on PalmInfocenter (www.palminfocenter.com), an independent Palm OS® community. In the survey, which generated more than 1,000 responses in four days, 73 percent of the participants said that they meet people or strike up conversations as a result of their handheld or smartphone, and a weighty 67 percent claimed that their handheld or smartphone plays a role in their love life.
>
> The palmOne Romance Survey tells a story not yet captured by trend watchers and academic studies—savvy couples and singles on the dating scene use technology to organize dates and romantic time together, express feelings and simply communicate better.

Even minor holidays generate additional advertising in newspapers and magazines of all sizes, especially in the consumer press. Since editors and journalists must fill the larger news hole with lively stories that are different from those printed during the previous year's holiday season, a well-written, provocative press release with a holiday news hook can generate stories, especially if the release points to a new trend.

Note in the example the uses Palm made of a simple, fun survey posted for four days on its Web site. First, reading the survey keeps visitors on the site longer, possibly prompting them to look more carefully at featured products and offers. Next, the survey questions make the customer think about how useful the company's product is in daily life. Third, the customer interacts with the company by answering the survey, in effect declaring "love" for the product's use in his or her love life. The answers generate information for the Palm "lifestyle" feature press release and possible feature stories in the press during the Valentine's Day holiday season. Finally, respondents and even visitors who did not answer the survey questions may return to the Palm Web site to view the survey results. The best-case scenario for Palm is that people who were only shopping might be convinced to buy from Palm based on its newly discovered "lifestyle" usefulness. These sorts of leveraging and repurposing of written materials make public relations writing even more important and useful in the digital age.

Localizing a National Release

A national organization or a nationwide company with numerous locations can use digital distribution to make announcements that are relevant to media across the country. The following example is a feature release that can be localized for each media market; it is also an example of a delayed lead:

Contact: K. C. Kavanagh
(914)640–8339
[e-mail address here]

STARWOOD HOTELS GOES TO THE DOGS

Sheraton, Westin and W to Allow Dogs Brand Wide
Hotels Pamper Pooches with New Dog Beds
and Amenities

August 11, 2003—White Plains, NY—Sleeping dogs finally have a place to lie. In a hotel industry-first, Starwood Hotels & Resorts Worldwide, Inc. (NYSE:HOT) announced today that its Sheraton, Westin and W hotels will welcome dogs brand wide in the U.S. and Canada. Not only is there finally room at the inn for man's best friends, but each of the hotel brands will also pamper pooches with luxurious dog beds and amenities like plush robes, doggie toys and canine massages.

Every Dog Has Its Duvet

Starwood spent millions of dollars to make its hotel beds the best in the business from W's signature pillow top beds to the famous ten-layer Westin Heavenly Beds® and the brand new Sheraton Sweet Sleeper Beds. As part of its new *Starwood LTD (Love that Dog)* program, the company is introducing new luscious, comfy beds for its four-legged guests. Starwood's new dog beds are custom-designed oversized pet pillows by Eloise Pet Accessories, a doggie line described as "where style and fashion meet man's best friend." Eloise's pet accessories are favorites of celebrities including Daryl Hannah, Dyan Cannon and Debra Messing. Each brand worked with Eloise to design dog beds that mirror their hotels' human beds and guest room design. Westin's dog bed features a miniature Heavenly Bed duvet while W's take on the dog bed is a stylish and colorful checkerboard pattern and Sheraton's version is a classic, all-American red and blue design.

Besides the beds, each brand will also offer food and water bowls and temporary I.D. tags with hotel contact information. In addition, a traveling tip card will be provided to all guests traveling with their dogs upon check-in, thanks to a partnership with The American Society for the Prevention of Cruelty to Animals (ASPCA)®. Other amenities include plush doggie robes, leashes and collars at some Westin hotels and a pet check-in package at W hotels that includes a pet toy, dog treat and bone plus a special turn down treat on the dog bed. And some hotels are really going the extra mile to spoil dogs rotten. The five W hotels in New York City will take pet pampering to a whole new level by offering in-room doggie massages by a licensed dog massage therapist (especially beneficial for dogs who have traveled by planes in small crates).

Who Let the Dogs Inn?

So why is Starwood catering to canines? With 62 million dog owners in the U.S. and 29 million who hit the road with their dogs in tow according to the Travel Industry Association of America, dog owners are a market niche that's been underserved by the travel industry. Most upscale and luxury hotel chains have varied pet policies meaning some hotels welcome dogs while others do not. Starwood is changing that.

"We intend to become the most dog-friendly hotel company in the land, and not just allow dogs to stay, but actually pamper and spoil them," said Barry S. Sternlicht, Starwood's Chairman and CEO, and proud papa of Comet, a Jack Russell Terrier and Potter, a Black Labrador. "We believe that like dogs, dog owners tend to be very loyal, and will reward a company that loves dogs, too."...

The Starwood release can be localized to individual markets in the e-mail pitch to which it is attached; in the headline; in the first paragraph; and/or in the contact information.

The Delayed or Feature-Style Lead

Just as in feature news stories, press releases intended as soft news, or features often make use of the delayed lead, such as in the above release, which does not give the answer to "why" until the fourth paragraph.

With a delayed lead, the specific subject of the story doesn't come into clear focus until at least the second paragraph into the piece, after the lead sets the background and tone. Here's an excerpt showing a delayed lead in a release about a new product, a no-batteries-necessary emergency kit called Ready Freddy:

CONTACT: Andrea Nelson
Nelson Public Relations
NEWS RELEASE (310)277–3070
FOR IMMEDIATE RELEASE
NelsonPR@SBCglobal.net

Introducing Ready Freddy,
The first NO-BATTERIES-NECESSARY
Emergency Preparedness Kit

Los Angeles, CA (June 2005)—Most people never con-sider preparing for the possibility of a disaster—until it's too late. With this year's hurricanes, floods, power outages, and ice storms the need to be prepared is essential. Even the Department of Homeland Security suggests getting prepared. Whether in the home, car, boat, or RV, every person should get prepared and be ready for whatever disaster may be looming. And now the best way to get ready is with a *Ready Freddy Emergency Preparedness Kit.*

Ready Freddy Emergency Preparedness Kits are the first emergency kits available on the market requiring NO BATTERIES. In case of an emergency, most people never think about how they will power radios, flash-lights, or even their cell phones, but Ready Freddy has solved the problem forever.

Besides being completely battery free, Ready Freddy is enclosed in an easy to store backpack and is the most unique kit in that it is organized into five clearly marked and color-coded bags....

The release begins by addressing a general trend: the public's tendency to put off thinking about the possibility of a natural or human-caused disaster until it's too late to prepare. Only in the fifth sentence does the release announce the name of the product that can remedy the situation described: Ready Freddy. The release then goes on to describe the product's unique features and benefits, as well as its availability.

Here is another example of a feature-style release with a delayed lead, this one announcing the availability of public service announcements for radio broadcast:

> Campbellville, ON (PRWEB) December 22, 2005— Visiting family and friends is part of the holiday season. Changes in routines, crowded rooms, unattended food and excited children can often lead to miscommunication between the resident dog and guests. Doggone Safe offers tips to keep kids and dogs safe over the holidays. Public service announcements for radio are available for live reads or as WAV files for download from www.doggonesafe.com.

This release goes on to detail the safety tips available in the downloadable files, so that an enterprising (or rushed) local radio personality can use the tips without even going to the Web site. As always, the key for public relations writers is to make the information easily available in as many affordable forms as can be anticipated being useful to the target media.

Quotations

Quotations are used to lend personal authority to a statement your client wishes to make. They are a standard element in public relations writing, particularly news releases. When drafting a news release on a new product, for example, you must often invent a comment from a product manager on the features of a new product or perhaps on its application in the marketplace.

Your made-up quotation will invariably have to be approved by that person. Even if your quotation is taken verbatim from its source, however, it should be approved by that source before it is released.

Journalists quote people directly, and any modifications the journalists make to these quotations are put in brackets or otherwise explained. In public relations writing, however, because you are often called on to make up quotations (for which you must always receive approval from the person the words are attributed to), bear in mind that the substance and tone of the quotation should be in keeping with the needs of your client. Here is a release excerpt with a quotation appropriate to its source:

Barack Obama, Russell Simmons, B. B. King, Harry Belafonte and Isaac Hayes Lend Their Voice to AOL Black Voices Celebration of Black History Month

January 30, 2006
AOL Black Voices, the premier site for African-American culture and community, celebrates Black History Month with an interactive look at the lives, stories and contributions of significant African Americans in history (http://blackvoices.aol.com/black_news/black_history_month). Through a partnership with The HistoryMakers, the nation's largest African American video oral history archive headquartered in Chicago, IL, users can watch video interviews from significant figures including Senator Barack Obama, Russell Simmons, B.B. King, Harry Belafonte and Isaac Hayes, among others.

"As one of the most comprehensive news organizations bringing Black culture and information to millions of people each month, AOL Black Voices is thrilled to focus a six week campaign looking at the contributions of Black Americans," said Nick Charles, Editor in Chief, AOL Black Voices. "Through video, audio and exclusive articles, we

are bringing our community closer together to debate
and rejoice in the rich history of black people." [AOL 2006]

Note that this release is timed to reach the media when they
may be searching for new material to cover in connection with
the month-long focus on black history each February.

Quotations should provide only relevant information. As a
public relations practitioner, you must remain keenly aware of
the interests of your audience and your client. Don't clutter a
news release with unneeded facts.

Photos, Samples, and Review Copies

Whenever appropriate, you should state that a photo or color
slide, a sample, or a review copy of the subject of the release
is available on request or downloadable from a specified Web
address (if it is not already enclosed with the release). Music
critics complain that publicists will call and ask if they want
to interview band members. If a music critic has never heard
the band, has no idea what the group sounds like, and has not
received a compact disc, been directed to a sample on a Web site,
or been invited to hear the band perform, there is no chance the
reporter will know if he has an interest in writing about it, let
alone whether he wants to do an interview.

Make it as easy as possible for the journalist to experience
firsthand the subject of your press release. If the release is about
a speech, attach a complete text of that speech. If the release
is about a new fabric, attach a swatch. When a sample cannot
be enclosed, invite the reporter to a place where the subject
of the news release can be viewed or encountered. Make full
use of the capabilities of the Internet to provide compelling
photographs, video, and audio to help tell your story and for the
media to use as background information or as content for their
stories.

Style and Form

A consistent style and format give your news release a professional look. There are a number of guides or stylebooks on the market. Since you are most often sending your release to newsrooms, however, we recommend *The Associated Press Stylebook and Briefing on Media Law* (2004), which is used in most newsrooms across the country. The more your release and your approach to a story look like the work of a journalist, the better reception it will have.

All news releases must have four key elements:

1. *Date and embargo.* Include a date indicating when the release is issued and another date indicating when it should be made public. Any restriction on when the information may be used is called an *embargo*. An embargo is usually used when issuing information that can be released to the public only after a specified date and time. Embargoes can be tricky and should be used cautiously. If one member of the press ignores the embargo and breaks the story early, others will probably follow. If your release has no time restrictions for going public, mark it "For Immediate Release."

2. *Contact.* Include the name, telephone number, and e-mail address of the person to whom inquiries should be directed. For breaking stories of great urgency, you may also want to include a cell phone or home phone number if media may need information during nonoffice hours.

3. *Headline.* The headline at the top of the release summarizes the story and catches the reader's attention. When the story is complicated, use a subhead as well. Headline information is drawn from the body of the release, because the release must hold up as a complete thought without the headline.

Headlines are important, Although editors almost always write their own headlines, the ones you write are nevertheless important. For one thing, they help direct an editor's view of your subject. For another, they are your billboard. Based on your headline, editors decide whether to keep reading.

When using e-mail to pitch your story or distribute the release (or both), put your headline in the subject line to entice the editor to open the e-mail and read your release. Your short e-mail pitch may then include the lead paragraph of the release. It should also include the availability of other story resources, such as the names of the people available for interviews and offers of samples when applicable.

4. *Letterhead.* Use the official letterhead of your company or the client you're representing. The letterhead lends credibility and professionalism to your presentation, and it often contains useful information, such as the fax number and address.

These elements can be arranged several ways in a news release. Here are two examples of the most typical and accepted styles:

Block Style

Contact: John Doe   Month, date, year
(202) 555-1234   For Immediate Release
          HEADLINE GOES HERE

Use Subheads When Stories Are Complicated

The text of the release begins here in
paragraph form ....

Newspaper Style

          For Immediate Release
          HEADLINE GOES HERE

Use Subheads When Stories Are Complicated

[CITY, month, date]—The text of the release starts here, in
paragraph form ....

When you use newspaper style, insert a six-digit code at the end of the release to indicate the full date. For example, the code for May 29, 2008, would be 052908.

Some press releases carry the date and embargo on the top and list the contact and telephone number at the bottom.

Each public relations office has its own style for laying out the essential elements of a press release. What is important is that all four elements—date and embargo, contact, headline, and letterhead—are present.

Here are some additional points of style in formatting press releases:

- Format all copy to print double-spaced in 11- or 12-point type in a clear typeface such as Courier on standard eight-and-a-half by eleven-inch paper.
- Leave reasonable margins of at least one inch on all sides of the paper.
- When the press release continues for more than a page, include the word *more* or *continued* as a footer at the bottom of the page to lead readers onward.
- Use short paragraphs. Don't be afraid to use one-sentence paragraphs.
- Use capitalization sparingly, though conforming to your company's or client's style. Given the choice, use lowercase for titles such as vice president and chief executive officer. A common rule of thumb is to capitalize a title (for example, John Doe, Senior Director, Sales) but lowercase a position (John Doe is the senior director of the sales department).
- Be consistent in style. If your company or client has a style guide, use it. Otherwise, refer to *The Associated Press Stylebook and Briefing on Media Law*.

The Q&A

If your release presents a complicated story, you may find it useful to attach a question-and-answer sheet (Q&A) that anticipates questions reporters will have. Sometimes such a sheet is helpful to have for your own internal use in responding to inquiries from the press or to provide to the executive who will be doing a telephone interview.

Here is an example of a Q&A used during the publicity for the publication of author Walter Dean Myers's young adult novel *Shooter*:

1. What inspired SHOOTER?

I view school shootings as a type of suicide in which the shooters carefully plan a scenario that will leave them dead either by police bullets or by their own hand. When I heard about the Columbine incidents as well as the other school shootings, I wanted to explore the reasons for the suicides—what conditions made these boys want to take their own lives? The exploration of the bullying and of their futile attempts to connect with a rejecting world resulted in SHOOTER.

2. The story is revealed through interview transcripts, press clippings and diary entries. Why did you write SHOOTER in this format?

There was an actual panel assembled to investigate the shootings and the dangers that could be detected prior to the incident. I thought the panel was concentrating too much on the inner life of the boys, and not their environment. I wondered what kind of panel I would have formed and what conclusions they would form.

3. How do you feel about the characters in the book? Are any or part based on kids you have met?

I have great sympathy for kids who don't fit into the neat boxes of a perfect world. I also know how difficult it is to help them. All of the kids in SHOOTER are based upon young people I have met.

4. What do you hope SHOOTER accomplishes?

I hope SHOOTER raises the issues and gives young people the knowledge that their bullying episode is not unique while presenting an opportunity for them to discuss bullying publicly.

5. Based on your interviews, to what extent is bullying a part of American society?

I was surprised to find how common bullying stories were among troubled teens. I believe that bullying is, in too many schools and neighborhoods, an integral part of American society ("A Q&A with Author Walter Dean Myers," 2000).

In most cases for clarity and ease of reference, a Q&A should ask and answer only one question at a time.

Photos

Photographs are an important way to document and publicize a subject. Although the mechanics of submitting photographs to publications have changed in the digital age, the four principles of gaining photo coverage in connection with a press release or as stand-alone coverage of an event remain the same:

1. The image must be animated, compelling, and professional in quality.
2. The caption and photo headline must concisely and accurately convey the five W's (who, what, where, when, and why).
3. A photo credit must identify the copyright holder of the photograph.
4. The photo should be sent in the publication's preferred digital format and file size, which should be verified before sending.

Many publications run photos supplied by public relations offices if the photos meet certain standards of professional quality.

Whenever possible, you should hire a professional photographer and not attempt to use your own snapshot or one taken by another amateur.

If you send an interesting, high-quality digital photograph with your news release, there is a good chance the editor will decide to run it with the story, giving your story bigger play. At most publications, it is rare that an editor will assign a staff photographer to shoot photographs to accompany a story generated by a press release.

Because readers are more likely to look at photos than read text, you should always be considering newsworthy photo opportunities that tell a story. Dignitaries, celebrities, and public officials are usually considered newsworthy by the trade and consumer press. Photos of senior management such as presidents and key executive officers are often considered newsworthy by the trade press.

Except for product photos, which are primarily static shots, photos featuring people in action are always more interesting than posed shots. Think of ways to bring the action and intensity of a sports shot to other types of stories. For example, Exhibit 2.1, a photograph of John Lasseter and Brad Bird, is a much more compelling accompaniment to a business acquisition story than a traditional head shot.

Avoid submitting standard head shots to publications, except for photos that accompany appointment releases or at the request of the editor.

When people are to be featured in photos, always try to have them doing something rather than staring into the camera. At photo sessions or during events, encourage people being photographed to be naturally active, depending on the situation. Avoid "grip and grins," posed shots of people shaking hands or holding an award.

For internal executive purposes, however, the more clichéd shots can serve a purpose. For example, the typical photo of a celebrity visiting a school for an inspirational school assembly

Exhibit 2.1 Creative Genius

John Lasseter (left), founding member of Pixar Animation Studios, and Brad
Bird, writer and director of Pixar's hit film *The Incredibles*, are pictured at
the premiere of the film in Hollywood in October 2004. The Walt Disney
Co. has agreed to acquire Pixar Animation Studios in an all-stock transaction
worth $7.4 billion. (Allstar/Globe Photos, Inc., photogrpaher: Graham Whitby-
Boot/Allstar)

shows the school principal shaking hands with the important
visitor, perhaps with a child or two lined up beside them. This
setup makes an adequate memento for a participant. Therefore,
the tactful public relations representative or photographer will
make sure to record this standard setup. The resulting photograph,
however, will probably not be printed anywhere as "news."
Exhibit 2.2 shows another way to shoot the photo: both the
photograph and the caption tell the story more vividly than a
grip and grin.

Photo Captions

The subjects in photos should always be identified and described
in a caption included in both the digital photo file and the cover
e-mail. A photo caption is best written in the present tense and

Exhibit 2.2 Still Got the Moves

Boxing legend Muhammad Ali greets children at the Royal Albert Hall in London, after serving as a presenter at the second annual World Sports Awards in 2001. (Dave Benett/Globe Photos/Getty Images)

active voice. Choose one verb that best explains the action and circumstance in the photo and state the basic five W's.

Headlines for Photo Captions

Photo captions that are stand-alone art—meaning they do not accompany a story—usually carry a headline. For example, the photograph, headline, and caption in Exhibit 2.3 tell a complete story. When a photo is used to accompany a story, a headline is not necessary.

Groups of people shown in photos are usually identified in order from left to right. If the names in a caption need titles as well, use semicolons to separate the subjects in the list:

Pictured from left are board members being sworn in: John Smith, vice-president, marketing; Bill Anderson, treasurer; Charlotte Brown, public relations director.

Exhibit 2.3 Passing of the Torch

Sir Roger Bannister, a former athlete best known as the first man to run a mile in less than four minutes, begins the Olympic Torch Relay for the 2004 Games at the Wimbledon Tennis Club. (SanWordley/Alpha/Globe Photos, Copyright 2004)

Photo Credit and Copyright

Each digital photo file and cover e-mail should include a photo credit that identifies the copyright holder. The photo is usually credited to the photographer, who retains any rights to the photograph for which you do not specifically negotiate and pay. Some organizations such as a movie studio doing a publicity shoot will pay for full buy-outs of rights, and then the photo credit reads, for example, "Warner Bros." Accurate records of copyright should be kept for all photos to avoid an inadvertent reuse in the future that violates the signed agreement with the photographer.

Submission of Photographs

Most publications want photographs submitted as a digital file with a cover e-mail that includes a copy of the caption covering the five W's. The e-mail should also include your full name, the organization, and all contact information, including alternate numbers.

Although preferred formats vary, most publications want to receive photographs as digital files, so that the time-consuming scanning process is already done and the photograph is ready to be sized and cropped to fit their needs. The Associated Press, for example, advises starting with an image of about ten inches in the longest dimension (think of the old standard of an eight-by ten-inch photo). The image should be scanned at about 200 dpi (and no more than 300) and saved as a JPEG file of about 1 megabyte. The caption and photo credit should be included in the JPEG file.

Media Kits

A media kit, also referred to as a press kit, is an organized, comprehensive package of information on a client. Media kits are often compilations of several of the kinds of public relations writing discussed above.

Items in a media kit vary, depending on the client, but standard contents may include hard news releases and feature news releases; a Q&A; biographies and backgrounders (discussed in Chapter Four); photos of the key executives or products; and lists of goods manufactured, achievements, honors received, or films or records released. Sometimes media kits include annual reports, brochures, or publications, such as those discussed in Chapter Ten. Finally, media kits can include CDs or DVDs with material about the client, including previous media coverage and B-roll, secondary video clips without sound, such as shots of company headquarters, which a news outlet can use to fill out a story.

Photocopies of other articles already published about the client can be particularly useful in press kits. They can influence editors to do stories while at the same time allowing them to avoid duplication by finding a new angle. Make sure such copies always include the date they originally appeared and where they were published.

A media kit helps a journalist by making background information readily available, thereby saving research time. Public relations offices get very busy, and you won't always have time to compile a kit every time you need one. Prepare standard kits in advance so that you can send them at a moment's notice or add elements for special needs.

Media kits are also frequently put together for a special event. If, for example, you're holding a media conference to announce award recipients, the media kit will most likely include short biographies of the award recipients, background on the awards and their sponsor, and, when applicable, samples of what warranted the award (for example, photographs, artwork, or essays).

Sometimes media kits are compiled in response to breaking stories. In those situations, they may contain reports, court records, and other documents that support or refute a claim.

Media kits are often packaged in custom-printed folders with the client's logo on them. This presentation is attractive but not mandatory. A less expensive kit can be packaged in a glossy, colored pocket folder with laser labels available at a standard office-supply store.

Here are the elements included in the media kit when *Daily Variety*, the venerable Hollywood entertainment trade newspaper known for its snappy headlines and self-coined lingo, announced a redesign of its logotype and layout:

- A press release about the publication's redesign with the headline, "Slick Sheet Shocks Showbiz."
- A tip sheet for a media/celebrity party celebrating the new design.

- A "Headline History—Daily Variety Style" with vivid examples and their subheadlines or "translations," dating back to 1935, for example:
  - August 30, 1935: "CHILLERS NOW DUE FOR ICING, World Censors Warn Studios on Horror Pix"
  - September 17, 1986: "'DUCK' COOKS PRICE'S GOOSE" (The failure of *Howard the Duck* leads to Frank Price's dismissal as Universal studio head.)
- A corporate backgrounder on Cahners Publishing Company, the publication's corporate owner.
- Biographies of the publication's editors and the top executives of the corporate owner.
- Repro (reproductive quality material) of the redesigned logotype and of the new and old front pages.

The media kit for the Ready Freddy Emergency Kit included these items:

- The press release reprinted previously in this chapter
- A full-color product sheet picturing the emergency backpack and its six color-coded internal packs, enumerating the contents of each
- A DVD of a television commercial
- A DVD of television news coverage
- Clips of previous news coverage

Approvals

To prevent misstatements of fact or divulgence of inappropriate information, a series of approvals is necessary before a news release—or public relations material of any sort—is sent to the media. The line of copy approval can be quite long, and several rounds of rewrites and approvals are frequently needed before copy can be released. Be accommodating, and rewrite according to suggestions and comments from those approving the copy. If you disagree with a change that makes a substantive difference, tactfully and succinctly explain your point of view. Perhaps you can suggest an alternative phrasing that both of you are comfortable with.

In a corporation, there is likely to be a series of people in management who must read and approve your copy before it can be released. In most companies, a high-ranking member of the legal department is part of the review process. Because anything released to the media becomes part of the company's public image, the approval process often goes to the top of the corporate structure in both the company you represent and its parent company, probably up through the senior officer of corporate communications and, in many corporations, the CEO. These corporate officers want to know in advance what will appear in tomorrow's papers. The motto for public relations personnel within a company and those at an agency representing a client is: NO SURPRISES.

In an agency, your copy is usually first approved by your supervisor and then sent to your client, where it must go through the company's established approval process before it can be sent to the media.

Because of the labyrinth of approvals through which a document must travel, it's a good idea to ask for dated initials on approved copy or to save e-mail approval responses to a special file. These copies will help avoid confusion later as to who saw what when. Don't be insulted or discouraged when your copy is altered. It doesn't necessarily mean that you haven't done a good writing job. There is simply a lot of rewriting that has to be done in public relations, and clients often have specific ideas they would like to see communicated through your writing.

There may be times when you feel your client is making copy changes that will not advance his or her goals or communicate them as clearly as you would wish. You must be the judge of when and whether you should point them out. Your dual role is to serve your clients' needs as well as the needs of the target media.

Remember that a single mistake or a single lie in a press release or in any subsequent verbal interaction with a journalist will cost you your hard-earned credibility and reputation. Accuracy and truth are paramount.

Never send a news release to the media before it goes through all necessary approval stages. No surprises!

Chapter Recap

The guidelines that follow are the most important ones to keep in mind while researching and writing a news release:

1. Make sure your subject is newsworthy.
2. Make sure the release will advance your client's objectives.
3. Summarize the entire story in the first paragraph. If the story is a feature, make sure the first paragraph will capture and hold readers' interest.
4. Write the release in the pyramid news style.
5. Answer all the logical questions the release is likely to raise.
6. Attribute the announcement to an official source.
7. Check all information for accuracy.
8. Include a date and embargo (the date the news may be released), contact, telephone number, e-mail address and headline.
9. Provide copy that is formatted to print double-spaced in a clear typeface with adequate margins.
10. Provide lively photographs in the format preferred by the publication, and include well-written captions that tell the story and provide accurate photo credit and copyright information.

11. Release an announcement only after you have obtained all the necessary approvals. Your chief executive officer wants no surprises.

12. Never forget that any inaccuracies in your written and verbal interactions with a journalist will damage your reputation and destroy your credibility as a future news source.

3

THE PITCH: CREATING MEDIA INTEREST

The goal of most public relations work is to gain media interest in your story. The first step toward media coverage is usually a pitch—a concise summary that sells your story idea to a receptive editor, journalist, or segment producer, in the case of television and radio news and magazine shows.

The process for presenting a good pitch can be broken down into stages:

1. Analyze the subject, and identify the target.
2. Call the editor.
3. Write your pitch. Begin with a reminder about your telephone conversation. Then write a catchy lead and brief, informative text. Wrap up the pitch, and say you will follow up.
4. Follow up.

Stage One: Analyze the Subject, and Identify the Target

The key to a good pitch is the hook, or news angle, it offers. To find that hook, you must understand the subject you're pitching and then consider the needs of the journalist who will receive the pitch letter.

If you're trying to promote a story about a new high-definition digital video camera, for example, the first step is to understand all you can about that camera and what makes it newsworthy and different from all others. Most of this information will be readily available to you, but if it's not, seek it out. This may mean telephone calls to engineers who designed the product or salespeople who understand its position in the marketplace. Most importantly, you must know the image of the product that your client or boss wants presented to the press: innovative, rugged, sleek, easy to use, refined, or "the professional's choice," for example. Identifying this angle is a key element of creating a brand image and may require a number of conversations with a team including engineering, design, marketing, and sales.

Once you understand why your product is special, you then turn to the target media. If, for example, you want the trade magazine *Videography* to write about this high-definition digital video camera, your approach should be technical and in depth. If instead you want *USA Today*, a consumer newspaper, to write about it, your approach will be entirely different, geared more toward general information.

Assuming *Videography* is the target of your first pitch, you must find out who specifically at the magazine would write an article about the product you are pitching, and you must know what types of articles are published in *Videography*. If you can, study an issue of the magazine, and note the editorial contact telephone, address, and Web site or e-mail contact for your media list to send future press releases.

If a copy of the publication is not available in your company's office, do an online search for the Web site by using the magazine's title, perhaps paired with "publication." The *Videography* Web site has a link to the editorial calendar. With monthly periodicals, often referred to as "long-lead press," the magazine comes out during the month prior to the cover date; deadlines for editorial content are two to three months ahead of the cover date, and stories need to be pitched six to eight weeks ahead of the actual deadline. Therefore, you will need to be looking four to six months into the future for the projected feature articles. Deadlines for some portions of the magazine, usually containing shorter items such as technology updates, are closer to the publication date. As a rule, the more comprehensive an article you aim for, the earlier it needs to be pitched.

After carefully studying the editorial calendar and three or four issues of the magazine and analyzing the product you're pitching, you should now be ready to start developing a pitch suited to *Videography*.

Stage Two: Call the Editor

In some cases, you will know who the editor is, but most often you won't. Call the publication, and ask who covers stories on high-definition cinematography. Once you know the person to call, you can make a brief phone pitch: a one- or two-sentence summary of your story idea.

When you make the call, introduce yourself using your first and last name, and explain why you are calling—for example, "My name is John Smith, I'm calling from XYZ Public Relations, and I represent General Electronics." Explain that you have information on a new high-definition digital video camera that exceeds the expectations of cinematographers devoted to using film and that you think it would be a good story for a feature article in their upcoming March issue on high-definition cameras and lenses.

Editors who have time to talk will encourage you to elaborate on your ideas. Many, however, will ask you to send more information to them so they can look it over. Their time on the phone is limited, so get to the point quickly and be brief. Having notes in front of you will help. If the editor directs you to someone else on the staff, your opening line to that person will include that you were "referred by the editor."

If an editor rejects your story immediately, listen carefully to the reasons (if they are offered). You can learn what will be better suited to that editor's needs the next time. Then thank the editor, and get on to your next call.

When the editor encourages you to send more information, ask how she prefers to receive it. Confirm the spelling of the editor's name and the e-mail address, fax number, or mailing address, depending on the preferred method of receipt and the type of material you are sending. Obviously a product sample would need to be sent by messenger, overnight package service, or priority mail. (You may want to make a separate call to ask the receptionist to confirm a street delivery address for overnight delivery versus a post office box for ordinary mail.) Your credibility will be hard to reestablish if you get anything wrong.

You now have the right recipient, as well as the right angle of approach.

An editor who consistently receives good ideas and timely, useful information from you will begin to be more responsive to your efforts to make contact. But if an editor frequently receives inappropriate pitches and releases from you or you consistently approach the publication just after it has done feature articles on similar products, most of your material will end up in the trash.

Stage Three: Write Your Pitch

The written pitch often determines whether an editor or reporter pursues the story. Because most editors and reporters are extremely busy and don't have much time for telephone calls, they often prefer to receive extended pitches and background material by e-mail, fax, or mail. A letter saves time, can be read at the person's convenience, and is a polite, unobtrusive way to present your ideas.

Pitches are used for all kinds of reasons: as cover letters or e-mails attached to press releases, as invitations to events, as requests for endorsements or contributions, and so on. The most typical pitches are sent by a public relations representative to a journalist.

In addition to suggesting a newsworthy story idea, good pitch letters offer substantive background information, help in setting up interviews, and, when appropriate, samples of the product you are pitching.

In short, not only do you suggest a good story idea, but you also make it easy for the reporter to cover the story in depth by anticipating questions and providing research, background, bios, and previously published articles on similar topics.

Form and Tone

Pitches should always be presented neatly in standard business form on official letterhead or with your own or your company's standard e-mail signature.

The pitch reflects your—and your client's—level of professionalism and competence. Grammar and punctuation should be perfect. If your pitch is sloppy, an editor might infer that your information is also sloppy and might discount your ideas. Forget all the shortcuts and bad habits you've developed text-messaging and e-mailing friends, and write in complete, properly punctuated and capitalized sentences. Before sending the pitch, make sure that you reread it carefully in addition to using your spell-check program. (Reading an e-mail aloud to yourself can be a handy way to catch errors as well.)

Unless you are friendly with the person to whom you are writing, do not use a highly personal tone, and certainly do not address him or her by first name. But don't make the pitch too stuffy or formal either. Most of the time, you will be writing to editors and reporters you don't know or don't know well. Be professional and polite in your approach, and you won't go wrong.

Following is an example of a pitch template provided by the U.S. Food and Drug Administration to local agencies partnering on a March 2004 Health Education Kit targeted to the Gulf Coast:

(NAME OF YOUR AGENCY)
LAUNCHES EDUCATIONAL CAMPAIGN
Warns the Hispanic Community about Raw Oysters

Have you ever eaten a raw oyster? If you or someone you know has, the enclosed information could save someone's life.

The U.S. Food and Drug Administration is issuing a warning to the Hispanic community about the risks of eating raw oysters contaminated with a bacteria that lives in the waters of the Gulf coast. In the last two years, nine Hispanic men died in the U.S. from eating raw oysters contaminated with the bacteria, *Vibrio vulnificus.*

It is imperative we get the message out to the community about this issue as soon as possible because as the weather gets warmer the amount of bacteria in the water increases. Also, as you know, raw oysters are a favorite food among Hispanics, especially Hispanic males.

A[n] [name of agency] representative will be available for interviews next week on [insert date/s] to speak to you. Please consider scheduling an interview to discuss this important topic.

Enclosed is the following information:

• Press Release
• Vibrio vulnificus Fact Sheet
• Myths about raw oysters
• Cooked oyster recipes
• Feature article

For more information, please contact:
(Name, Organization, phone, e-mail)

In this next pitch, Stephanie Cohen, senior manager of marketing and communications at Korn/Ferry International, offers an expert for an interview for an announced feature article:

Subject: Succession Planning Expert Interview

Hi Roberta,
I noticed that you're planning a feature on succession planning for the magazine's October issue. If you're looking for expert insights, please let me know if you would be interested in speaking with Scott Kingdom of Korn/Ferry International.

Based in Chicago, Scott is Global Managing Director of the firm's Industrial Practice, which covers the aerospace, automotive, energy, industrial products, and industrial services sectors. Functionally, he focuses on senior-level assignments for chief executive officers, presidents, and functional heads of sales, marketing, and finance.

He can speak extensively about trends in succession planning, particularly as they relate to the industrial markets. He can also discuss Korn/Ferry's recently released research on succession planning, the top-line findings of which you can find here: http://www.kornfery.com/Library/Process.asp?P=PR_Detail&CID=1004&LID=1

Please let me know if you'd be interested in speaking with Scott and I'll be happy to make the arrangements.

The following pitch, also from Stephanie Cohen, attempts to inspire interest in writing about a proprietary process:

Dear Sandra,
I see that you are planning to cover the emerging issue of preemployment assessment in your October issue.

I hope that you'll consider including Korn/Ferry International and our innovative assessment tool, Search Assessment, in your coverage.

Studies have shown that the main reason people are unsuccessful on the job is due to a lack of behavioral and/or cultural fit with the organization, not a lack of skills. To prevent this, Korn/Ferry, the premier provider of executive search, has developed Search Assessment, a proprietary assessment process designed to complement the executive search process and help organizations determine, before an employment offer is made, which individuals will succeed and why.

We tapped into Korn/Ferry's database of several hundred thousand searches to develop Success Profile—specific profiles in leadership for executive positions across most industries and functions.

Please let me know if you'd like more background on Korn/Ferry's Search Assessment process or if you're interested in speaking to a Korn/Ferry executive to get additional information. Looking forward to your thoughts.

Notice the common elements in these pitch letters: they're short (no longer than one page), to the point, catchy, and full of information. Reporters are inundated with public relations material every day. Pitch letters therefore must reach the right person, get to the point, intrigue the reader, and contain substantive information.

Writing a Catchy Lead

The opening paragraph of a pitch letter is the best chance you have to interest an editor. You have only the time it takes an editor to reach for your faxed letter in the in-box and lift it from the desk to rivet his or her attention and prevent it from being tossed directly into the trash. If you pitch by e-mail, and most people do these days, your window of opportunity is even briefer; your subject line must arrest the editor's habitual "Delete" response.

As with all other good copy, the lead of a pitch should be enticing and informative; it should make the editor want to read on. Here are some good opening paragraphs and subject lines.

This one is directed to the editor of a financial publication:

Did you know that while 95 percent of female chief financial officers would recommend the career to other women starting out now, only 61 percent of them expect to finish their careers in the CFO function? These are only some of the surprising and interesting results of a recent survey of female CFOs undertaken by the executive search firm Korn/Ferry [Korn/Ferry International 2006].

Here is the subject line of an e-mail pitch to a technical publication:

Hi-Def Digital Camera Wows 23 Feature Film Cinematographers

Following is the lead of a sample pitch provided by the U.S. Centers for Disease Control and Prevention for use by community organizations in pitching local media:

The mosquitoes are biting—and thousands of people are putting themselves at risk of getting ill with West Nile Virus (WNV). Mosquitoes carry the virus. A single bite from an infected mosquito can cause severe disease with life-altering consequences. In some cases, especially among older adults, WNV can be fatal. Since 1999, almost 17,000 cases of WNV have been reported to the Centers for Disease Control and Prevention.

Each of these examples focuses on a subject that could interest the editor. Each also contains impressive facts and figures, and each is intriguing to someone who covers those fields.

The first sentence is often the hardest part of a pitch letter to write. One of the best ways to formulate an opening line is to single out the most newsworthy aspect of the subject you are pitching, and state it simply. If, for example, you are pitching a story on the world's first self-cleaning solar roof panel, your opening sentence could very well be, "Turn On the Sunlight (TOTS) has developed the world's first self-cleaning solar roof panel."

If you are pitching a case history, an interview, or a survey, you need to build up to the pitch with a provocative opening. The pitch from Korn/Ferry is a good example of this type of opening line: "Did you know that while 95% of female chief financial officers would recommend the career to other women starting out now, only 61% of them expect to finish their careers in the CFO function?" It's a catchy opening, urging the editor to read on and find out where this fact came from and where the pitch is going. This lead is an example of how to make a dry subject interesting.

When writing an opening line, try to come up with something fresh and intriguing. Don't use the first paragraph to give a lengthy history of the company you are pitching or explain who you are. (Your name, title, and contact information should be listed at the end of every e-mail or letter.) And don't tell the editor about his or her readership. Many novice writers make the mistake of opening a pitch letter with something like this: "The readers of *Videography* are interested in the latest developments in the video industry." That sentence only reiterates the obvious. Certainly a reporter for *Videography* will know what the magazine's readers are interested in. Don't waste time by pointing that out.

Compose Brief, Informative Text

Once the opening paragraph has caught your reader's attention, the rest of the letter must flow smoothly and logically. If your opening line is, "Turn On the Sunlight (TOTS) has developed the world's first self-cleaning solar roof panel," your next sentence should take a natural step of detailing the facts behind that claim. Thus, the second sentence might be this: "The effect of this patented technology means that TOTS' panels will continue working at 100 percent efficiency, even in smoggy city and foggy coastal environments where pollution and mineral deposits can quickly lower solar collection efficiency by 30 to 50 percent. TOTS' breakthrough means more solar electricity generated, more fossil fuel conserved, and more money saved, according to John Doe, Vice President of Product Research for Turn On the Sunlight. Doe contends that the new panel. . ." Stick to the facts, and avoid using adjectives, especially words like *unique*, *greatest*, *phenomenal*, and *incredible*, which are overused and rarely true.

If you look at the sample pitch letters in the beginning of this chapter, you will see that they all flow smoothly and head toward an ultimate purpose, whether it is for the editor to read a product description, request an interview with an expert, or write about a company's proprietary process.

The middle section of a pitch letter is often where the story information, or "meat," is found. This is where you expand on the central idea. It is here that you explain how Chi-Chi Thin uses proprietary technology to consolidate four bulky communication and computer devices into one ultra-thin, ultra-chic titanium MobComm, this year's must-have Christmas gift; how Google uses Internet beta releases of its new products and upgrades to allow its own customers to discover and report bugs; or what five principles Toyota Motors is using to manage U.S. manufacturing plants to maintain an edge over its Detroit competitors.

When you have several crucial points of information to get across, it is often helpful to list them in bullet form—that is, to indent and set them off with bullets or some other typographic device. The bullet technique is quite effective because it allows editors quickly to see what kind of information you're offering. For example, look again at the FDA's pitch template on the dangers of Gulf Coast raw oysters. After an opening hook, the pitch presents the facts, and then the last paragraph uses bullets to save time and space in listing the resources available to an editor interested in pursuing the issue, including an already prepared feature article, which might very well be attractive to the editor of a small Gulf Coast newspaper with limited staff resources. Here's an example, also from Stephanie Cohen, from a pitch to a specialized human resource publication on staff outsourcing:

> I noticed that *HRO Today* is planning a feature on out-sourcing temporary and permanent staffing for your July/August issue. I hope you'll consider highlighting Futurestep, a subsidiary of Korn/Ferry International and a leading provider of RPO [recruitment process outsourcing] solutions.
>
> As you likely know, analysts are projecting the world-wide RPO market to reach $35 billion by 2008. While many firms are entering this highly lucrative market, Futurestep is highly unique on a number of fronts:
>
> 1. Our history and affiliation with Korn/Ferry International, founded in 1969 and the world's largest executive search firm
> 2. Our reach, with offices in 15 countries across Asia/Pacific, Europe and the Americas
> 3. Our holistic solution, which includes middle management search, project recruitment, managed services, interim solutions and assessment technology.
>
> Bob McNabb, CEO of Futurestep, is extremely knowledgeable about RPO and is in the finishing stages of writing what we believe is a seminal article on the trend (an early draft is attached). It includes a case study from one of our major clients, Telecom New Zealand.
>
> Very much looking forward to your thoughts.

Through use of techniques such as numbered lists and bullets, you can pack in a large number of hard facts clearly and concisely.

Whether you use bullets or straight prose, always keep your letter short. Rarely are you justified in writing a pitch letter longer than one page or an e-mail longer than three or four short paragraphs. When you have finished a draft, ask yourself a few questions:

- *Is there any redundancy in the letter?* Redundant phrases plague business correspondence. There is no room for saying something twice in any type of public relations writing. For example, do away with phrases like "Seventy-five *different* countries"; saying "seventy-five countries" is enough. Similarly, phrases such as "unique and different," "new and innovative," or "at the forefront of the cutting edge" are all redundant.

- *Is there any information that is not vital to the story?* When you are developing a pitch letter, it's easy to include information that is not germane. Reread the letter carefully to make sure everything you've written is absolutely central to the pitch.

- *Is there a faster way to get to the point?* Don't waste time leading up to the subject of a pitch letter. By the third paragraph, the editor had better know why you've written. Wrap It Up, and Say That You Will Follow Up.

There are standard lines for ending pitch letters. Each writer has a preference, but most end their letters with sentences such as Cohen's, "Looking forward to your thoughts," which implies further conversation. Others prefer to state more explicitly, "I'll call you in a couple of days to see if you're interested."

Stage Four: Follow Up

It is best to follow up a pitch letter with a telephone call to see if the reporter received the material and is interested in the story.

As the reporter begins to shape the story, be prepared to offer assistance with further resources, such as interviews with senior management. Offer only someone who can add to the story and whom you can deliver within the reporter's time frame.

Disappointing a reporter by overpromising is a sure way to kill the story that you've worked hard to pitch and place. Therefore, you must clear the possible interview with the executive in advance. You might start by telling the highest-level person involved with the project that you've pitched a story about the high-definition video camera to *Videography* and they seem interested. "If the story goes forward, I recommend that we offer an interview, and of course, the reporter's first choice would be you. What's your availability?" The executive may not be willing to do the interview. The decision may depend of the status of the executive, the relative importance of the publication or the article, or previous interactions with the specific journalist.

If the executive is not willing or not available within the projected time frame, ask who else might do the possible interview, whom the publication would be interested in talking to, and who is familiar with the technical issues. When you speak to that executive, conveying the wishes of his boss, he or she will be both flattered and eager to oblige if he or she will be available before the reporter's deadline. You can then comfortably offer the interview to the reporter.

When you call, you can tell the journalist, "I'm calling to make sure you received the material, and I was wondering if you would be interested in talking to Ms. CEO for your story?" In today's world of ubiquitous voice mail, be prepared to leave effective and tantalizing messages, such as, "I have a possible senior-level interview that might be helpful for your story." The more you can promote one-on-one conversation with the journalist, the more subtle influence you can have on what is included in the story, what is emphasized, and what is downplayed.

Always remember that reporters are extremely busy and may not have time even to take your call. Use discretion to identify whom to call and when. For example, editors on morning newspapers are on deadline in the afternoon, so the best times to call them are usually between 10:00 A.M. and noon. Radio and television editors have varying deadlines, but one rule is safe: never call right before airtime.

As we've shown, the pitch e-mail and pitch letter are crucial to effective public relations. Take the time to prepare them correctly. Then ensure their effectiveness by following up with an offer to provide additional information, and possibly an interview with the highest-level executive who is familiar with the areas that will interest the readership of the publication.

Chapter Recap

Here are the stages for successful pitches:

1. Analyze the subject, and identify the target.
2. Call the editor.
3. Write your pitch. Begin with a reminder about your telephone conversation. Then write a catchy lead and brief, informative text. Wrap up the pitch, and say you will follow up.
4. Follow up.

4

THE BIOGRAPHY
AND BACKGROUNDER

Bringing Your Subject to Life

Public relations biographies, often referred to as bios, follow two forms. The first, newspaper style, offers background information in a simple and comprehensive way organized as an inverted pyramid, with the most recent and most important information given first. The other is a feature biography, which is more like a magazine story or personality profile.

Whereas biographies are written on people, backgrounders, while similar in form to biographies, are written on companies, products, and places. Obituaries, frequently called obits, are essentially bios, with the lead offering details about the person's date and cause of death.

Biographies and backgrounders are often accompanied by fact sheets that simplify complicated information by breaking it down into various categories. Histories of events, products, or companies are often presented in time lines, which are chronological lists of information.

A company or organization's public relations writer typically writes a news release for every new employee or promotion to a level that would interest the industry's trade media (as discussed in Chapter Two). Thereafter, the press announcement is kept on file to provide to journalists and others as needed. When someone is promoted, the previous press announcement can be quickly rewritten to reflect the upgraded title and job duties while the background and work history stays the same. Media releases are usually reconfigured into bios, or biographies for only the most senior executives.

It is now customary, particularly for companies with publicly traded stock, to post the biographies of senior management and boards of directors on the company Web site. Typically these biographies are posted under headings such as "About Us" or "Our Company" or "Corporate." Companies often avoid posting biographies of second-line and less senior management as an impediment to personnel raids by competitors and headhunters.

This chapter discusses the creation and structure of news and feature bios, obits, backgrounders, fact sheets, time lines, and bibliographies.

Biographies

Writing an effective bio has ten steps:

1. Work from a sensibly constructed outline.
2. Command authority with the lead.
3. Clarify, simplify, and condense.
4. Vary language and sentence structure.
5. Connect thoughts.
6. Attribute quotations.
7. Back up all your claims.
8. Use one tense.
9. Assume nothing on the part of the reader.
10. Proofread carefully.

The structure of biographies is similar to that of appointment releases, discussed in Chapter Two. Although the content of each bio will differ depending on the person it is written about, the framework for all bios is similar and generally conforms to the following outline:

- Opens by identifying the subject by name, title, and other relevant attributes
- Summarizes the scope of the person's activities

- Offers educational and professional background on the person
- Saves personal information for the end, if such data are to be included at all

Here is an example of how easily the appointment release in Chapter Two on pages 20-22 becomes a newspaper-style bio with a minor adjustment to the lead:

> Dan Henson, 44, chief marketing officer of General Electric reporting directly to GE Chairman & CEO Jeff Immelt, is responsible for customer satisfaction and enhancing the capabilities of GE's 45,000+ sales and marketing professionals. Henson's goal is to drive sales and marketing excellence, sales force effectiveness, enterprise accounts, strategic marketing, advertising, branding and communications.

The person's age and other personal details are optional.

Feature bios are written in a more relaxed style and read more like a magazine story, with additional elements of human interest, usually delivered through quotations from the subjects themselves, as in this one from www.Samata.com:

> "I remember being embarrassed, thinking I couldn't possibly do those strange positions the right way," says Dr. Larry Payne, Ph.D., founding director of the new yoga certification program at Loyola Marymount University in Los Angeles. "My muscles were tight and I was wired from the stress of my job. Then a dear friend insisted I go to a yoga class, he virtually dragged me there!" Larry's description of his first yoga experience sounds unlikely for a man later named "one of America's most respected yoga teachers" by the *Los Angeles Times*.
>
> Living a high-stress life as an advertising executive in Los Angeles in the late 1970s began to take a serious toll on Larry's health. "Eventually I developed

high blood pressure and a serious back problem," says Larry. Over the next two years, orthopedic specialists, physical therapists, and prescription drugs failed to bring him relief. It wasn't until that first yoga class that Larry felt freedom from the pain, if only for a few hours. "It was a life-changing experience, and I was eager to share it with the people around me." And that's just what he did.

Larry is now the founding president of the International Association of Yoga Therapists and founder of the corporate yoga program at the J. Paul Getty Museum. He is also cofounder of the yoga curriculum at The UCLA School of Medicine.

But first, he had to learn. In 1980, Larry's initial step on his new path was to attend a retreat run by the late Dr. Evarts Loomis, one of America's founding fathers of holistic medicine. Larry later embarked on a year-long world tour—a sabbatical that spanned eleven countries—to immerse himself in the philosophy and techniques of yoga. Larry's experiences in India became pivotal. Says Larry: "There I trained as a yoga teacher and had the fortune to study with many of India's foremost yoga masters, including my teacher of twenty years, T.K.V. Desikachar."

In 1981, Larry returned to Los Angeles fully certified and cast off his life as an advertising executive to become a full-time yoga teacher. In that same year, Larry founded the Samata Yoga Center—Samata meaning perfect balance or equipoise in Sankrit.

Larry earned a master's degree and then a doctorate in fitness education, with an emphasis in Hatha Yoga, from Pacific Western University. With a background in psychology, he also completed graduate work in physical therapy at Cal State University at Long Beach. Now an internationally respected yoga teacher and back pain specialist, Larry has helped thousands of people recover from chronic back pain and other debilitating conditions.

Taking his message of the healing powers of yoga to a broad audience, Larry became the first yoga representative ever invited to attend the World Economic Forum in Davos, Switzerland, where in 2000 he introduced world leaders to the benefits of yoga.

His pioneering efforts have been well recognized throughout the world. Larry received Outstanding Achievement Awards for yoga in Europe and the United States and the Golden Lotus Award from South America.

He is the coauthor of *Yoga Rx* (Broadway Books), *Yoga for Dummies* (John Wiley & Sons), and *The Business of Teaching Yoga* (Samata International). Most recently, Larry released six instructional DVDs as part of the Yoga Therapy Rx series with a focus on a healthy back and immune system.

Larry resides in Los Angeles, California, and practices in Marina del Rey and Malibu and sums up his approach as "no pain, all gain!"

This feature bio contains all the information on the subject's history, but adds another dimension by way of his own reflections, including an opening comment.

Obituaries

An obituary is the same as a biography, except that the lead of the obit offers details about the date and, usually, cause of the person's death.

A bio can easily be converted into an obit by changing the lead to include details of the person's death and adding appropriate quotations, as in this excerpt from the Discovery Channel's official obituary for Steve Irwin:

Discovery Communications is deeply saddened by the tragic and sudden loss of Steve Irwin, the Crocodile

Hunter. Steve was beloved by millions of fans and animal lovers around the world and was one of our planet's most passionate conservationists. He has graced *Animal Planet*'s air since October 1996 and was essential in building *Animal Planet* into a global brand.

Steve was killed during a filming expedition for *Animal Planet* on the Great Barrier Reef. While we are still collecting specific details, it appears that this was a rare accident in which Steve swam over a stingray and was stung by its barb in his chest. A doctor on board *Croc One,* Steve's research vessel, was unable to resuscitate Steve, and by the time a rescue helicopter reached him, he had died.

DCI Founder and Chairman, John Hendricks said, "Steve was a larger than life force. He brought joy and learning about the natural world to millions and millions of people across the globe. He was a true friend to all of us at Discovery Communications. We extend our thoughts and prayers to Terri, Bindi and Bob Irwin as well as to the incredible staff and many friends Steve leaves behind."

This company-issued obituary press release includes quotes from other top executives and details of the company's plans for tributes to Irwin. Then the obituary presents details about Irwin's life and background that are typically found in company biographies.

A recent *New York Times Book Review* of *The Dead Beat* by Marilyn Johnson summarizes the newspaper obituary form:

A tombstone is the conventional first-sentence appositive sandwiched between the name of the deceased and the declaration of death. It is followed by what she calls the bad news (how it happened), the song and dance (the highlight or turning point of the person's life), the reverse shift (where the deceased came from), the desperate chronology (a recitation of events in the subject's life), a friar or two (colorful quotes) and finally the lifeboat (a list of survivors) [Stern and Stern, 2006].

This is another way of saying that very little adaptation is needed to turn a corporate-style bio into an obituary suitable for the business press. The facts of the person's work history are already included in reverse chronological order in a biography ("the desperate chronology"). The quotations from superiors about the person's specific abilities can be put in the past tense ("a friar or two"). With a little research or some tactful questions posed to someone in the grieving family, personal information that sometimes forms the last paragraph of the bio can be adapted to the "lifeboat" list of survivors. In most cases, close colleagues and family members will be very cooperative with the public relations writer's efforts to turn an existing bio into an obituary for timely release to the media.

Backgrounders

Backgrounders are written on inanimate subjects, places, and products. Here is an example of a corporate backgrounder on Steelcase, an office furniture manufacturer, used with permission from its Web site (http://www.steelcase.com):

The Steelcase Story

Who is Steelcase?

... a company dedicated to helping people work more effectively while helping organizations use space more efficiently.

Whatever you need to accomplish, Steelcase can provide you with the environment and the tools to do it better, faster and more effectively. That's because we're passionate about unlocking the potential of people at work. It's the fundamental principle on which our company was founded in 1912 and it remains our single-minded focus in the 21st century.

We make it our business to study how people work, to fully understand the ever-changing needs of individuals, teams and organizations all around the world. Then we take our knowledge, couple it with products and services inspired by what we've learned about the workplace, and create solutions that help people have a better day at work.

... a company with a rich heritage

Steelcase began in 1912 as The Metal Office Furniture Company in Grand Rapids, Michigan. We received our first patent in 1914 for a steel wastebasket—a major innovation at a time when straw wastebaskets were a major office fire hazard. That led to metal desks, and we've led the way with product and service innovations ever since. Today, our portfolio of solutions addresses the three core elements of an office environment: interior architecture, furniture and technology. We changed our name to Steelcase in 1954 and became a publicly held company in 1998.

For more about our history, see our milestones [a time line that is part of the backgrounder].

Steelcase was founded by people with a strong commitment to integrity and doing the right thing for their customers, employees, business partners, associates and neighbors. Their principles became the foundation of our company, passed on from decade to decade. Living our core values is essential to our identity, reputation and success today, just as it was in the past.

At Steelcase, we:

• Act with integrity
• Tell the truth
• Keep commitments

- Treat people with dignity and respect
- Promote positive relationships
- Protect the environment
- Excel

... a company with a global reach

Although we are still headquartered in Grand Rapids, Steelcase today is an international company with approximately 13,000 employees worldwide, manufacturing facilities in over 30 locations and more than 800 dealer locations around the world.

For a more detailed discussion of the Steelcase family, view our list of companies. Or see some of our key buildings.

This backgrounder succeeds for several reasons. It condenses lots of notable information into a concise essay, and it offers the information simply, clearly, and painlessly. Let's examine each paragraph separately.

Paragraph 1: The big picture. The lead defines the subject of the bio right away (Steelcase) and makes an important statement ("dedicated to helping people work more effectively while helping organizations use space more efficiently").

Paragraph 2: Summary of scope and philosophy. The second paragraph describes the company's priorities, research, and development.

Paragraph 3: Background. The third paragraph explains the process the company goes through in creating its products.

Paragraph 4: History. The fourth paragraph summarizes the company's history, followed by a reference to another Web page containing a more complete history, which is formatted as a time line. (Titled "Milestones," this time line is discussed later in this chapter.)

Paragraphs 5 and 6: Further details. These paragraphs discuss the company philosophy, its impact on various constituents, and the provisions of the company's pledge of integrity.

Paragraph 7: Conclusion. The backgrounder ends with the "boilerplate," the standard, company-approved summary that explains some basics about the company, such as where its U.S. offices and factories are located.

This particular backgrounder uses an unusual literary device not often found in corporate writing: a recurring phrase and variation to highlight the outline of the backgrounder and promote a sense of connection: "... a company dedicated to helping..." and "... a company with a rich heritage," and, toward the end, "... a company with a global reach."

A reporter doing a deadline story about a company does not have time to wade through eight or nine pages of material. This backgrounder works because it offers only the most important information and does so concisely.

Notice that the language and sentence structure are varied, each sentence is a complete thought, and all sentences and paragraphs are logically connected to the ones preceding and following them. The writer does not assume that the reader already knows anything about the company. Although this piece uses both the present and past tenses, it reserves the past tense strictly for historical events. When it writes about the present time and generalizes about the company's philosophy, it sticks to the present tense.

In public relations, you are often in the storytelling business. All good stories have beginnings, middles, and ends, and all are interesting as in the example of this Steelcase backgrounder. By the time you are ready to write, you should always know much more about your client than you'll be able to fit into the bio. Your job as a public relations writer is to learn everything you can about your client and then extract the most useful and important details to create a brief, coherent story.

If you consistently provide bios that are clear, concise, interesting, and truthful, journalists, investors, and other readers will come to trust and use the research and background information you provide.

Writing the Bio

Outline

All good writing starts with a good outline. It doesn't have to be detailed, but it should be logical and complete. An outline is a map showing exactly where you are going and how you will get there. No writer, no matter how accomplished, should skip this all-important first stage.

Command Authority with the Lead

If you are going to get and keep your reader's attention, you must summarize the whole story with impact and authority in the first sentence and paragraph. The reader will know immediately from the lead whether the writer is in full control, has the facts, has a realistic perspective, and will make the reading experience worthwhile.

To write the lead, try pushing all your notes and written material aside. Step back from the details and ask yourself, "What does all this add up to? What is the larger meaning of this story? Is there one stunning fact that stands out beyond all the others—and does the fact relate to everything else in this story?"

You might also ask yourself, "How would I tell this to a friend, conversationally?" In other words, how would you generalize about the topic? That may help you say it more simply. A good lead captures the essence of the biography without saying it in specific details.

Clarify, Simplify, Condense

Your job is to express ideas and information in the clearest and most logical way, with economy of language. Take the complex, and make it simple. The reader's reaction to confusion is always the same: boredom. Bore or confuse your readers, and you lose them. Be precise in choosing every word. Make sure the words you use mean exactly what you need to say—not almost, not overstated or understated. Also, make sure that each word and each sentence advances your story. It should not repeat information or just take up space. If a message can be communicated through an executive's quotation, let the quotation say it, without using the information again in the text. That will help the story tell itself. Use examples whenever possible. Use simple, declarative sentences.

Vary Language and Sentence Structure

One of the most common mistakes beginning writers make is that they don't vary their language and sentence structure enough, which makes their copy monotonous. Notice if every sentence you write is in the order of noun, verb; noun, verb; noun, verb. That comes out sounding like "Dick runs fast. Jane runs faster." A corporate example is, "John Doe was appointed president of the St. Louis Chamber of Commerce in 2006. He had served as vice president for five years previously. Doe is from Missouri." Boring, right? Here's a better way to condense that information and vary the language and sentence structure: "A native of Missouri, John Doe served as vice president of the St. Louis Chamber of Commerce for five years, until his appointment as president, in 2006."

When you are writing at length about one subject, find a variety of words to identify it. For example, if you are working on a bio of a novelist, you may want to refer to that person occasionally as a *writer* or an *author*. You do not want to use *novelist* six times in the same paragraph, page, or story. Reading your copy aloud and listening to your words may help you identify repetitions and awkward phrases. Rewrite accordingly. Do not, however, force the use of synonyms at the expense of accuracy. For example, don't confuse *profits* with *funds* or substitute *revenues* for *earnings*. (A thesaurus can be a dangerous tool; use it with discretion.)

Connect Thoughts

Make sure that each sentence is connected to the one before and the one after and that each paragraph flows logically from the one it succeeds. Transitions can come in many forms, such as comparisons, contrasts, analogies, or just the natural sequence of information. But information should never be introduced out of context.

Attribute Quotations

When you quote someone directly, attribute the quotation. Even if your biography covers only one person and your subject is the only person quoted throughout, you still must let the reader know who is speaking. Break quotes in natural places, not before the meaning or significance of the statement is clear. For example, "'I will be forced,' says John Doe, 'to retire at age sixty-five'" is not a good way to interrupt the quotation for attribution. Better wording is, "'I will be forced to retire at age sixty-five,' says John Doe." If you cite a quotation from a source—say, a newspaper article—always identify where and when it was published.

Failures to attribute quotations, paraphrases, and original ideas are thefts of intellectual property—plagiarism. Such thievery reflects badly on you and your client or company, and it can lead to embarrassment and various punishments for all involved.

Back Up Your Claims

When you make generalizations, substantiate them with facts. Attribute your claims to a source or a standard of measurement. For example, you can't merely say that your company is the largest. Largest according to what? Annual revenues? Number of employees? Amount of sales? Largest in the state, nation, world, or industry? Be specific in qualifying statements. A performer may be the best soprano in America, *according* to *Opera News* magazine; a cable network may be the fastest growing over the past six months as *evidenced* by A. C. Nielsen ratings; or a company may be the world's largest manufacturer of microchips, with annual sales of $35 billion.

Use One Tense

Beginning writers often switch haphazardly between present and past tense. Choose one tense, and try to remain in that tense throughout. Whenever possible, write in the present tense.

Assume Nothing

Do not assume your reader knows what you are writing about or what you are trying to say. You can never be sure your writing is clear until another person has read your copy and has no questions about anything you've written. Identify all names, even if they are famous (for example, *actress* Gwyneth Paltrow, *comedian* Jon Stewart). Also, define any technical terms you use. Clue readers in on all references.

By the time you write a biography or obit or backgrounder, you will know the subject intimately, but your reader will not. You must bring the story to the reader quickly, simply, and in a lively manner.

Proofread Carefully

Careful proofreading of all public relations writing is essential. Double-check the spelling of all names and the accuracy of dates and facts. Do not rely solely on computer spell-check programs, because they do not flag a correctly spelled word that is wrong in the context of the sentence, such as an incorrect verb tense, subject-verb agreement, or homonym.

Study and refer often to Appendix B in this book, a grammar reference, until you are certain you know the difference between frequently misused and often confused words. Nothing undercuts your authority faster than referring to Superman (the Man of

Steel) as the "Man of Steal." Such newsroom howlers also undercut the reputation of the public relations profession as a whole (not as a "hole"). So learn the difference between sound-alike terms, and never rely on a spell-check program for proofreading. Read and reread your copy word by word before printing it or clicking Send.

Fact Sheets

Fact sheets are a marvelous way to break down complicated information into easily grasped, bite-size pieces so that reporters and editors can easily find specific information that will be useful to them.

Here is a fact sheet on the Web site of SmartDraw.com, a software company:

SmartDraw.com Corporate Fact Sheet

Company: SmartDraw.com

Founded: 1994

Headquarters: San Diego, CA

Corp. Structure: Privately held by founders and employees. Financially self-sustaining and profitable since inception.

Statistics: SmartDraw.com websites are in the top 0.1% of the most frequently visited websites on the Internet. Each month, our websites receive 2 million visitors who download more than 300,000 software trials. More than 70% of customers buy their Smart-Draw.com products online.

Mission: To provide easy-to-use business graphics software.

History: In 1994, CEO/programmer Paul Stannard founded SmartDraw.com to sell his new diagramming software over the Internet. He received his first order less than 12 hours after opening for business. On the strength of the product, with no investors, no debt, and no outside funding, the company grew rapidly to become the Internet's #1 source of business diagramming software.

The company continues to explore new ways to provide innovative software over the Internet for users in all corners of the globe.

Products: SmartDraw
SmartDraw Legal Solution

Market: Anyone who needs to draw a diagram or manage digital images. More than half of Fortune 500 companies use SmartDraw.com products.

Major Customers: AMC Inc., BBC Scotland, Butler Memorial Hospital, California Institute of Technology, Carnegie Museum of Art, Coca-Cola Beverages, Coldwater Creek Inc., Colorado Department of Education, Cook County Public Defenders Office, Florida Department of Agriculture, Hewlett-Packard, Kent State University, Lockheed Martin, Los Angeles Community College District, Missouri Gaming Commission, New York State Department of Corrections, Nike, Nortech International, Phillips 66, Raytheon Company, Texas Instruments, Trek Bicycle, TRW, U.S. Bureau of Census, U.S. National Park Service, U.S. Coast Guard, Virginia Department of Transportation.

Awards: Technology Fast 50, 2004, Deloitte & Touche Technology Fast 50, 2003, Deloitte & Touche Inc 500, 2002, *Inc Magazine* Technology Fast 50, 2002, Deloitte & Touche Best Business Program, 2002 SIAF People's Choice Award, 2001, SIAF/CNET "Most Votes" Smart Choice Award, 2001, *Smart Computing Magazine* Technology Fast 50, 2001, Deloitte & Touche Best Business Program, 2000, *PC Magazine*/SIAF Best Business Program, 1997, Shareware Industry Awards

Best Business Program, 1996, *PC Magazine*/SIAF Best
Graphics Program, 1995, Shareware Industry Awards.

Private companies such as SmartDraw are under no obligation
to disclose their financials; public companies with stockholders
are likely to be more specific about their numbers, since the
figures are already made available to the public in quarterly earnings announcements and Securities and Exchange Commission
filings. A fact sheet on Valero Energy's Web site, for example,
includes Annual Revenues; Total Assets; Number of Employees;
Number of Retail Sites; Number of Wholesale Markets; and
Products.

The categories you choose for your subheadings on fact
sheets depend on the subject matter and target audience. A U.S.
Department of Agriculture fact sheet on farming in Alaska offers
information in the following categories:

- Population
- Income
- Education
- Employment
- Farm Characteristics
- Farm Financial Indicators
- Top 5 Commodities
- Top 5 Agriculture Exports
- Top 5 Counties in Agricultural Sales

Time Lines

When a chronology of developments or events is useful information, it is usually presented in a time line. The Steelcase Web
site features two distinct time lines, each divided by decade. The
first, labeled "Milestones," is a capsule history that focuses strictly
on business developments, beginning with some amusing antique

pictures of the founders and early twentieth-century products. The second Steelcase time line, titled "Timeline of Achievements," focuses on the company's record of social responsibility and public recognition. The section for 2006, through June, reads:

2006—Michigan Department of Environmental Quality 2006 Neighborhood Environmental Partners Gold Award—This award recognizes the company's efforts to initiate local projects that work towards raising environmental awareness and the quality of life within Michigan communities.

Habitat for Humanity of Kent County Corporate Donor of the Year Award—Steelcase recognized for project participation, volunteer effort, financial and materials support for Habitat projects, including making factory space available to build frames for housing in New Orleans.

Riverkeeper Annual Benefit Honors Steelcase— Steelcase was recognized for its efforts to preserve the environment and the country's waterways. Steelcase was the only company honored at the event this year.

Steelcase Joins EPA's Climate Leaders Program—By participating in this voluntary industry-government partnership aimed at developing long-term, comprehensive corporate climate change strategies, Steelcase has pledged to continue reducing its corporate-wide greenhouse gas (GHG) emissions.

Both of the Steelcase time lines organize and shape numerous facts about the manufacturing of everyday products, in this instance, office furniture, in a way that is readable and interesting. The time lines convey the image of a long-established company that has moved forward with the times, while safeguarding the environment and contributing to the community.

Bibliographies

It can sometimes be useful to include a bibliography with a bio or backgrounder, offering a list of articles that have been published by or about the subject. Such a reference list saves the reporter a lot of time by allowing quick retrieval of a needed article. Bibliographies are customarily included in media kits in the arts. Among other subheadings, they may include works written by authors or created by artists; lectures and participation in panel discussions; gallery exhibitions and museum shows of artists; and reviews of plays, dance pieces, or exhibitions.

Here are selections from a bibliography from an online media kit for comic book artist and academic A. David Lewis, which are listed alphabetically under the subheadings Articles, Essays and Presentations:

Comic Book Scriptwriting (XWRI 104-01) — Georgetown University SCS course, Summer 2004.

Ever-Ending Battle symposium — International Journal of Comic Art vol. 8, issue 1, Spring 2006.

"Fingeroth, Lewis, and Superman on the Couch" — Comicon.com's The PULSE feature link.

"Four Bearers: On the 40th Anniversary of the Fantastic Four" — Comic-Con International: San Diego 2001 Souvenir Book.

"Keys to the Kingdom" — Popular Culture Association Annual Conference, Spring 2002 link.

"Kingdom Code" — Popular Culture Association Annual Conference, Spring 2001.

"Kingdom Code" — International Journal of Comic Art vol. 4, issue 1, Spring 2002. [http://captionbox. net/media.htm].

Links take the reader or reporter to the full text of the items listed, allowing for efficient background reading and research.

Chapter Recap

Writing a biography or backgrounder has ten steps:

1. Work from a sensibly constructed outline.
2. Command authority with the lead.
3. Clarify, simplify, and condense.
4. Vary language and sentence structure.
5. Connect thoughts.
6. Attribute quotations.
7. Back up all your claims.
8. Use one tense.
9. Assume nothing on the part of the reader.
10. Proofread carefully.

Fact sheets organize complex information by category, time lines organize developments and events chronologically, and bibliographies organize publications or sources alphabetically or chronologically.

5

SPEECH WRITING

From Your Pen to Their Lips

In an age dominated by digital communications, public speaking remains a powerful tool to inform or persuade a group of people. It is an effective way to gain recognition and show leadership in one's company, community, or profession. In fact, public speeches often help set policy and act as a catalyst for action.

Good speeches are provocative and memorable; they should also be easily understood and moving. The best speeches gain a life well beyond their moment of delivery by influencing the audience, whether their purpose is to inspire, motivate, or encourage thought.

Each speech should fit the personality of the speaker, the occasion of the speech, and the composition of the audience. A speech has to give the audience confidence in the speaker. A speech allows the speaker to be accessible and make an emotional connection with the audience; it is a chance to be more than just a corporate officer or political figurehead.

Every day, hundreds of speeches are given at a wide variety of events—from groundbreaking ceremonies and Wall Street analyst meetings to award dinners, congressional sessions, and graduations. Public speaking is certainly not confined to politicians. Executives are also frequently called on to make speeches that offer prime opportunities for positioning them and their company as leaders in the industry or the community. Usually the public relations writer drafts the text of a speech.

In the United States, several thousand corporate speech writers earn high on the pay scale for public relations employees.

Very often, however, public relations generalists are also asked to write speeches. Whether it is one's exclusive specialty or only an occasional assignment, speech writing usually involves the writer with top management, major policy, and behind-the-scenes decisions. In addition to in-depth research, speech writing can require traveling to investigate or report on a subject or to be on the scene where the speech will be delivered in case there are last-minute changes.

Most executives are not professionally trained public speakers, and for some, the very mention of a speech makes them nervous. Many speechwriters have their own share of anxiety when it comes to preparing the speech. The better the preparation, however, the less hazardous the whole process will be for the writer and the speaker alike.

Ad-libbing doesn't work. Each year during the Academy Awards ceremony, we see seasoned actors go to pieces and stumble through acceptance speeches that are not scripted for them. The old show business saying, "If it ain't on the page, it ain't on the stage," summarizes the need for ample research, preparation, and rehearsal as safeguards to successful speeches.

Speech writing is a radical departure from other forms of writing. Many of the greatest literary treasures would make terrible speeches if they were read aloud. They may *read* well, but they don't *hear* well. In speech writing, the rules of written English must be replaced with those of conversational English. Writing for a listener is entirely different from writing for a reader, but a good writer can do both:

- Just as every story pitch is customized to fit the style, format, and focus of the media outlet you're soliciting, so too is each speech uniquely tailored to suit the speaker, occasion, and audience. That means there is no precise formula for writing speeches. The key steps speechwriters can take to ensure a coherent, appropriate script are:

- Begin the project by interviewing the speaker for ideas and speaking style.
- Learn about the place of delivery and the composition of the audience.
- Focus on a single theme.
- Obtain the speaker's approval on the theme and the outline before writing the speech.
- Write for the human voice and the vocal rhythms of the speaker.
- Think of pleasing the audience, not just the speaker.
- Keep in mind any controversy surrounding the speaker.
- Remember the importance of rehearsal, and participate in the teleprompter rehearsal.
- Draft answers to anticipated questions, another form of the Q&A for internal use only.
- Hear the speech delivered.
- Research ways to recycle the speech so that it reaches a wider audience than those in attendance.

In the following section, we'll look at these eleven general steps to approaching, preparing, and following through with a speech. In the second part of this chapter, we'll examine the technical guidelines for writing the spoken word.

Speech Writing I: Eleven Steps

Step 1: Interview the Speaker

Before you do anything else, talk to the person for whom you're writing the speech. Put yourself in a reporter's role. Take notes, and tape-record the session. The more you learn at the first meeting, the less rethinking and rewriting you'll have to do later. Nevertheless, even the most experienced writers rewrite their speeches. Three to six drafts are not unusual, and often many more are required as the speaker, as well as colleagues and trusted consultants, add, refine, delete, and reshuffle passages, anecdotes, and phrases.

Notice how the speaker speaks. What is the person's style and manner? Is he or she precise, measured, and soft-spoken? Aggressive and harsh? Choppy or long-winded? What are the speaker's rhythms, and where is the emphasis? What kind of language choices are made: erudite or slang? Your script must follow the speaker's natural pattern of voice and expression. If you tape-record your conversation, you can replay the tape later, carefully analyze the answers to these questions, and take notes on other details during the interview.

Following are some important areas to cover in the interview with your speaker.

Discuss the Audience. Who will attend the speech? Will it be a trade group or the general public? How much background will you need to provide? Will there be company employees only, or will they bring their spouses? The nature of the occasion will dictate the tone of the speech. A U.S. Senate hearing is not a Friars Club roast. A meeting of the Securities and Exchange Commission is quite different from a meeting of the Screen Actors Guild. Think about your audience members—their ages, backgrounds, reference points, interests, dispositions, and attitudes.

Discuss Topics. Ask the speaker what topics might work for the speech. Have the speaker define the important issues facing the industry at the moment. Perhaps a particular news item or article stands out, suggesting an area of concern. Find out personal convictions and perhaps what really bothers the speaker. Don't panic if you both draw blanks. You may have to do more thinking about a topic and some additional homework before you're even ready to suggest an idea.

Discuss Attitude. How does your speaker feel about giving the speech? Is it a treat or a chore? What happened the last time he or she gave a speech? How did the speech go over, and how did the speaker feel about it afterward? If the speech was a success, ask where you can find a copy, so you have a model of what this speaker feels comfortable with.

Discuss Length. Determine how long the speech should be. Rarely can any speaker hold the attention of an audience for more than twenty or twenty-five minutes. In speech writing, less is more. "The Gettysburg Address" is a good historical example: Abraham Lincoln delivered it in three minutes. Edward Everett, his predecessor on the platform, spoke for two and a half hours. Which speech is remembered? Always know the time limit before you start researching and writing the speech. When you begin to write, keep this guide in mind: on average, six double-spaced pages with ample margins will take about ten minutes to say; three pages, about five minutes; and so forth.

Step 2: Interview the Sponsor

Talk with the people sponsoring the event at which your speaker will appear. Learn every detail: What time of the day or night will the speech be given? Will there be other speeches, and if so, by whom and on what topics? Will any other activity be competing with the speech? What will the audience be doing during the speech: Standing or sitting? Eating dinner? Having drinks? Studying printed material? Listening to a translation? What will the audience have been doing before the speech, and what will the audience be doing after it? What is the context of the occasion? Is it a one-time affair or a regular event? Attendees at regularly repeated events develop expectations, so you might ask the sponsor for samples of prior, successful speeches.

Whenever possible, visit or view the site where the speech will be given. Rhetoric that might work well in a large auditorium or amphitheater could be disastrous in an intimate, twenty-person conference room. As a speechwriter, you'll need to write differently for audiences that are captive, as opposed to audiences that are free to come and go.

Step 3: Choose the Topic

When you emerge from the first meeting with your speaker without a decision on what the topic of the speech will be (which happens frequently), it is up to you to suggest a few possible subjects. At this point, the speechwriter goes from being an interpreter and translator to being a creator of ideas.

Where Do You Get Ideas for a Speech? In developing ideas for speeches, it helps to know a little bit about a lot of things. Do a lot of reading, and try to keep up with everything that's happening. Taking a definitive stand on a current controversy or looking at an old or new issue from a unique, or very personal, point of view are ways to turn an ordinary speaking occasion into a memorable event for the audience and the speaker.

Not all speeches invite unlimited possibilities for topics. There will be occasions that dictate what is appropriate to talk about. For example, if the occasion is the opening of a new factory, it would be logical to comment on what the new facility means to the company and the community. Or if an executive is unveiling a new product, it would be appropriate to talk about it.

Many occasions offer the opportunity for the speaker to demonstrate industry or community leadership, perhaps influencing opinions and opinion makers without ever mentioning the speaker's corporation. Such was the case with the University of Virginia's School of Law commencement address given by Bob Wright, chairman and CEO of NBC and vice chairman and executive officer of General Electric on May 19, 2002. Just five months after Enron declared bankruptcy on December 3, 2001, Wright's address, "Enron and the Inflexible Obligations of the Legal Profession," raises ethical and moral questions that go beyond the bounds of a single corporation or profession and speak to the country's founding values:

> Where were the lawyers? Well, they were at the table—with the accountants and the executives.
>
> Where are they now? Well, they're at the table, sitting before Senate hearings and in federal courtrooms, answering questions about shredding. Shred bad term papers, credit card offers, wild frat party photographs—but *never* shred evidence.
>
> The legal issues involved here will take years to unravel. But it seems to me the ethical issues are quite clear. Two weeks ago, federal regulators released e-mails written by Enron lawyers describing business practices that while perhaps not illegal certainly raise serious ethical questions. One lawyer wrote that "Enron gets paid for moving energy to relieve congestion without actually moving any energy or relieving any congestion."
>
> The revenues Enron booked from such practices came straight out of the pockets of California consumers. This is not just, as another lawyer called it, "taking advantage of arbitrage opportunities."
>
> Where were the lawyers? Were they complicit in supporting, justifying, and condoning trading tactics that are at best unethical, and at worse, illegal? Did greed trump their sense of fairness and justice? [Wright, 2002a]

The speech struck a chord that was replayed frequently as the perpetrators of corporate fraud at the turn of the new century were forced to defend their actions to the justice system.

Wright's address was influential beyond the law school graduates and their families who heard it in Charlottesville that day.

The address received press coverage and was reprinted in the University of Virginia alumni magazine and in *Vital Speeches of the Day*. Without Wright ever mentioning the names of his company, NBC, or its corporate parent, GE, he positioned them as ethical and upstanding, as leaders in the moral arena and as the antithesis of Enron.

How Many Ideas Can Fit Comfortably in a Speech? Like an essay, a speech should focus on one main idea or thesis that can be summarized in one or two sentences. The anecdotes, examples, statistics, and other details that make up the body of the address should illuminate and support the main theme and serve to make it understandable and memorable to the various constituencies in the audience.

When Do You Proceed with Research and Outlining? Your interview of the speaker and the event sponsor, as well as your general knowledge of current events and company and industry issues, should suggest a number of ideas to choose from. Present your two or three best ideas to the speaker, asking that he or she make the final choice. Never proceed to the outline stage without an explicit approval.

Be aware that some executives discover what they do want to talk about only when presented with ideas that they can reject, so don't be ego invested in your own ideas.

You will know the right topic when the speaker becomes excited and starts throwing out examples, facts, figures, and anecdotes. Be ready to take notes, and the bulk of your research will be done before the meeting is over. If none of the topics sparks a fire in the speaker, say that you'll come back with some more possibilities. A speech has no chance of interesting an audience if it doesn't interest even its speaker. Such a speech would be a disaster for everyone concerned, but the one blamed will be you—the speechwriter. In contrast, if the speech is a success, the speaker will receive the kudos.

Step 4: Research and Outline

After the topic of the speech has been approved, you are ready to research the subject and outline the structure and format of the speech. Good writing is based on thorough research and a careful outline, and speech writing is no exception.

Research. Check all references and resources available to you on the subject of your speech and any subjects closely related to it. Use a library or data bank to look up articles and books that relate to the topic. Check your office files for material that might be useful, review past speeches your client may have given on any associated subjects, and talk with people in your department and industry to get their thoughts on and reactions to the topic. If the chosen topic is industry specific or company specific, you should ask for permission to interview one or two people who report directly to the speaker and are thoroughly in command of the details of the operations or process.

On subjects that are timely or controversial, information can change quickly, so make sure you are up to date. Don't make your speaker look foolish by not being current, and make certain your facts are irrefutable. Your research is not finished until you completely understand the topic and have more information and background than you'll be able to use.

Even in the research stage, the ego of the speechwriter needs to be subdued. Your goal is to write the speech that the speaker himself or herself would write—given your talent and your time. Speechwriter is no job for an egotist.

Outline. There are numerous ways to structure a speech, regardless of its content and length. The elementary three-part format of essays—introduce what you're going to say, say it, and then summarize what you've said—is a good general format for speeches. The choices within that structure are almost limitless.

Here is a sample of a basic outline for a speech a company president might give to sales representatives at an annual sales meeting:

1. Welcoming remarks
   - Cordial greetings
   - Purpose of meeting
2. Report card on company growth
   - Sales figures this year
   - Sales figures compared with those of last year
   - Goals for coming year
3. Role of sales reps in relation to employees in other departments
   - Comparative remarks
   - Achievements
   - Goals for the future
4. Conclusion
   - Challenges ahead
   - How to meet them

An outline for a speech doesn't have to be intricate, but the more detailed and well organized it is, the more helpful it will be by pointing to where and how specific ideas and information will be used.

Unlike readers, listeners cannot go back if they missed or didn't understand something. Help the listener by summing up complicated points, and make sure the meaning is crystal clear.

The listener always needs help in knowing where the speech begins, where it's going, and when it ends—and so does the writer putting it together.

Step 5: Make It Conversational, Keep It Simple, and Keep It Light

Speeches should be based on conversational language. The less formal, bloated, and academic the writing is, the better the speech will be.

There are phrases and idioms that look like slang in print but are wonderful when said aloud. For example, colloquialisms—expressions that are characteristic of familiar, informal conversation—should be used in speeches. In his Stanford University Commencement Address in May 2005, Steve Jobs, the CEO of Apple, opened in this way:

> I'm honored to be with you today for your commencement from one of the finest universities in the world. Truth be told, I never graduated from college and this is the closest I've ever gotten to a college graduation.
>
> Today I want to tell you three stories from my life. That's it. No big deal. Just three stories. The first story is about connecting the dots.

Notice that the change in the level of rhetoric from "honored" and "finest universities" to the conversational "That's it. No big deal" makes it seem as if Jobs is suddenly speaking to each graduate individually.

When writing a speech, ask yourself how the speaker would casually say this to a person sitting next to him or her on a train. That should help you express the information more conversationally in the speech.

Keep the material simple and light but not trite. Using humor and anecdotes helps keep a speech light, but beware of jokes. Most public speakers do not have the timing and delivery of stand-up comedians, and most are not natural storytellers either. But if humor can flow naturally out of the subject and is appropriate to all considerations, then it can be helpful: For example, near the beginning of his speech titled "Labor Issues Relating to the Free Trade Agreement of the Americas Symposium" at the University of Richmond on October 5, 2001, Ambassador Richard Fisher said:

> In the August 22nd edition of *The Washington Post,* there was an article by Robert Samuelson recalling Alfred Kahn. Fred Kahn was Jimmy Carter's head of voluntary price controls during that awful period in the late 1970s when inflation was raging out of control and interest rates were headed through the roof.
>
> Fred was a no nonsense guy. One day he gave what I thought was a darn good speech. He told it like it was: if we didn't get inflation under control, he said, we would tumble into "recession." Or maybe a "deep, deep depression." Well, the alarm bell went off all over the White House. Kahn was called to the President's woodshed and told in no uncertain terms to never use the word "recession" again. He never did. Instead he used the word "banana." "If we don't lick this wage-price spiral," he would say, "we are headed for a big banana."
>
> Well, to borrow from Harry Truman, in Washington, there is a lobby for almost everything. If you call someone a jackass in Washington, the jackass lobby complains. Sure enough, within five minutes of Fred Kahn's speech he received a complaint from the banana producers. So he shifted to "kumquat."
>
> Ladies and gentlemen, if what we were facing before the tragic events of September 11th was not a global recession, we were facing one of the worst "kumquats" I've seen in 30 years of business and two terms in government.

Thus, Ambassador Fisher was able to lighten a serious examination of the dismal state of the world economy in the aftermath of the September 11, 2001, terrorist attacks. His next sentence was a direct transition to the meat of the speech, "Let me give you the stark statistics," but substituting "kumquats" (the fruit with no apparent lobby) for "deep recession" at a few key points in the speech lightened the effect of the grave economic statistics he was presenting and also gave the speech a satisfying sense of organic unity.

Never resort to joke books. Humor must be organic to work. The classic, awful opening of a speech is when the speaker tells an irrelevant little joke and then says, "But seriously, folks..." Some executives resist using humor and anecdotes. They'll say, "I don't do humor; this is a *serious* speech." But you don't have to be pompous to be dignified. Being serious doesn't mean being dull. Injecting personal feelings, maybe even self-deprecating humor, is a way to attract and hold the attention of the audience.

The Lead. There are many ways to grab the attention of listeners at the start of a speech. You don't have to open with an arresting question, a compelling anecdote, or an inflammatory statement that shocks or startles—but it's not necessarily bad if you do. More often, good speeches start with a salutation, the speaker's gracious acknowledgment of where he or she is, who is being addressed, and why. For example, Paul C. Reilly (2003), chairman of the board and CEO of Korn/Ferry International, began a speech in China by saying:

> Good afternoon and thank you for having me here today. It is always a pleasure to come to Beijing, and I am particularly pleased to be addressing this group of MBA students, because you truly represent the future of Chinese business leadership.

Often a speaker will begin with an amusing, self-deprecating comment to put the audience at ease by showing that the speaker doesn't take himself or herself too seriously. For example, when

Bob Wright (2002b) of NBC spoke on "Restoring Trust: The Work of America," he began:

> Thanks, Charlie [Menges]. It's a pleasure to be here to speak to the Legatus organization and its guests. But first, you can't invite a television executive anywhere without having to watch a videotape. I brought a short one that relates to my theme today.

In addition to humor, a short videotape or a powerful (and relevant) visual image on a slide can also be effective ways to capture the audience's attention. (See Chapter Six.)

A more straightforward approach can be used as well, diving right into the subject, as illustrated by Reed Bolton Byrum then president and CEO of the Public Relations Society of America, who began a speech to his organization's Western District Conference in March 2003 like this: "There is a crying need for strategic leadership in the communications industry. It should be at the top of the agenda of every serious professional and every corporation and institution."

We advise not using famous quotations, unless they can be seamlessly integrated into the speech, as demonstrated by the moving conclusion to Bob Wright's speech to high-level Catholic business executives, which quotes both the Bible and the pope:

> In 1981, Pope John Paul II issued his encyclical on the subject of human work. This document presents the position of the Church on work in a way that sheds light, I think, on our current situation.
>
> In the Book of Genesis, Adam and Eve are told by God: "Be fruitful and multiply, and fill the earth and subdue it."
>
> To the Pope, the expression "subdue the earth" has a particular meaning. It refers to the way each and every human being takes part in the giant, ongoing process whereby man uses all the resources of the earth to

make things for human use: to grow food, to build housing, to invent new CAT scans, to design improved jet engines, and even to create TV shows—although the Pope doesn't mention NBC specifically.

His point is that "subduing the earth" is a synonym for human work, which is not only fundamentally creative and ethical—but is mandated by God. We can translate those lines from Genesis like this: "Be fruitful and multiply... and get to work."

Indeed, the Pope goes further. In the eyes of the Church, the act of work, of contributing your talents to a business, of making things of value, is analogous to the very first act of creation—God's creation of the world.

In other words, when we work, from a theological perspective, we are reflecting the very action of the Creator of the universe. As the Pope writes, "Man's work is a participation in God's activity."

This is worth remembering as we go about our daily lives. Honest and ethical work, no matter how monotonous or alienating, is dignified by God and connected to His creativity.

I think you'll agree that some types of "work" don't fall in this category: accounting fraud, for example. Or setting up sham transactions to book phantom revenue. Or manipulating markets.

Think how the state of American business would be improved if employees everywhere, from top executives to the mailroom, asked themselves: "Do my actions at work contribute to the creation of value? Does my work reflect the creativity and integrity of God himself? Or is it a sham transaction?"

In the Book of Genesis, each day of creation ends with the words: "And God saw that it was good."

> My prayer is that one day soon we'll be able to look across corporate America, look at every industry and every company and every boardroom, and be able to say these words as well. Because—fundamentally, essentially, theologically—the work of America is good [Wright, 2002b].

So although the general rule should be to avoid using quotations, a more precise rule might be: use a quotation only when you can weave it into the fabric of the speech so that the quotation enhances the meaning and the emotion you want your speech to convey.

Conclusion. The end of a speech must be self-evident. The audience needs cues that it's almost over and the speaker expects applause. There are numerous ways to signal the end of a speech. The speaker can say, "Before I leave you this evening, I'd like to review the main point..., " or "To conclude, I'd like to summarize...," or "I know you're eager to hear the other guest speakers—and so am I—but before I finish, I'd like to say..."

The best speeches have a unifying theme throughout, and the end of a speech should have a natural tie to the beginning. The main points should be summarized at the end of the speech.

Whenever possible, leave an audience with an optimistic feeling. Point to what can be achieved, what challenges lie ahead, and what rewards will ensue. Steve Jobs's speech both signals the end and offers a sense of optimism:

> Stewart [Brand] and his team put out several issues of *The Whole Earth Catalogue,* and then when it had run its course, they put out a final issue.

> It was the mid-Seventies and I was your age. On the back cover of their final issue was a photograph of an early morning country road, the kind you might find yourself hitchhiking on if you were so adventurous. Beneath were the words, "Stay hungry, stay foolish."

It was their farewell message as they signed off. "Stay hungry, stay foolish."

And I have always wished that for myself, and now, as you graduate to begin anew, I wish that for you. Stay hungry, stay foolish [Jobs, 2005].

What does the whole speech mean to the speaker? What does the speech mean to the audience? As with Jobs's speech, those answers, stated simply, are usually points you should write into the conclusion.

Step 6: Personalize the Content

It's important to please the speaker for whom you're writing, but that's not the only opinion that counts. The speechwriter has to consider the audience. Will anybody really want to hear the speech? Will anybody truly care? If you have personalized the content of the speech to the audience, the answer will be yes.

Personalizing the speech and injecting emotion into it can be challenging, especially when you're dealing with lots of plain facts. But analyzing how the information affects the people listening to it should help you personalize it. If you have a diversified audience to reach, break down how the subject affects each group that is listening.

Step 7: Confront Controversy

Whether to address controversial subjects related to a speaker will always have to be decided on a case-by-case basis. But if your speaker has been invited because of that issue, you can't possibly avoid it. Confronting controversy can be a good way to clarify misinformation, offer background perhaps not covered in the press, or disarm a hostile audience. You do not want the audience thinking about one subject while your speaker addresses another, and you never want your speaker's credibility compromised. If a contentious subject is likely to come up in a question-and-answer period later, it's better to bring up the subject first and tackle it head-on.

Step 8: Test the Speech, and Encourage Rehearsal

As soon as you've finished the first draft of the speech, read it aloud. Notice where your tongue gets twisted or you run out of breath, and rewrite accordingly. Then read it to someone else and ask to be stopped wherever the meaning isn't clear or confusion arises.

Before you show the speaker your first draft, test the speech by writing a news story based on it. If you have trouble writing even a paragraph or two, it may suggest that the speech is not very interesting and needs more work.

When the speaker is ready to review the speech, try to be there to listen. Find out what is not communicated clearly enough or where the speaker may feel uncomfortable. Also, make it your business to check any audiovisual, video, or other materials that will accompany the speech. Participate in technical rehearsals whenever possible. (See Chapter Eight.)

A speaker using a teleprompter needs enough practice that the operator learns to follow the speaker's pacing, and the speaker learns to trust that the operator will speed up and slow down as needed. The speaker—not the operator and not the machine—determines the pace.

Step 9: Draft Answers to Anticipated Questions

Help your speaker by anticipating questions and comments the speech is likely to raise. Some speeches are followed by a question-and-answer period with members of the press or the general audience, and the speaker should not be surprised or caught off guard by any of the questions. Supply related information if it is likely to be requested. When a speaker does not have specific information available on the spot, it is perfectly okay to have him or her say, "I don't have that information at the moment, but I will be happy to check on it and get back to you."

Step 10: Attend the Speech

Whenever possible, the speechwriter should be present when the speech is given. Short of that, the writer should review a video or audio recording of the speech. There is a great deal to be learned by hearing the speech delivered; it can always be better the next time around.

It is also helpful to hear people's reactions directly following the speech. Speechwriters often comment that the most valuable reviews are heard in the restrooms afterward.

Step 11: Recycle the Speech

If the press is attending the speech, it is usually a good idea to have a copy of the speech available (sometimes it is distributed before the speech is given), along with a press release summarizing the most important points.

Speeches can also be compelling content when posted on the company or organization Web site, and in fact, many organizations post actual video or audio so that the visitor can experience the speech almost as the original audience did, complete with the speaker's gestures and intonations. Consider also making speeches available online for downloading and Podcasting. The speech in written, video, or audio form can become part of the organization's online archive for future reference by both the media and others.

Some speeches announce a corporate theme that can be amplified in or adapted to other media. According to NBC Universal's head of executive communications, William Bartlett, Bob Wright's speech, "Technology and the Rule of Law in the Digital Age," delivered to the Media Institute Friends and Benefactors Awards Banquet, in Washington, D.C., on October 27, 2004, was "Bob's first major speech on the issue of IP [intellectual property] theft as it affects not just the media industry but all industries. This has been a recurrent theme for us as a company since this speech, and I work it into almost every public appearance by Bob and other top execs. A short version of this was printed in *Broadcasting & Cable*, and a revised and updated version was published a few months later in the *Notre Dame Journal of Law, Ethics & Public Policy*. [It was] also reprinted in *Vital Speeches*" (e-mail from W. Bartlett to M. Aronson, June 19, 2006). In addition to finding their way into newspaper stories, speeches can be reprinted in internal publications, excerpted in trade and consumer magazine articles, taped for radio and television uses, and submitted to newsletters on current speeches, such as *Vital Speeches of the Day*, which publishes the full text of eight to ten speeches twice a month, and *Speechwriter's Newsletter*.

Speech Writing II: Technical Guidelines

The following suggestions on format, grammar, and construction in speech writing will help speakers read the speech more effectively and listeners hear the speech more clearly:

- Never trust your speaker with an outline; write everything out, including all cues. If he or she is to hold up a plaque or point to a screen, for example, write those directions into the script, using parentheses.

- Write out dollar amounts ("twelve million dollars," not "12 million" or "12,000,000"). Don't make your speaker count zeros.

- Submit copy that is clean and double-spaced and has reasonable margins. Your speaker may want to make notes. You may wish to use a large typeface. Some speakers like to have their scripts typed in all capital letters. There is, however, a danger that punctuation can get lost.

- Underline emphasized words.

- Repeat nouns instead of using pronouns ("The school is in trouble"; "The school needs your support") to remind listeners of the subject and bring their attention back to it should their minds wander.

- Write in parallel phrases and sentences: "Being here today gives me a chance to thank you, a chance to greet you, and a chance to bring you up to date"; "This is a government of the people, by the people, for the people."

- Use simple words and simple declarative sentences. Short, crisp sentences are the most dramatic form of writing; forget big words and flowery language. Avoid tongue-twisters. Substitute common words for less used ones, for example, *especially* for *particularly* and *stubbornness* for *obstinacy*.

- Beware of homophones—words that are pronounced alike but are different in meaning, such as *pier* and *peer, sew* and *sow*. (Consult Appendix B when you have a question on usage.)

- Keep the subject and verb together. Good: "Having learned of the new schedule, John arrived at class on time." Poor: "John, having learned of the new schedule, arrived at class on time."

- Don't overload sentences with subordinate phrases and clauses. Clear, simple wording can transform lackluster speakers into attention getters.

- Be specific, use examples, don't exaggerate, and don't overdramatize. Avoid overstated rhetoric and stick to basic, clear expression.

- Beware of quotations. A common first impulse is to refer to *Bartlett's Familiar Quotations* for a famous remark on the subject of your speech, but such quotes usually do not work. When a well-known quote is appropriate and worth using, set it up correctly, like this: "As President Kennedy said in his inaugural address, and I quote, 'Ask not what your country can do for you; ask what you can do for your country.' End quote." Indicating when you are using a quotation is essential.

- Avoid plagiarism. Not fully attributing a quote to its original source is plagiarism. Plagiarism is one of the worst sins of any kind of writing and can lead to public embarrassment. There have been recent, visible examples of plagiarism in speeches. U.S. Representative James A. Gibbons, Republican of Nevada, plagiarized his February 2005 speech from one given in 2003 by Beth Chapman, Alabama's auditor (SourceWatch, n.d.). Bryan LeBeau, a dean at the University of Kansas City—Kansas City, based part of a 2003 commencement address on a decade-old speech by another academic. According to a *Columbia Daily Tribune* article, LeBeau admitted that "he failed to use the same principles of attribution in his speech that he does in his published materials" ("UMKC Dean Admits Plagiarism of Speech," 2005). Online search engines and antiplagiarism programs frequently used by colleges make plagiarism, whether premeditated or "accidental," more likely than ever before to be discovered. Punishments range from embarrassment to career suicide. Don't plagiarize.

Chapter Recap

Here again are the eleven basic steps to writing a speech that is interesting and timely and makes a useful comment on something of importance to the audience:

1. Interview the speaker.
2. Interview the sponsor.
3. Choose a topic that excites the speaker.
4. Research and outline.
5. Make it conversational, keep it simple, and keep it light.
6. Personalize the content.
7. Confront controversy.
8. Test the speech, encourage rehearsal, and participate in any teleprompter rehearsal.
9. Draft answers to anticipated questions.
10. Attend the speech.
11. Recycle the speech.

6

MULTIMEDIA AND POWERPOINT PRESENTATIONS

Many speeches today are accompanied by PowerPoint slides, photo montages, and even specially produced short films or videos. Flip charts on an easel, transparencies shown using an overhead projector, slides with graphs and pie charts, and snazzy computer-generated PowerPoint slides are tools to illustrate important points. Used correctly, these visual aids can help explain numbers, proportions, and relationships. Used incorrectly, they divert the audience's attention from the speaker, so that the speaker's voice is reduced to a voice-over or soundtrack. As a result, for many members of the audience, listening to a complex message during a multimedia presentation can be as difficult and confusing as trying to understand a disembodied voice speaking in a foreign language on the telephone. Therefore, never let technology upstage your speaker.

When you are preparing to write a multimedia presentation, you need to decide what your main goals are by asking yourself the following questions. Are you trying to:

- Illuminate?
- Convince?
- Convert?
- Celebrate?
- Entertain?
- Pass the time until dessert is served?

Having your goals clearly in mind will help you decide how much and what kind of media can be put to the most effective use in your multimedia presentation as visual aids to communication.

Illuminating Difficult Subjects

Audiovisual presentations of financial and other business material are a way of life in the corporate world. All too often, however, they are confusing, overly long, and poorly paced. Your goal as the writer and producer of a business presentation should be to put across the material as clearly and concisely as possible. Don't get carried away trying to enliven dull subject matter. Your audience will expect to be informed, not entertained, and they will be impressed by your presenter's grasp of the material, not by his or her sense of humor or showmanship.

A Few Words About Taste

Because business presentations tend to be dry and because business (especially finance) has until recent years been run almost exclusively by men, business conferences and meetings have traditionally had the tone of a men's club smoker, if not a stag party. Before you put together your first presentation for such a meeting, remember: times have changed.

Most companies now prize diversity in the workforce all the way up to the composition of the boards of directors; discrimination is illegal. Companies are now liable and can be sued for having a hostile work environment, elements of which can be ethnic and sexist jokes, personal remarks, or references to what body parts a speaker finds particularly attractive or unattractive.

Humor can be a useful tool. A little levity in the midst of a complicated presentation can be as welcome as a cold drink on a hot day. But before you insert any humor into your work, stop to ask yourself, "Is it appropriate? Is it in good taste?" And (last but not least), "Is it funny?" The downside risk, as they say in business, far outweighs the risk of being boring. (See Chapter Five, Step Five, for more on the topic of humor.)

When it comes to using humor, personal anecdotes, famous quotations, and visuals, another good rule is: when in doubt, leave them out.

A Philosophy of Slides and PowerPoint

Some people love slides. Their presentations, however brief and however seemingly simple, are awash in slides—one after the next that illustrate the most minor point or change of topic.

Slides and PowerPoint have their place. They can simplify complex material, or instantly make clear something that would take much longer to explain in words. But just as a speech should be no longer than it has to be to cover the topic, slides and PowerPoint should be used only when needed.

A Few Words About Rehearsal, Delivery Stance, and Not Insulting the Intelligence of Your Audience

Audiences want to hear the speakers, not watch them read. Speaking to an audience means maintaining a certain level of eye contact, which means that rehearsal is essential, even if the speaker is using a teleprompter. By the time your speakers deliver their presentations, they should be so familiar with them and so natural in their phrasing that audience members believe they are talking directly to each person individually.

Nothing weakens the impact of a speaker's personality and dispels the illusion of intimacy more quickly than putting the entire text of a speech on PowerPoint slides that the audience can read while the speaker speaks the text. Even worse, with the words right up there on a screen, nervous speakers, especially those who haven't practiced enough or are uncomfortable with making eye contact with the audience, often turn toward the screen, and therefore turn their back on the audience, and read the speech aloud.

People are not interested in watching someone stand sideways looking at and reading from the screen. Besides, almost everyone in the audience will be able to read the text on the screen faster than the speaker can read it aloud to them. The audience will always beat the speaker to the point and be bored by the time the speaker catches up.

You might ask, "What about putting just the outline on the PowerPoint slides?" Certainly PowerPoint, which users can easily learn in a few minutes, encourages an outline format. Most PowerPoint users, however, simply break sentences into phrases and make each phrase a bullet point. Once again the audience members see almost exactly what the speaker is saying and think to themselves: *Why is the speaker droning on? Doesn't he [or she] think we're smart enough to read?*

A Few Words about TMI and TMI (Too Much Information and Too Many Inputs)

PowerPoint slides are so easy to make—just type and click—that many writers make too many of them and load them with too much information for audience members to absorb in the time that they're on the screen. But the most damaging problem with PowerPoint presentations is that people really cannot pay attention to two things at once. They cannot watch the speaker closely to absorb meaning and nuance and concurrently read words projected on a screen nearby; they cannot extract the meaning from seeing a bar graph while simultaneously listening to a speaker's amusing anecdote; and they cannot understand one set of words being spoken and at the same time comprehend a different set of words appearing on a screen.

Despite the percentage of people who pride themselves on multitasking, most people cannot do two intellectual tasks well at the same time. The upshot is that most PowerPoint presentations and many other sorts of multimedia are visual distractions, not visual aids. They put the audience members' brains on overload. Presented with too much information and too many inputs, people simply tune out in self-defense.

Today, it's easy to use flashy technology, as a tempting substitute for substance and clarity. Therefore, as you write multimedia presentations, the biggest challenge is to harness powerful multimedia tools so that they are truly visual aids in communicating your ideas.

A Few Tips for Using PowerPoint and Slides

To avoid audience overload, use these guidelines in your multimedia presentations:

- Limit the number of slides.
- Limit the amount of text on each slide.
- Use slides for important subheadings and simple visuals.
- Prepare the way for a complex slide, for example, by describing the elements of the study it summarizes.
- Use the unveiling of a new slide to vary your pacing by pausing a few seconds for the audience to view the slide.
- When presenting a graph or chart, clarify the category represented by each axis or by each color in a pie chart.
- Consider using a pointer or laser pointer to highlight each element of the chart as you talk about it.
- When you move on to a new point or topic, insert a company logo or better yet, on PowerPoint cue the B key for a blank screen, so the audience will look back at the speaker.

When writing for multimedia, remember that the speaker needs to be watched to be understood, to have an emotional impact, and to leave the audience with a lasting impression. Don't let your technology upstage your speaker.

The Script

Your text in a multimedia presentation will look and read very much like a speech (again, see Chapter Five), but with the addition of cues and references to any other media you are incorporating. Leave a wide margin on one side of each page, and insert cues where appropriate. Your finished copy will thus serve as a running script for your presenter, as well as a list of audiovisual and related cues for the person who is handling the technical side of the presentation. (If the media you are using are complicated, you may want to prepare a separate technical outline.)

Few speakers who cue their own slides can resist looking over their shoulders to make sure the slide changed when they pushed the button. This breaks their concentration and their eye contact with the audience. Whenever possible, someone other than the speaker should cue the elements of even simple audiovisual presentations.

Exhibit 6.1 provides an example of a column-format multimedia script, a portion of a lesson on "Understanding the Hazard Communication Standard (HCS)" for workplace safety education developed by the U.S. Department of Labor's Occupational Safety and Health Administration (OSHA). As a lesson plan, the script offers only an outline for the speaker, an approach we strongly recommend against for the complexity of most public relations presentations.

Following is an example of a multimedia script, before it is input into a teleprompter in two columns, with the media cues in the left column. The hypothetical QQQTV network presents its fall line to an audience of advertisers in New York to convince them to purchase ad time during QQQ's new fall lineup. Here is an excerpt from the CEO's presentation:

We've got an exciting new fall television season coming up. When you see the new schedule that Network President Sue Smith has put together, we think you'll

Exhibit 6.1 Column Format Multimedia Script

Time (minutes)	Subject Outline	What to Do	Aids/Cue
1:00	Introduction	Introduce yourself **Circulate** attendance sheet **Introduce** topic: Understanding the Hazard Communication Standard (HCS)	Slide No. 1: Title slide
3:00	Overview of lesson	Overview of lesson **Ask** if anyone present has heard of or is familiar with the HCS	Slide No. 2: Purpose of HCS
		If parts of HCS have already been implemented at your site, **remind** participants	
		State the purpose of the standard: . . . to ensure that the hazards of all chemicals produced or imported are evaluated, and that information concerning their hazard is transmitted to employers and employees.	
		Explain that hazards are communicated through container labeling and other forms of warning, material safety data sheets, and employee training	
Time unknown		NOTE: If you have obtained a video outlining the HCS, show it now	Video (optional)

(continued overleaf)

Exhibit 6.1 (continued)

Time (minutes)	Subject Outline	What to Do	Aids/Cue
2:00	Learning objectives	State the following course objectives: * Employees will be able to identify the purpose of the HCS * Employees will recognize the 5 main sections of the HCS * Employees will indicate (in a quiz/orally) how and where hazard communication information is available at their site * Employees will recognize (in a quiz/orally) who is responsible for this function at their site	Slide No. 3: Learning Objectives
3:00	Identification of responsible staff	**Describe** who is responsible in your workplace for: * Identifying hazardous chemicals * Preparing and implementing the written program * Making sure that in-plant containers are labeled, tagged or marked with the identity of the material and appropriate hazard warning * Ensuring adequate labeling of shipped containers if you are a manufacturer, importer or distributor * Obtaining/maintaining MSDS information and training programs	No. 4: Who Is Responsible On Slide No. 4, fill in the names of responsible staff, either on the computer or, if using overheads, with a marker slide

5:00	Identification of hazardous chemicals in the workplace [see paragraph (b) in the HCS for exemptions]	**Explain** that the HCS covers all chemicals that manufacturers/importers have evaluated and classified as hazardous. This evaluation is described on the material safety data sheet issued by the manufacturer. They can include:	Slide No. 5: Identification of Hazardous Materials
		* Liquids in containers	
		* Substances in pipes	
		* Chemicals generated in work operations such as welding fumes and exhaust fumes	
		* Solids, gases and vapors	
		Explain that if there is no hazard, the rule does not cover the chemical.	
		Show an example of the chemical inventory from one of your work sites, if available.	
		Ask the class if they can think of examples of hazardous chemicals from their various work sites.	

Source: U.S. Department of Labor Occupational Safety and Health Administration (2003).

agree that QQQTV is the best buy in network television. Why? Because we offer you the best continued access to the demographics you want to reach.

(Pause)

(Slide: Momentum in ratings)

For the full 30-week television season, QQQTV is the only network with real growth in all key adult demographics. At QQQTV, and only at QQQTV, the audience you'll reach is growing and expanding in the most desirable demographics.

(Slide: A18–49)

In adults 18–49: QQQTV is up 8%. In contrast, the other networks are down, except for PPP television. Their bright spots are confined to two nights, and they are up only 1% in adults 18–49 over their entire schedule.

(Slide: A18–34)

In adults 18–34, none of the other networks show a gain. In contrast, among adults 18–34, QQQTV is up a hearty 11%.

Let's talk about half-hour wins. During the previous year's TV season, QQQTV was number one in adults 18–49 in only one of our half-hours.

How things have changed.

(Slide: Half-hour wins—A18–49)

For the just-completed television season, QQQTV shows ranked number one in their time periods in adults 18–49 for 10 half-hours.

And on top of that, QQQTV had more half-hour wins than the two traditional leaders combined among adults

18–49 in head-to-head competition. That's growth. Not smoke and mirrors. Real growth.

(Slide: Half-hour wins—A18–34)

In adults 18–34, QQQTV delivered winning time periods for its advertisers in 12 half-hours. This was achieved despite some disappointments with the new shows we launched last year.

None of the other networks matched our growth performance this season. QQQTV has always been a great way to reach the younger demographics. We still are, and we're getting even better.

As Sue presents our fall schedule and shows you clips of our exciting new shows, you'll see how she has positioned both the new and the returning shows to maximize their chances for success.

(Pause)

No matter how good our shows are, of course, their value to you depends on the strength of our distribution system.

If there's any doubt in your mind that QQQTV can deliver huge numbers right now with the right programming, let me show you something interesting:

(Slide: 2nd highest-rated program)

These are the three highest-rated telecasts this past season.

That's right. The second-highest-rated broadcast of the entire season was on QQQTV.

The Big Sports League championship with a 28.6 household rating was second only to the Super Bowl and ahead of the Academy Awards.

(Slide: QQQTV Sports)

The BSL broadcasts have been a tremendous success, both creatively and in the ratings. And we are really just starting to build this franchise.

It is my pleasure to introduce the man who gave the Big Sports League the QQQTV touch, helped deliver that 28.6 household rating for the championship, and earned us our first four sports Emmys in the process: Please welcome our president of QQQTV Sports for QQQTV.

Lengthy multimedia programs require careful pacing. The CEO's portion of the program is all business—facts and figures to make a logical, intellectual case for the advertisers to buy time on the network. The sports portion of the program that follows appeals to the audience's emotions with video clips, including one of a rousing pregame show's opening sequence, as well as a custom video package of interview clips with players and fans.

The "New York up-fronts," as these spring presentations to advertisers by all of the television networks are called, are complex, day-long marketing and public relations events (see Chapter Eight) that also require writing press releases as well as elaborate sales kits that include bios and backgrounders for each show on the schedule. The presentation itself builds in excitement and emotional appeal to the unveiling of the lineup and culminates with the president of the network introducing a cavalcade of stars. For the personal touch, the celebrities then circulate and socialize with the advertisers at a lavish cocktail party. The multimedia presentation, however, is the centerpiece of the network's sales process.

Coordinating Text and Slides

If every slide in a multimedia presentation has a purpose, then logically, your script must make that purpose clear. In other words, once you put a slide up on the screen, you have to talk about it in some way. Nothing confuses and exasperates an audience more than watching slides flash past while the speaker talks about something else entirely. It's hard enough following one line of thought without having to juggle two or more at the same time.

If a slide shows company revenues from 1992 to what is estimated for 2012, the text must in some way deal with that subject while the slide is on the screen. This doesn't mean repeating, "As you can see in our next slide..." or similar phrases. The slide belongs on the screen as long as it pertains to what is being said, and then it should come off immediately.

Impact and Continuity

Lowering and raising the house lights again and again is clumsy, and the repeated transitions from light to dark to light can irritate the audience. If portions of your script need no slides, you can use filler slides of your company logo, general topic slides, or, better yet, the blank black screen cued by the B key on PowerPoint. When your slides and video clips are finished, bring the lights back up. In the dark, people tend to doze. In most cases, the final segment of your presentation should focus solely on the speaker for maximum understanding and impact.

Putting It All Together: Rehearsal

Rehearse, rehearse, rehearse. There is a mysterious law of the universe that says any audiovisual machines, computerized systems, and laptop hookups you fail to check well in advance of your presentation will fail to work when you need them. Technical difficulties are embarrassing for the speaker and painful for the audience. Most multimedia presentations are controlled by computer and high-tech configurations of digital equipment. The more technology you use, the greater is the likelihood of technical foul-ups.

What couldn't go wrong? Ask Microsoft. In July 2006, it presented securities analysts and the media with a multimedia demonstration of its voice recognition technology. "Dear Mom," the speaker said. "Dear aunt," the computer wrote on the screen for all to see. Business channels replayed the clip repeatedly for days afterward while Microsoft's competitors crowed. The stock did not get the boost the company had hoped for, and the buzz on the upcoming release of the new product turned more negative than before the big PR push. Tech check and tech rehearsal are essential, no matter what your business is.

Rehearsal allows you to check on the flow of the presentation. Are the slides in order? Are the slide cues in the right places in the script? Can your presenter see the script with the lights down? Does slide 1 appear while topic 1 is being discussed and disappear immediately after? Are videotapes rewound to the correct starting points?

Proofread the finished slides, and check the arithmetic. Unless you're making the presentation yourself, you can't be certain there will be no mistakes. What you *can* ensure is that the people doing the talking go in as well prepared as you can make them. A good presentation is like a successful play: the audience's response is immediate. Thorough preparation earns you your share of the credit.

Audiovisual Presentations

Certain audiovisual presentations are intended to create an emotional response in the audience. Complex audiovisual presentations generally run from one to seven minutes and can use up to one hundred projectors simultaneously. Sometimes the choice of slide images is suggested by a script; other times, the presentation may be all images and music, with no words spoken at all. The main advantage of an audiovisual presentation over a film is that slides can be changed easily up to the last minute, whereas film or video editing is more complicated and time-consuming.

Chapter Recap

When scripting audiovisual business presentations, adopt these guidelines:

- Follow the principles of speech writing discussed in Chapter Five.
- Keep the material clear, concise, and in good taste.
- Create a script that shows the timing of each slide in relation to the text.
- Make sure there is a clear purpose for each slide.
- Limit the number of slides.
- Limit the amount of text on each slide.
- Use slides for important subheadings and simple visuals.
- Prepare the way for a complex slide, for example, by describing the elements of the study it summarizes.
- Keep a slide on the screen only as long as it is directly relevant to the text.
- Use a logo, a general subtitle, or a blank black slide as a filler.
- Rehearse.
- Proofread slides, and recheck the arithmetic.
- Recheck the audiovisual and computer equipment, slides, and tapes.
- When the slides are finished, turn on the lights.
- As much as possible, keep the focus on your speaker, especially at the end.

7

WRITING FOR BROADCAST

Communicating with Video and Sound

People now receive much of their news and information from television and radio, so getting your story covered by broadcasters is an important way to spread your message. Writing for broadcast follows the principles covered thus far in this book: your ideas must be timely and newsworthy, your information must be accurate, your story must interest the intended audience, and your message must be stated clearly and concisely. In addition, broadcast news releases, pitch letters, and electronic media kits impose special considerations, which are covered in this chapter.

The most important difference is the style. Broadcast style is more concise and more conversational than print style. It writes for the ear or the eye, or both. Also, broadcast stories are most effective, and therefore most likely to be picked up by the media, when they use video and sound.

The ability to pitch stories for broadcast media and write scripts for video stories to be digitally distributed has become crucial to public relations writers. The changes from over-the-air to cable and satellite and the switch from analogue to digital delivery have greatly increased the number of outlets for news and informational coverage. Consumers' upgrading from slower-speed dial-up Internet connections to higher-speed DSL, cable broadband, or optical also means that companies and even individuals can deliver video directly to a consumer or target audience by e-mail or make it available on a Web site for viewing, downloading, or Podcasting. With the transition to digital delivery, broadcast writing skills are more important than ever before because there are now so many more outlets for broadcast-style stories.

Pitch Letters and News Releases

When writing news releases and pitch letters for broadcast segments, whether for local news programs, network talk shows, or cable programs, follow these guidelines:

- Do your homework.
- Pitch to the sound and video capabilities of radio and television.
- Use a concise, conversational broadcast style in your pitches and news releases.
- Write the lead or the e-mail subject line as a tease.
- Offer the facts, but don't write the script.
- Keep it short and appropriate.
- Determine the category.
- Produce video news releases (VNRs) and promotional films to control your message.
- Repurpose your broadcast-style stories for the Web and Pod casting.

Do Your Homework

The opportunities to advance your client's objectives through broadcast story placements have increased tremendously in the past decade. There are now more than eighty-five hundred radio stations and more than seventeen hundred local television stations in the United States as of March 31, 2006, according to the U.S. Federal Communications Commission. Entertainment programming such as the late-night talk shows broadcast by major television networks and ubiquity of cable channels have opened numerous opportunities for wide-ranging sorts of stories and expert appearances; twenty-four-hour cable news and business channels need experts with insights about current events and business, as well as exclusive stories of interest to their viewers. In addition, there are now niche cable channels for special interests, ranging from home improvement and cooking to horse racing and golf, any of which may be receptive to an appropriate product pitch or an expert or author interview.

The switch to digital and high-definition television now allows stations to split their assigned bandwidth into multiple channels, which bring with them new advertisers and require original content. Many of these channels target niche audiences, sometimes in targeted zip codes. Again, these new channels and niche markets offer opportunities for story ideas initiated by public relations writers. Broadband Internet has also opened up numerous new ways to deliver information, news, how-to features, and entertainment.

Content is now king, and your public relations pitches, news releases, and stories are the building blocks of content that is both timely and cost-effective for budget-strapped programming outlets. The challenge, as always, is to offer material that is fresh and perfectly suited to the outlet's format and target audience. Do your homework by learning as much as you can about the show you are pitching, and avoid scattershot press releases that will probably be relegated to the trash.

Pitch to the Sound and Video Capabilities of Broadcast Media

There is a fundamental difference between writing for print media and writing for broadcast media: in print, you are ultimately reaching readers, whereas in broadcasting, you are reaching listeners and viewers. To succeed in writing for the broadcast media, you must change your mind-set to think first of sound and video rather than the printed word. Most importantly, your style must be concise yet conversational.

Radio news and features are based on actualities, a term applied to the literal sound of anything other than the radio announcer's voice. Most often, an actuality is a sound-bite from an interview with another person. An actuality, or ambient sound, can also be the sound of traffic, music of a band in a parade, or the siren of a fire engine en route to a fire. Radio reporters often use actualities as background for their reports. Radio is based on sound.

Television is based on moving pictures and sound. In television, what is shown on the screen is generally more important than what is said. The TV picture literally tells the story; the words simply reinforce it.

Broadcasters need stories that suit their medium. Audience surveys during the 1990s showed that the audience for local television news was shrinking; that less frequent viewers no longer cared about the many stories on "the weather, accidents, crime, education and high school sports"; and that even frequent viewers of local news "didn't care much about two of those topics: accidents and high school sports" (NewsLab, n.d.).

Recent, more refined research shows that in telephone surveys, people underestimate how much local news they watch, probably because they are now in the habit of multitasking, especially during news broadcasts, for example, by simultaneously reading the newspaper or working on the computer (NewsLab, n.d).

If we may speculate for a moment, perhaps television news is now being treated like a radio broadcast, because the predominant local news image is either an anchor desk and newsreader or a video clip that has already been broadcast numerous times that day on the twenty-four-hour news channels or the local newscast's teases with the tagline: "More at eleven."

The viewers' sense of having seen it all already presents public relations writers with opportunity and challenge. The opportunity is in the local news director's search for a story with fresh visuals. Therefore, you should mention the availability of a live interview, on-site taping, or preexisting video or audio in every story proposal to broadcasters. The challenge is to come up with a visual opportunity that will compel the station's news director or assignment editor to assign the story and compel the viewers to drop their knitting and actually watch instead of just listening.

In television, the visual appeal of a story is sometimes as important as its news or information value. After you've grabbed the attention of the news director in your letter or release, you must suggest ways to make your story visually exciting. For example, if you issue a news release announcing the results of a new survey, a broadcast reporter will be reluctant to cover it. If, however, you can offer an interview with an expert knowledgeable about the study, your chances for broadcast coverage are much greater.

If you're pitching a story about a television show or a theatrical production, invite the television crew to cover a rehearsal; if you're pitching a story on a manufacturing business, invite the television crew to visit the factory or plant to record the process by which the product is made. TV cameras are particularly suited to recording processes, demonstrating how something is done, or showing an event as it happens. Action is what television reporters look for. Similarly, radio reports need sounds to convey action and immediacy.

In your broadcast story proposals, you should suggest opportunities to tape the subject. For example, if it's Jane Doe, High School Mentor of the Year, whom you are trying to get TV and radio reporters to cover, your pitch might be written this way:

> Subject Line: Who's the city's best role model for teens?
>
> The Professional Women's Association has chosen Jane Doe, head of Internet innovations for Capstone Technology, as its Mentor of the Year. Jane's outstanding mentoring has been keeping at-risk girls in school for six years.

Ms. Doe will be accepting the award next Tuesday, May 10, at a noontime luncheon in the Garden Room of the Regency Hotel. You are invited to attend and tape her acceptance speech. Ms. Doe will speak about plans to include at-risk boys in the Mentoring program.

Ms. Doe will also be available for interviews both prior to and after the luncheon. Also, a "day-in-the-life" coverage could be scheduled for when she is mentoring a student on the job.

Attached are Ms. Doe's biography, as well as background on the Mentor of the Year Award, the mentoring program, and the Professional Women's Association. I'll call you next week to see if you can attend the luncheon. Meantime, call [phone number] or e-mail me, if I can help in any way.

Sincerely,

[Name and title]

This pitch offers the news director several ways to obtain the video or audio needed to shape an interesting broadcast story.

Use Broadcast Style for Your Pitch and Backup Material

Broadcast writing is ultimately a skill requiring great condensation. A broadcast writer must learn to summarize vast quantities of information in a short, conversational form. To illustrate the difference between magazine writing and broadcast writing, here is a lead paragraph from a *National Geographic* magazine story about dance excerpted on the magazine's Web site:

From ballet to break-dance, from the hora to hip-hop, this country stays moving on the dance floor. . . .
Planets spin. Lightning leaps. Atoms dance. And so do we. From the first kick of a baby's foot to the last "Anniversary Waltz,"

we dance—to internal rhythms and external sounds. Before the written word, humans spoke the language of dance. It's as ancient as the 3,400-year-old image of a man with a lute, dancing on a clay plaque discovered in northern Israel [Newman, "Shall We Dance?" 2006].

That's a good magazine lead, highly descriptive and detailed. This *National Geographic* story is also promising as a television feature story because of the interesting possibilities for visuals that range from striking dances with contrasting musical styles to interviews with anthropologists, dance historians, choreographers, and regular people who just love to dance. For television, the story would be written much differently, including offering pronunciation tips for tricky names by underlining stressed syllables, perhaps something like this:

Before the invention of writing, we humans already knew how to record our triumphs and tragedies ... in dance. Today, dance styles in America are as diverse as our ethnic origins, regional accents, and ages.

Here is Local University's chairman of the anthropology department, John Doe. (Video Interview)

(Voice-over video of last year's rodeo) This week Denver will celebrate Frontier Days with the National Rodeo Championships.

Dance is also a big part of the celebration:

The National Square Dance Festival brings 1,000 couples to do-se-do on the Denver Broncos' home field. (Video interview of a Square Dance Festival couple in costume, ending with them demonstrating "swing your partner.")

Also this weekend, the visiting Big City Ballet company dances Agnes de Mille's "Ro<u>deo</u>," Martha Graham's "Appalachian Spring" and George <u>Balanchine</u>'s "Western Symphony." (Promotional video of BCBallet's "Western Symphony" hoe-down scene.)

For those who prefer to do it themselves, dance halls in Denver and all across the country offer line dancing and Texas two-step every weekend. (Voice over video of line dancing at a local western bar.) See our Web site for more information about Frontier Days, ballet tickets, and local spots to Texas two-step.

Notice how quickly the broadcast lead summarizes the entire story.

Write the Lead or E-Mail Subject Line as a Tease

The lead sentence grabs the reader's attention and compels him or her to continue reading. For broadcast purposes, the lead should be sharply honed into a tease, a short, tantalizing promo for a story to induce the viewer to stay tuned in. A story for the evening news will be teased during the afternoon talk shows, and the end of the early evening news will tease a story being prepared for late-night news. Other teases, particularly ones for breaking news, air during popular prime-time programming.

Our e-mail subject line for the story about mentoring is written as a tease: "Who's the city's best role model for teens?" So is the lead of our pitch about dance: "Before the invention of writing, we humans already recorded our triumphs and tragedies."

By teasing your story with a great subject line or lead sentence, you gain assignment editors' attention and show that you speak their language and are aware of their needs. Newsrooms may "receive literally hundreds of press releases each day," according to an assistant news operations manager for a busy Atlanta local station (Funk, 2006). To gain broadcast exposure, your writing must stand out from the pile.

Test whether your lead sentence works as a tease by reading it aloud and following it with the phrase, "Film at eleven," "The answer at eleven," or "Details tonight at eleven." For example, imagine you represent a consumer interest group that believes that popular, icy summer drinks that are promoted as healthy are actually loaded with calories. Your broadcast news release lead might read: "Your 'health' cooler may be making you fat." [Details at eleven.] Or say you represent an organization that has received a large challenge grant from a local business that will donate two dollars for every one dollar raised from the community. Your subject line might be, "A local company wants to make you a better citizen." [Find out how at eleven.]

Offer the Facts, But Don't Write the Script

The best broadcast writers tend to write in short, declarative sentences using action verbs. And while it is a good idea to write this way and make your lead snappy in a broadcast tease style, it is not a good idea to present a public relations pitch in the form of a script. All reporters and newsrooms have their own style of writing and reporting, and you do more to irritate than interest them if you try to supply a prewritten story.

You can, however, help a broadcast reporter by rounding off numbers ("nearly $10 million was raised," not "$9,693,292 was raised") and paraphrasing titles ("Jack Smith, head of the network," rather than "Jack Smith, executive vice president and general manager of the network"). You can also help the reporter, as well as your story's chances, by avoiding pomposity ("firestorm of controversy"), overdramatization ("major break-through"), cop-speak ("fled on foot"), nonconversational word choice ("estranged husband"), and clichés ("at the end of the day"). Abe Rosenberg (2006), a writer at KTTV Fox 11 in Los Angeles, keeps an evolving list of these and other tediously repeated phrases that he calls "groaners."

Keep It Short and Appropriate

Radio and television news coverage is often referred to as a "headline service" because of its brief treatment of subjects and events. Your broadcast proposals must also be brief and to the point. In addition to condensing information, your material must be tailored to the show you are sending it to and the length of the treatment it is likely to receive—anywhere from thirty seconds on radio to one or two minutes on television.

If you've done your homework, you will know the needs of the broadcast outlet you're pitching. You can shape your pitch to make it attractive to your target station rather than sending a one-size-fits-all-but-fits-nobody-very-well press release.

Local news stations, for example, want a local story or a local angle or local expert interview related to a broader story. For Veterans Day, for example, offer an interview with your client, a local veteran who has started a nonprofit organization to aid veterans dealing with post-traumatic stress syndrome.

Like newspaper editors, many broadcast news and entertainment show editors and talent bookers prefer telephone queries before any written material is sent. Being brief and concise is just as important on the telephone as it is in writing. Again, don't take it personally if you get told no. The job of these experienced professionals is to know instantly if a story or interview is right for their show, so don't argue or try to talk them into a story they don't want.

There are no universal criteria for what makes a story or guest eligible for broadcast coverage. Even two local news shows in the same market may have different formats and philosophies. One may have an entertainment or soft news focus, with an emphasis on in-studio interviews. The other may be more devoted to hard news, with an emphasis on field reports. For the former, an actor in a new film would be an ideal subject; for the latter, only a mayor or governor might do.

Nationally, for example, both *The Tonight Show with Jay Leno* and *The Daily Show with Jon Stewart* are late-night programs taped with a live audience. Both rely on in-studio interviews, but the emphasis and the type of guests interviewed on each are different. Leno usually interviews celebrities who are making the rounds to publicize new movies or television series; occasionally he also interviews a person with an odd hobby or unusual accomplishment that will appeal to his middle-American, middle-aged audience. *The Daily Show* specializes in "fake" news and topical humor, but has one interview segment. Exposure to the young, hip audience and viewership makes the show's interview chair a must-sit destination for politicians wishing to appeal to youth and for authors if they are verbally agile enough to spar with Stewart. It's important that you recognize such differences between similarly formatted shows before you write broadcast story proposals.

Determine the Category

News stories tend to fall into seven categories:

- The meat and potatoes of local news that viewers seem tired of: weather, accidents, crime, education, and high school sports
- Crises and natural disasters
- Medical stories concerning health and well-being
- Economic stories that affect ordinary people
- Good Samaritan stories about people who have done something positive for their communities
- Clever or humorous stories that entertain rather than just inform
- Celebrities and entertainment

The Mentor of the Year story fits the Good Samaritan category, and the dance story falls under entertainment. Before you call to pitch a broadcast news story or write a release or pitch letter, check to see which of the seven categories the subject fits into and what video or audio opportunity it offers. If your story doesn't qualify in some broad sense, perhaps you need to review the way you are presenting it.

Creating Scripts for Electronic Media Kits

Some forms of broadcast public relations writing require a script. Among them are public service announcements, video news releases, and promotional films.

Broadcast scripts have their own technical language, which is usually abbreviated. Here are some of the most common shorthand examples:

B-roll	scenic pans, ambient sound, interview responses (all without the reporter)
CHYRON	text on screen
CU	close-up
ECU	extreme close-up shot
LS	long shot
MS	medium shot
OC	on camera
PKG	reporter package or VNR package, a self-contained story on video, usually running 1:15 to 1:45 minutes
SOT	sound on tape
VO	voice-over

Public Service Announcements

A public service announcement (PSA) is a short spot between ten and sixty seconds in length that television and radio stations broadcast at no charge to the sponsor. Nonprofit organizations place the most PSAs on the air, but commercial organizations may also promote nonprofit activities, causes, or events using PSAs.

It is through PSAs that broadcast stations fulfill their obligation, as outlined by the Federal Communications Commission (FCC), to serve the community and public interest. PSAs usually publicize community events and health or safety tips. The people at radio and television stations who decide what gets aired in the form of a PSA usually have titles such as public affairs director or public service manager.

A PSA can be submitted on paper in script form, or it can be produced on audiotape for radio or on video for television. Sometimes the public relations representative provides the PSA both as a script and on tape.

Here is a radio script provided to local Parent Teacher Associations for distribution to radio stations on their own letterhead:

:60 SECOND SPOT LIVE COPY (ANNOUNCER):

DID YOU KNOW THAT ADOLESCENTS AND YOUNG ADULTS ARE AT INCREASED RISK FOR A POTENTIALLY DEADLY DISEASE CALLED MENINGOCOCCAL MENIN-GITIS (PRONOUNCED MEN-IN-JO-KOK-UL MEN-IN-JI-TIS)?

IN FACT, ONE IN FOUR TEENS INFECTED MAY DIE. ANOTHER 20 PERCENT SUFFER PERMANENT DISABIL-ITIES INCLUDING ORGAN DAMAGE AND LIMB AMPU-TATIONS.

NEW VACCINATION RECOMMENDATIONS HAVE RE-CENTLY BEEN APPROVED FOR TEENS AND COLLEGE STUDENTS WHO ARE AT AN INCREASED RISK FOR CONTRACTING THIS DISEASE. IMMUNIZATION AND GOOD HYGIENE MAY HELP PREVENT MOST CASES IN TEENS AND YOUNG ADULTS.

TALK TO YOUR CHILD'S DOCTOR ABOUT IMMUNIZA-TION OR VISIT W-W-W- DOT-N-M-A-U-S-DOT-O-R-G.

A PUBLIC SERVICE MESSAGE BROUGHT TO YOU BY [INSERT PTA NAME] PTA AND THE NATIONAL MENINGITIS ASSOCIATION [National Meningitis Association, n.d.].

The script also included two shorter versions, a fifteen-second and a thirty-second spot.

Here is the script by the Ontario Office of the Fire Marshal and the Ontario Ministry of Natural Resources for a PSA provided on audiotape to Canadian radio stations as part of Wildfire Prevention Week in 2005:

Sound effects: Crackling wood fire, owl hooting, crickets, music

CHILD: Please, Dad, can I roast just one more marshmallow?

DAD: OK, but then we have to put the fire out and get to bed.

ANNOUNCER: A camping trip doesn't seem complete without a cozy fire. But with the romance comes responsibility.

Build your fire on bare dirt or rock.

Keep a one meter area around your campfire free from anything that burns and never leave it unattended.

Always keep a pail of water and a shovel handy.

And, before you leave, please make sure that campfire's out.

Dead Out.

A public service message from your local fire service [Ontario Office of the Fire Marshall, Ontario, 2005].

The following is a sample television PSA script to be produced in minority and Caucasian versions:

Pennsylvania Diabetes Spots (2 X:30)
(African-American & Caucasian)

Open with blurry scene. Scene comes into focus to simulate putting on reading glasses. Establishing shots afterward.

Senior flips on radio to sentimental music. She sets down coffee mug and starts flipping through photo album.

V/O: You've spent a lifetime making memories.

As she approaches last "modern" photo, V/O resumes.

Take care of yourself for the memories yet to come.

Senior Inserts new photo into album as next line of V/O reads.

If you have diabetes, talk to your doctor about the A1c test and an annual dilated eye exam. Control your diabetes ... for life.

INSERT GRAPHIC: A1c Test, Dilated Eye Exam

Closing "reflective" scene.

Brought to you by Quality Insights of Pennsylvania, the Commonwealth's Medicare Quality Improvement Organization.

INSERT GRAPHIC: Quality Insights of Pennsylvania Logo

INSERT SMALL DISCLAIMER: *Paid for by Quality Insights of Pennsylvania under contract with the Centers for Medicare & Medicaid Services, an agency of the U.S. Department of Health and Human Services* [Quality Insights of Pennsylvania, n.d.].

The pages of broadcast scripts can also be divided into left and right sides, with the text on one half only, as this example shows (Youngman, 1986):

Visual/Sound Ideas	Voice Script
Sounds of hitting, shouting, or arguing (could be made by slapping a pillow with a stick or belt).	Anger that's out of control can cause you to hurt the people you love.
Photograph of a family or child with the glass frame broken.	Anger can destroy families.
Doll with tear running down the face.	Young children are especially vulnerable when parents are angry. Abuse may be the unexpected result.
Show the publication.	If you find yourself absolutely furious, or out of control with your family, contact your county Extension Office for the fact sheet "Dealing with Anger and Creative Parenting," a self-study course.

The two-column format helps the writer keep sentences short, and therefore more easily spoken, with plenty of opportunities for breathing. For television, the page division also allows one side to be used for noting what is on the screen (video) as the text is being read (audio). A one-page, double-spaced, typewritten script on the right side equals approximately thirty seconds of spoken copy.

Video News Releases and Promotional Films

A video news release (VNR), also referred to as an electronic press release (EPK), is a client-sponsored video that presents a controlled message using a news angle and broadcast style. Generally a VNR runs between ninety seconds and two minutes, the usual length for a reporter package in television news. A VNR is a public relations tool that provides information and footage broadcasters can easily use.

The use of VNR by broadcasters, however, is controversial because of instances in which stations do not disclose that the source of the footage is, for example, a pharmaceutical company or a government bureau with a political agenda. The Public Relations Society of America (n.d.) has clear ethical standards for the creation of VNRs:

1. Organizations that produce VNRs should clearly identify the VNR as such and fully disclose who produced and paid for it at the time the VNR is provided to TV stations.

2. PRSA recommends that organizations that prepare VNRs should not use the word "reporting" if the narrator is not a reporter.

3. Use of VNRs or footage provided by sources other than the station or network should be identified as to source by the media outlet when it is aired.

News organizations are responsible at their end for upholding ethical standards for disclosing the sources of VNRs they broadcast, so the public should never be confused, much less purposely deceived, about the source of information and video.

For the most part, a VNR is used as a filler on a slow television news day or as a feature story. Many television reporters say they use a VNR only if it covers a subject they're interested in and there's absolutely no way they can shoot it themselves.

From the public relations writer's standpoint, here are three basic uses for a VNR:

- To promote a product or service by tying it to a newsworthy event
- To disseminate information quickly in a crisis (see Chapter Thirteen on the importance of providing B-roll—secondary video shots such as one of corporate headquarters and other alternate positive video)
- To publicize a corporate announcement

The running time of electronic press kits can be longer than VNRs. Both VNRs and EPKs can provide video with and without voice-overs. Those without voice-overs may be accompanied by a suggested script. The goal, as always in public relations, is to make it as easy and convenient as possible for a media outlet to do the story that you and your company or client want the public to know about.

Here is an example of a script for a video news release:

Full script and background

YOGA THERAPY FOR HEALING COMMON AILMENTS

SUGGESTED STUDIO INTRO: Tired of backaches and assorted body aches and pains? How about exercise you hate doing? Or maybe stress is just getting the best of you? There appear to be some new answers in the ancient wisdom of Yoga for beating all these health issues and more.

VIDEO	AUDIO
Group Yoga class	**SOT/VO:** YOGA—IT'S FIVE THOUSAND YEARS OLD AND IMPORTED FROM INDIA. AND IT'S ONE OF THE HOTTEST EXERCISE TRENDS IN AMERICA TODAY. BUT DID YOU KNOW IT CAN ALSO HELP YOU FIGHT DISEASE AND COMMON AILMENTS, AND RECOVER FROM INJURIES?
Picture of "Yoga Rx"	A NEW BOOK CALLED "YOGA RX" SHOWS HOW YOGA THERAPY CAN BE USED TO TREAT EVERYTHING FROM BACK PAIN TO ASTHMA, AND HIGH BLOOD PRESSURE.
Book authors Larry Payne, Ph.D. and Richard Usatine, M.D. walking in garden 1-on-1 Yoga therapy	ACCORDING TO AUTHORS DR. LARRY PAYNE AND DR. RICHARD USATINE, YOGA OFFERS NATURAL PRESCRIPTIONS FOR RELIEVING PAIN AND CREATING AN OVERALL SENSE OF WELL-BEING.

TOTAL RUNNING TIME—:33

VIDEO	AUDIO
SOT: RICHARD USATINE, M.D., coauthor of "Yoga Rx"	**SOT:** Dr. Richard Usatine No matter what your medical condition Yoga is incredibly safe to use. (:05)

Picture of UCLA Medical Center Group Yoga class	**SOT/VO**: WORKING TOGETHER AT THE UCLA SCHOOL OF MEDICINE, THE TWO DOCTORS DEVELOPED THE FIRST YOGA COURSE EVER OFFICIALLY OFFERED TO MEDICAL STUDENTS IN AMERICA. (:14)
SOT: RICHARD USATINE, M.D., co-author of "Yoga Rx"	**SOT:** Dr. Richard Usatine "As a family physician, I see so many of my patients suffering from stress related problems. I take my prescription pad and I write a prescription for yoga therapy." (:10.5)
Group Yoga class	**SOT/VO:** DOCTORS AND OTHER HEALTH PROFESSIONALS AGREE THAT YOGA THERAPY IS AN IMPORTANT AND SAFE METHOD TO ACHIEVE BETTER HEALTH.
SOT: JAMIE SHAW, physical therapist and Yoga teacher	**SOT:** Jamie Shaw "I tell my students if you can breathe, you can do yoga. And if you can breathe and do yoga you can make a change." (:06)
SOT: MARTY CALLNER, chronic back pain sufferer	**SOT:** Marty Callner "Before I did yoga there wasn't a day that went by when I wasn't in pain.

Since I've been doing yoga, I have no pain, zero pain in any part of my body." (:11)

SOT: LARRY PAYNE, Ph.D., co-author of "Yoga Rx" 1-on-1 Yoga therapy

SOT: Larry Payne "You don't have to be athletic, strong or flexible to do Yoga. All you have to do is concentrate and breathe." (:07)

Asthma and arthritis sufferer doing Yoga 1-on-1 with Yoga therapist Larry Payne SOT: HERB BERNARD, chronic back pain sufferer

SOT/VO: THE GOOD NEWS IS THAT IT'S NEVER TOO LATE TO START PRACTICING YOGA. (:04) **SOT:** "I've had back pain ever since I was a kid. At the age of 65, approximately, I started doing yoga. I'm 75 now. I'm free of pain." (:13)

SUGGESTED STUDIO TAG: Ironically enough, according to the Yoga Journal magazine, there are more people doing Yoga in America—some 28 million—than in all of India where it all started!

FOR MORE INFORMATION ABOUT THIS TOPIC, YOU CAN WRITE FOR OUR HEALTH FACTS. SEND A SELF-ADDRESSED, STAMPED ENVELOPE TO THIS ADDRESS: (YOUR STATION'S ADDRESS ON SUPER).

AUDIENCE INQUIRY: For additional information on Yoga:

International Association of Yoga Therapists, 2400A Counter Center Drive, Santa Rosa, CA 95403 or on the Web at http://www.iayt.org

Samata Yoga Center, 4150 Tivoli Ave., Los Angeles, CA 90066 or on the web at http://www.Samata.com

TOTAL TIME—1:48 OUTCUE: "... I'm free of pain."

Produced By: Merry Aronson (818) 760-1502 or Merry@MerryMedia.net

YOGA Rx SOUND BITES

There are :02 at the top and tail of each bite.

BITE #1—Chris Briscoe—testimonial from an asthma sufferer (:17 sec)
SOT: "For 25 years I took asthma medication, everything you could take. When I started doing Yoga 12 years ago, it all changed. I could eliminate my medications and I could breathe well and I use it every day."

BITE #2—Larry Payne, co-author of "Yoga Rx" (7.5 sec)
SOT: "You don't have to be athletic, strong or flexible to do yoga. All you have to do is concentrate and breathe."

BITE #3—Larry Payne, Ph.D., co-author of "Yoga Rx") (:11.5 sec)
SOT: "We are living in very stressful times. Everything is going faster and faster and faster. Yoga is a lot about quieting your mind."

BITE #4—Larry Payne, Ph.D., co-author of "Yoga Rx" (:10 sec)
SOT: "The title 'Yoga Rx' means a natural prescription for health incorporating the ageless wisdom of Yoga with the modern science of medicine."

BITE #5—Marty Callner—testimonial from a chronic back pain sufferer (:20 sec)

SOT: "I tried everything. Yoga is the only thing that worked for me and I was not easily converted to Yoga. But when I started it I could see the results immediately. Within the first day I did Yoga my back started to feel better. After two or three sessions I haven't had back pain since and that was almost two years ago."

BITE #6—Richard Usatine, M.D., co-author of "Yoga Rx" (:15.5 sec)

SOT: "Many illnesses are caused by stress or aggravated by stress. Yoga is a powerful method of stress reduction that allows the person to combine the power of the mind and the body for self-healing."

BITE #7—Richard Usatine, M.D., co-author of "Yoga Rx" (:15 sec)

SOT: "No matter what your medical condition Yoga is incredibly safe to use. Yoga is a way to strengthen the body, increase flexibility and use the mind-body connection and diminish pain and feel good once again."

BITE #8—Ingrid Kelsey—testimonial from an asthma and arthritis sufferer (:25.5 sec)

"Asthma makes you tighten up and after Yoga practice I feel relaxed and I can breathe and instead of tightening up more when I feel an attack coming on I relax and breathe deeply. As far as the arthritis is concerned, the stretches actually do away with the pain."

B-roll (TRT 1:24)

Group Yoga class

Larry Payne, Yoga therapist doing 1-on-1 Yoga with Ingrid Kelsey (asthma & arthritis sufferer);

Chris Briscoe (asthma sufferer); Richard Usatine (co-author of "Yoga Rx" and back pain sufferer); Jessica Levinson (auto-immune disease sufferer).

"Yoga Rx" book cover

This VNR offered television news directors two options: to use the video with a prerecorded announcer's voice narrating the story or to use just the video so that each station could use its own announcer's voice-over.

Electronic press kits for major motion pictures often include up to forty-five minutes of material, typically with these components:

- Movie trailers of various lengths
- Sound-on-tape interviews with cast members, the director, producer, and perhaps an important department head, such as the makeup designer on a horror film
- Film clips of various lengths
- Behind-the-scene footage shot during filming
- Outtakes—those amusing mistakes and bloopers that happen during filming

EPKs for films have become lengthy and elaborate. Film studios now know that almost any specials and interviews shot during production for promotional stories leading up to a film's release can be repurposed (with or without additional editing) for use as bonus material on the DVD release. Fans love an inside look, so much so that film distribution companies now typically leak or premier certain trailers and specials on fan-oriented Web sites to build excitement long before a film is scheduled to open.

In addition to VNRs and EPKs, there are broadcast versions of many of the public relations writing forms discussed in this book. For example, a client may want a film produced to tell the company's history (the backgrounder), explain benefits to employees, inform customers about its services or tell the financial community about its growth and future prospects (the brochure or annual report), or show community involvement (the PSA). Companies and organizations also create films for regional or national meetings, celebrations and award ceremonies, and seminars and other educational purposes.

Many large public relations firms have in-house departments that work exclusively on film and video presentations. Smaller firms and clients hire independent production companies to do the production.

Promotional films are often termed *industrials*, *trailers*, *teasers*, *promos*, and *previews*. Scripts are sometimes written after the tape is shot; other times, they are drafted well in advance of production. Whichever way the script is created, it is almost always a highly collaborative effort that goes through many hands and many drafts.

Repurpose Broadcast Stories for the Web and Podcasting

The digital age presents multiple opportunities for leveraging stories in additional formats to reach different or wider audiences. Also, the major challenge of maintaining a Web site is to post fresh material often enough to lure repeat visitors, a topic discussed in Chapter Ten. The Web started as a print medium. This has changed because of faster Internet connections and other technological advances, easily used online audio and video players, the capacity of a variety of handheld devices to receive or download digital audio and video files, and the viral and word-of-mouth success of video as a marketing tool on the Web. Now Web posting can bring widespread public exposure to VNRs, promotional films, and full-length interviews that were edited to twenty-second sound-bites for television news stories. In any case, the person in charge of a company or client's Web presence usually welcomes your broadcast-style material.

Public relations firms and freelance writers often request permission from clients to post outstanding examples of their broadcast material on their own Web sites to keep their Web presence fresh and to impress prospective clients with their broadcast writing skills.

Chapter Recap

Every public relations agency and department has its own style of script writing and formatting for each type of broadcast writing. The main point to remember in writing broadcast scripts is that the words will be spoken and therefore must be written in a short, conversational style. And when writing video scripts, you must always consider what will be pictured on the screen and how the words will relate to the images.

In review, the guidelines to writing broadcast news releases and pitch letters are as follows:

- Do your homework by knowing the content of the show you are pitching.
- Pitch to the sound and video capabilities of radio and television.
- Use a concise, conversational broadcast style in your pitches and news releases.
- Write the lead or the e-mail subject line as a tease.
- Offer the facts, but don't write the script.
- Keep it short and appropriate.
- Determine the category.
- Produce video news releases and promotional films to control your message.
- Repurpose your broadcast-style stories for the Web and Podcasting.

8

SPECIAL EVENTS

The Art of Getting Noticed

As a public relations representative, you are often responsible for creating events that bring attention to your client or cause. In proposing and planning an event, the most important question to ask yourself is, "Will anybody care?" The next question is, "How can I make them care more?"

Sometimes you need only your local community to care; other times, you want the entire country to take notice. As you read news stories, listen to radio reports, or watch television news programs, try to determine how many news items come from a public relations event. Examples of such events range from contests, parades, and fashion shows to political conventions, debates, protest marches, concerts, and ceremonies of every kind. The news conference, the junket, and the publicity tour are the most widely used vehicles to inform the media, which in turn inform the public.

In this chapter, we examine these special events and the writing skills required for creating invitation copy, media alerts, photo opportunity alerts, media kits, speeches, event time lines, introductions, and talking points, as well as anticipated questions from the media and drafts of possible answers. Your public relations writing is crucial in both creating an event and making it special enough to garner widespread media coverage and public awareness.

News Conference

Perhaps the most common public relations event is the news conference. To hold a news conference essentially means to gather the media at a designated place and time so that they can hear a significant and newsworthy announcement and ask questions. This is one of the most straightforward methods of generating publicity.

The most important part of a news conference is the announcement being made. Regardless of how much hoopla accompanies a news conference, if the announcement is not newsworthy, the coverage will be minimal at best. Even worse, the media will be angry that you wasted their time and left them with an empty news hole that they had budgeted for your big story.

Covering a news conference consumes about four hours of time for the reporter, plus camera and sound crew for broadcast (travel, setup, one-hour event, additional interviews and B-roll, breakdown, and travel). What the media want in exchange for this commitment of time and staff—besides strong coffee, fresh pastries and bagels, and orange juice—is something beyond the story they would get by saying, "Just send us the press release." This "something else" is the challenge for public relations. You'll be asked, "What else do you have for me?" or, more likely, you'll be told, "That's old news. We've done that story already. What else ya got?"

At the minimum, press events should be designed to generate interesting photographs for the print media and great video footage and a sound-bite that the broadcast competition doesn't have. In addition to the speeches, copies of which you will thoughtfully provide in the media kit that the press will receive whether or not they attend, the journalists expect "something else." A Q&A itself can be the "something else" (news), when a free give-and-take allows reporters to ask hard-hitting questions—for example, when a normally publicity-shy CEO banters with the press and gives answers that seemingly are off-the-cuff.

Of course, before the event, you anticipate the most obvious or troublesome questions and provide the speaker with possible answers. You probably also help the spokesperson rehearse answering reporters' questions in a relaxed style that seems impromptu. If your speaker is not willing to take reporters' questions, don't call your event a press conference. (See Chapter Thirteen about the use of official statements in crisis situations.)

Other times, "something else" might be photographing an interaction with someone famous, such as a governor, national political figure, renowned researcher, the inventor or designer of a new product, or a sports star or entertainment celebrity. Nonprofit organizations, as well as consumer product companies, like having celebrity spokespeople, because wherever they go, cameras and media coverage follow, like Little Bo Peep's sheep.

Invitations to large charity events often list a celebrity committee, some of whom lend their names to the cause but don't actually attend, much to the disappointment of attendees who are unfamiliar with the double-booking and last-minute-cancellation habits of prominent people. A news event, however, should deliver what it promises: news. Otherwise a no-show can become part of the story.

Before you list someone from the world of entertainment, politics, or sports on your invitation to a press conference, be sure that the person and his or her staff and public relations representative are definite about availability and commitment. If you have any doubt, your invitation might read "Larry Davidson and special guests" or "and a few surprises." If you have a firm commitment by the day before the event, include the person's name in your notice to the Associated Press Daybook to attract camera and broadcast coverage. The AP Daybook compiles a daily listing of events such as press conferences and celebrity appearances that editors and news directors of organizations that subscribe to the listing can use when deciding which stories merit reporter and camera crew assignments.

Sometimes the best use of a celebrity's commitment of time to a charity is at an event announcement press conference that will generate ticket sales and advance donations.

Begin with a checklist. Because news conferences, like all other special events, are detail intensive, it is useful to make a list of all items that might need attention.

Imagine you will be holding a news conference to announce a credit-card-sized device that combines the capabilities of a cell phone, computer, wireless internet, television, satellite radio, and MP3 music player—the Sextet Communicator. Your checklist could look like this:

✓ Invitation list—press, celebrities, politicians, and others
✓ Time and date: possible conflicts
✓ On-site arrangements
  ✓ Venue rental
  ✓ Parking location and validation
  ✓ Security
  ✓ Menu
  ✓ Green Room location (a backstage area for speakers and guests) and refreshments
  ✓ Stage: Company logo, dais, podium, microphones, teleprompter, ice water
  ✓ Press needs: Sight lines, sound plug-ins, electrical, Internet
  ✓ Audiovisual, computer, Internet hookup, duplicate program media, and other electronic equipment
  ✓ Signage
  ✓ Staff communication devices
  ✓ Sign-in book
  ✓ Name badges
✓ Invitations
✓ Media alert
✓ Photo opportunity alert
✓ Book your own photographer and videographer
✓ Hire a media monitoring service

✓ Callbacks to invited press members to firm up attendance

✓ Associated Press Daybook

✓ Media kit
  ✓ Speeches
  ✓ Main announcement release
  ✓ Technology release
  ✓ Executive bios
  ✓ Company backgrounder/fact sheet

✓ Photos/captions (see Chapter Two)

✓ Event time line, emcee self-introduction, speaker introductions and talking points

✓ Possible questions from the media and drafted answers

✓ Staffing assignments

✓ Rehearsal

✓ The PR Newswire and the Business Wire

✓ Follow-up

✓ Postmortem

Now let's examine each item on the checklist.

Invitation List

Every event requires its own list of journalists who should be invited. In addition to the media, it is often appropriate to invite prominent industry figures, celebrities, or client-related management representatives, among others. Special considerations for the media list include the following:

- *Location.* It doesn't make sense to invite a TV reporter in Omaha to a news conference in Dallas. Invite only those people who would not have to travel unreasonably far.

- *Subject matter.* A food editor will not be interested in the Sextet Communicator announcement. Make sure you invite only journalists who would have an interest in covering the subject of the news conference.

- *Visuals.* Will television crews be able to tape a good story at the news conference? Does the event offer good photo opportunities? If you invite television crews and photographers, make sure you offer more than talking heads. (See Chapter Seven for information on broadcast publicity.)

Once you have considered these elements, it is helpful to divide your media list into categories. For the Sextet Communicator news conference, your media list could be divided into the following categories:

- General business publications
- Local newspapers
- Wire services
- Computer publications
- Audiovideo publications
- Music publications
- Broadcasting trade
- Science/technology
- Consumer publications
- Local and network television news programs

Time and Date: Possible Conflicts. When selecting the time and date of an event, you must consider several factors that could affect attendance. First, do not hold the conference on a major holiday or the day before or after a long weekend.

Next, as best you can, make sure the event does not conflict with other activities that will be drawing journalists that day. For the Sextet Communicator announcement, it would be disastrous to hold the news conference in a different city during the same week as the winter or summer Consumer Electronics Show, which attracts all of the major media covering consumer electronics. If the client releasing the Sextet is a small company, it would be wise to avoid announcing during the same news cycle that Microsoft or Apple announces a major new product. The news cycle for monthly publications is a month long, so try not to announce during the same month.

How can you know what the industry giants will be surprising the media with, and when? Research. Become familiar with your client's industry, talk to the technical people and the sales force, and in general stay informed, and you will avoid the most obvious conflicts. When you establish good relationships with reporters and editors, they can also be good sources for what else is going on. Any news conference, however, can be upstaged by breaking news, such as an earthquake or a blackout.

The time of the event is important. Deadlines for morning newspaper reporters and evening television news reporters are in the afternoon, so if you want them to attend, hold your event in the morning. But if your goal is to attract columnists, weekly and monthly magazine editors, or feature television reporters, you may want to hold a press party in the afternoon or evening. A press party is more relaxed than a news conference and, as the name implies, is more festive. It is usually held to celebrate or mark a special occasion, and food, drink, and entertainment are customarily provided.

On-Site Arrangements

Entire books have been written on how to throw a good party or produce a successful event. Because this book focuses on writing, we will not delve into the countless details in coordinating the on-site activities of a large event. We will, however, offer an overview of the basic items to keep in mind when planning an event.

Venue Rental. Always plan ahead in selecting a site for a media event. Common sites such as hotel banquet rooms are often reserved at least two or three months in advance, especially during busy convention periods and holiday times. Try to book a site at least two months in advance, and always visit the site before agreeing to host an event there. When selecting a site, keep in mind such factors as its reputation, the convenience of its location, room size, and accessibility for the media. While it is possible, and sometimes fun and appropriate, to hold a news conference or other event at an unconventional location, it is much easier to choose a venue such as a hotel or conference center that has an event coordinator, catering and serving personnel, chairs, podium, audiovisual equipment, and parking already on hand.

Parking Location and Validation. Nothing puts your guests in a worse mood than not being able to find convenient parking, and that goes times ten for the media, who need a secure location for satellite trucks and equipment. Arrange to pick up the tab for parking, and arrange for a way to stamp or validate the ticket for your guests' parking.

Security. You may want to arrange for security at the media's parking area to prevent theft or vandalism of their expensive equipment, near the guest check-in table to prevent crashers and stalkers, and assigned to the special guests first in the Green Room and then near the podium, especially if they are celebrities. Many venues want you to hire from their security pool or security company. At other times, you may want to draw from your own company's security staff.

Menu. The menu is an important consideration. Depending on the type of event and who will be attending, you will be selecting either a very elegant and expensive menu or simple coffee-and-pastry service. The food service is particularly significant at cocktail parties or festive galas.

Green Room Location and Refreshments. Arrange with the venue for a place where those on your program can relax and socialize while the press is arriving and setting up. A curtained corner of the main room is one possibility, but remember that anything the media see or overhear is fair game to end up in their reports. A separate room is preferable. Food, beverages, and comfortable seating are necessities. Flowers and snacks are additional niceties.

Stage. The point of your press conference is to create public awareness for your company, organization, or product. Therefore, your company name, logo, or product (or all three) should be clearly but discretely visible in every video and still image shot at the press conference. You will need either a specially created backdrop or banner or a legible logo that attaches to the front of the podium, or both; the venue should be prepared to provide ways to display your corporate identification. You want your speaker easily seen and heard by seated guests and print reporters, by still cameras arranged along the side or in the back, and by electronic media, often placed on raised tiers in the rear. Sight lines for everyone are usually enhanced by staging the speaker or speakers on a slightly raised dais. Since people tend to look most comfortable and most commanding when they stand to speak, a podium with a fixed microphone is the usual configuration for press conferences. Some energetic CEOs, however, prefer not to have a podium that can look like and function as a barrier. Wired with a portable microphone, the active CEO may prefer to walk around and work the crowd or at least move closer to the reporter asking a question. In this case, the speaker's platform typically has two stools: one for water and one for the speaker to perch on casually during questions or for a moment's rest. This arrangement enhances the possibility that photographers capture an interesting action shot—or a really awkward pose. (See Chapter Two for more on photographs.)

Staging is more complex if several people are speaking or being introduced. Until their turns to speak, they may be seated to the side of the speaker platform, behind a draped table with individual or shared microphones for the Q&A period, or in reserved front-row seats. When they speak, they stand at the podium with your corporate identification.

Press Needs. Good sight lines, lighting (no back lighting or bright windows behind your speaker), and sound are essential. To avoid electronic feedback, distortion, and background noise, radio and television reporters like to be able to attach their microphones directly to the podium. Because this arrangement puts *their* logo in *your* image, instead arrange for them to plug into the sound system fed by your microphones. The electronic press also needs plenty of electrical hookups, and the print press, which used to want a nearby bank of telephones to phone in their stories, now wants easy and fast Internet connections or wireless Internet.

Equipment. A broken slide projector or the inability to boot your speaker's laptop PowerPoint presentation can ruin a news conference. Always double-check your audiovisual and electronic equipment to make sure everything works, right up to the last minute before the event begins. Having backup equipment and alternate means of hookup and delivery is a good idea. If the room has an Internet connection and computer projection, for example, you should make the presentation accessible online on a Web site or through e-mail. You can also have duplicate copies on CD, DVD, or a USB device. Electrical power is particularly critical during product demonstrations. You will probably want on-site tech support if your event depends on a computer, projector, or electronic device. The press will have a story but not the story you want them to convey if, for example, Cool Tech's breakthrough Sextet Communicator malfunctions and works only in three modes—or none at all.

Signage. In addition to your prominently displayed backdrop or company logo, you will need plenty of clear signage outside the venue and inside on easels to direct guests and press to the parking and from the parking to the room.

Communication Devices. The public relations staff needs to be able to communicate easily with one another from their assigned positions: greeting at the main entrance and telling you when special guests and important press arrive; escorting special guests to the Green Room and introducing them to one another; in charge of the electronic press; in charge of photographers, print press, and electronic crews; handling the sign-in and distribution of badges; and so forth. Multichannel walkie-talkies (one channel for everyone and one channel for a private conversation) are the time-honored preference of film and television productions. The interchanges on the main channel keep everyone apprised of what's happening everywhere in the venue. Earpieces provide privacy and reduce noise pollution. Cell phones, which every staff member should also have, with all staff on speed-dial and conference call capability, are workable but less convenient. In addition to walkie-talkies, every staff member needs a list of important telephone, cell phone, and pager numbers, as well as e-mail addresses for instant communication and problem solving. For major events that require staff to display an access pass on a neck lavaliere, PR pros often clip on a laminated card with essential emergency contact information.

Sign-In Book. A sign-in book, or register, should be at the entrance to your event, and guests should be asked to enter their names and company or media affiliation. This book is invaluable for your follow-up work, since it contains the name of everyone who attends for easy press follow-up and for thanking guests. It also indicates those who did *not* attend who should be contacted and offered another way to cover the story.

Name Badges. It is helpful to have name badges for everyone attending and participating in a special event. Badges should be prepared before the event (use your participant and RSVP lists). Arrange the badges in alphabetical order at the sign-in desk for the event. For unexpected guests, bring along extra blank badges and a way to write or print names and affiliations.

Invitations

The invitation copy and presentation are a crucial part of generating attendance and media coverage for a special event. Some reporters receive up to fifty pieces of e-mail a day from public relations people. By necessity, they often sort it quickly, making fast decisions on whether to delete it or save it for a closer look. One of the best ways to make sure your invitation will be opened and read is to write the subject line as a tease.

An invitation is similar to a pitch letter or e-mail and should get right to the point. Essentially, it should answer the following questions:

- What is the purpose of the event?
- Where is it being held?
- When is it being held?
- Why should a reporter attend? What can the reporter learn on-site that cannot be conveyed on paper or by telephone? In other words, what is the "something else" that makes this an event that is special?
- Will any type of food or drink be served?
- Who should be contacted for more information?
- How does the reporter RSVP? Few will commit in advance; you will have to call them, but at least offer the opportunity for them to be polite.

Invitation copy condenses a lot of information in a small amount of space. For the Sextet Communicator announcement, your e-mail invitation might be written this way:

> Subject Line: What device will let you throw away your old portable electronics?
>
> You are cordially invited to attend the unveiling of the world's most comprehensive communications device on Tuesday, November 8, from 10:00 A.M. to noon
>
> Press Conference and Continental Breakfast
> Greentree Hotel, Palace Suite
> 123 Elm Avenue
> Chicago, Illinois
> RSVP: John Doe
> 312/555-1234
> john.doe@cooltech.com
>
> Cool Tech, America's foremost producer of cutting-edge portable electronics, will unveil and demonstrate its latest multifunctional handheld device. Larry Davidson, the president of Cool Tech, will be available to answer questions.

In some cases, the invitation copy should not divulge the news content of the news conference beforehand. This means you must be vague about the announcement but enticing nonetheless. In such a case, an invitation might read like this:

> Subject Line: An unveiling
>
> You are cordially invited to attend a news conference hosted by Cool Tech. The company will make a significant announcement on Tuesday, November 8, from 10:00 A.M. to noon
>
> Press Conference and Continental Breakfast
> Greentree Hotel, Palace Suite

123 Elm Avenue
Chicago, Illinois
RSVP: John Doe
312/555-1234
john.doe@cooltech.com

Cool Tech, America's foremost producer of cutting-
edge portable electronics, will unveil and demonstrate
its latest breakthrough. Larry Davidson, the president
of Cool Tech, will be available to answer questions.

The invitation copy will be written differently for parties, concerts, sporting events, and other affairs, but if you include the vital information listed above, your invitation is likely to produce results.

Media Alert

A media alert, also called a news advisory or a tip sheet, provides a brief summary of the basic facts of an event and is often used to follow up a printed invitation or replace it when there is no budget or time for one.

Media alerts should never be more than one page in length, and they should contain the same information as invitations. They should always answer the fundamental questions of who, what, where, when and why. More often than not, this information is printed in boldface type to stand out quickly to the reader.

Here's how a media alert for your Sextet Communicator conference might look:

Subject line: MEDIA ALERT FROM COOL TECH

CONTACT: John Doe
312/555-1234
john.doe@cooltech.com

What: **Cool Tech** will unveil the world's most comprehensive communications device.

Where: **Greentree Hotel**, Palace Suite, 123 Elm Avenue, Chicago, Illinois

When: **Tuesday, November 8,** from 10:00 A.M. to noon

Who: **Larry Davidson**, the president of Cool Tech, will be available to answer questions.

BACKGROUND INFORMATION

Cool Tech, America's largest producer of handheld electronics, had annual sales of $2 billion last year. In the past 18 months, Cool Tech has successfully introduced several new business and personal communications devices, including last Christmas's must-have gift.

All invitations or alerts should grab attention right away. They should never be long-winded or flowery.

Photo Opportunity Alert

A photo opportunity alert or photo tip sheet (also called a photo op) is a media alert customized to attract television or photo coverage. When you are sending media alerts or invitations to television reporters or print photographers, your copy must stress the visual aspects of the event. Thus, an alert for the Sextet Communicator announcement would be written with an emphasis on the visuals—or photo opportunities—offered by the new product—for example:

Photo Opportunity: Cool Tech will show a credit card–sized device that can replace all of your handhelds.

Good visuals can be tremendously effective. When Starwood Hotels launched a program making luxurious dog beds and pet amenities available to guests traveling with a pooch, Merry Aronson helped create an event made for the visual media. Here is the media alert issued by Murphy O'Brien Public Relations in Los Angeles:

Contact: [name, phone, e-mail]

WHO LETS THE DOGS IN?
STARWOOD HOTELS WITH
L.A. DOGGIE BED LAUNCH EVENT

WHAT: To kick off the introduction of Starwood Hotel's new luxurious dog bed program, celebrities, L.A. notables and dog-lovers are invited to bring their loyal companions for a walk down the red carpet where pooches can pose for doggie photo portraits and snack on gourmet treats.

Open to the public, this complimentary event will also include lunch stations, a Bow Wow bar for adults, and a Doggie Buffet for their canine pets. Leading Los Angeles–based photographer Brian Kramer will photograph the dogs in one of the hotel's poolside cabanas. Cloud Star and Three Dog Bakery will provide the gourmet doggie treats.

WHERE: The Westin Century Plaza Hotel & Spa 2025 Avenue of the Stars in Century City. The Rotunda, the round grassy knoll in front of the pool. Valet parking will be complimentary.

WHO: Participating L.A. area hotels include The Sheraton Universal, The Westin Century Plaza Hotel & Spa, Sheraton LAX and the W Los Angeles—Westwood.

WHEN: Wednesday, August 13, 11:00 A.M. to 2:00 P.M.

WHY: In response to the 62 million dog owners in the U.S. and 29 million who hit the road with their dogs in tow, Starwood has created new dog beds, custom-designed by Eloise Inc., a doggie line described as "where style and fashion meet man's best friend." Eloise's pet accessories are Hollywood favorites, and were recently featured in the movie *Legally Blonde 2: Red, White & Blonde*.

Westin's version features a miniature Heavenly Bed duvet. In addition, dogs stay for free at all Westin hotels.

HOW: Please RSVP [name, phone, e-mail].

* Additional information on the nationwide Dog Bed Launch and fun dog statistics available.

The visual opportunities are clear from the first paragraph of this general media release; nevertheless, a photo alert line could have been added:

PHOTO OPPORTUNITY: Celebrities and L.A. notables will walk their dogs down the red carpet and introduce them to Starwood's luxurious new custom-designed dog beds.

For some events, you will want to write two different invitations or media alerts: one for print media and one for broadcast reporters and photographers.

Book Your Own Photographer and Videographer

If showing a short film would be useful in your event, be sure to hire the filmmaker/editor well in advance. (See Chapter Six for information on VNRs and promotional films.)

You also need to book your own photographer and videographer under work-for-hire contracts, so that your client or organization will own and be able to use images of the event for your own purposes. Be sure that the people you hire are professionals and that they use equipment that produces broadcast- or magazine-quality images.

Photographs can be put to a number of uses, for example:

- Making them immediately available to media organizations that for some reason—such as breaking news—were prevented from attending
- Using them in external and internal newsletters and on the company Web site
- Using them in the company's annual report to shareholders
- Giving framed copies as souvenirs to participants for possible display on their own personal walls of fame, either in their offices or at home (see Chapter Two)

Having control of videotape of the event means you can use it in the future in a number of ways:

- A video news release, including excerpts and B-roll to distribute to the media, especially if breaking news diverts the news crews from your event (see Chapter Seven)
- Posting on the company or product Web site
- As part of an "industrial" to be shown at your national sales meeting or annual meeting of shareholders (see Chapter Seven)

Although hiring a photographer and videographer increases the cost of the event, it offers multiple ways for repurposing and leveraging the work and expense of producing the event.

Hire a Media Monitoring Service

Every public relations operation needs ways to evaluate its various activities, justify its expenditures, and track media coverage. Hire a media monitoring service to track coverage of your event for a specified time period. (See Chapter Fourteen on tracking and evaluation.)

Callbacks

Once your invitation or alert has been sent out, begin conducting callbacks several days before your event. Callbacks are necessary because people often do not respond to the invitations and because invitations and alerts can easily be overlooked, deleted, or lost.

After completing your callbacks, make an alphabetical list of everyone who will be attending. This is crucial for planning the amount of food to be served, the number of press kits to prepare, the number of seats to set up, the security check-in list, and name badges for attendees.

Keep an organized list as well of those not attending the event and their reasons. That information will help you plan subsequent events and avoid wasted effort. Send press kits to those interested in the story but unable to attend.

Associated Press Daybook

As a planning guide for news organizations that subscribe to its service, the Associated Press maintains a "daybook" listing local, regional, national, and international events. Assignment editors and reporters keep a watchful eye on the daybook, and you should always try to have your news event included. To be considered for the daybook listings, call the local Associated Press bureau when you are ready to e-mail an alert (no attachments) or fax a press release. Be sure to submit your daybook notice in time that it can be listed in the afternoon on the day before the event and in the morning on the day of the event.

A daybook alert for the Sextet Communicator announcement might look like this:

NEWS CONFERENCE ON MULTIFUNCTION HANDHELD

Cool Tech will unveil a breakthrough handheld communications device the size of a credit card that can replace all of your handheld electronics. The conference will take place in the Palace Suite at the Greentree Hotel from 10:00 A.M. to noon. Larry Davidson, president of Cool Tech, will be available to answer questions. Contact John Doe at 312/555-1234, john.doe@cooltech.com for further information.

A daybook listing reinforces the importance and visibility of your event for assignment editors. However, it does not substitute for personal reminder calls to the individual media outlets.

Media Kit

Media kits must be available at any news-oriented special event and any other kind of event for which you want news coverage. The kits contain all the vital background a reporter needs to write a story on your client. The easier you make it for a reporter, the better your chances are of coverage.

If you are responsible for publicizing an event or client in conjunction with a large-scale activity such as a music festival, convention, or a major sporting event, there will be a central pressroom or press box. You should have an adequate stock of media kits in this room so that journalists can pick up whatever information they might need. This is also true at trade shows, where there is a central pressroom with media kits from all participating companies to supplement the supply at the individual companies' booths on the floor.

Typically a media kit contains the following materials:

- News releases describing whatever is being announced.
- Biographies of any executives, celebrities, or dignitaries who will speak at the event. For a bio of someone outside your company, contact the person well in advance to have one sent or do a telephone interview so you can write one. The person must approve any bio you write or edit to suit your own specifications.

- Copies of any speeches delivered at the event.

- A fact sheet on any new product being announced.

- A backgrounder or brochure on the company or individual sponsoring the event.

- Photos and captions on a CD or DVD or the address of a Web site where they can be downloaded. You may wish to include a photocopy of an index page with thumbnail-size views so reporters and editors know what images are readily available. (See Chapter Two for information on photographs and captions.)

Event Time Line, Emcee Self-Introduction, Speaker Introductions, and Talking Points

As with press releases, media kits, and VNRs, producing an event allows the public relations practitioner a lot of control over the content and the images released to the media. You are the producer-writer of the event. The more clearly you are able to visualize both what you want to happen and also all the ways the event could go off track, the more control you will have. An awkward event usually represents a failure of imagination—yours! Even if something happens that you clearly have no control over, you will be blamed. So as much as possible, try to anticipate every detail and every contingency.

To prompt your imagination as you write the time line, ask yourself, "How do we build drama? Unveil the product? Make the evening news?" Also ask yourself, "What if?" Some of the answers to that question will mean adjustments in the timing or order of the program; others will require changes in staff assignments or hiring additional temporary staff.

Event Time Line. Your time line is for the major internal participants and staff so that everyone knows what should happen when and in what order. The final draft of the time line should mention assigned staff members by name in connection with specific responsibilities. Here is a possible time line for the 10:00 A.M. news conference for the Sextet Communicator.

7:30   Assigned staff members arrive at the Greentree Hotel with sufficient product samples for the unveiling and hands-on opportunity; product display unveiling stand and cover; company banner and/or logo for the front of the podium; press kits; guest lists and pens; badges for staff, press, and other guests and supplies to make extras; printed "Reserved" signs for front-row seats, as necessary; laptops, printer, paper, stapler, tape, paperclips; and walkie-talkies.

Speechwriter arrives with latest versions of all speeches, copies of which are already inserted in the press kits, as well as a laptop and perhaps another printer to make last-minute changes in speeches, talking points, and Q&As.

Room and equipment check: Company banner hung behind the speaker or logo attached to the podium, lighting that will not interfere with photography and videotaping, microphone working, audio levels adjusted, speech input into the teleprompter, computer and projection equipment functioning.

Final adjustments with catering and venue staff (water for speakers, attractive arrangement of the food on one side of the room), final parking validation arrangements.

Final review and revisions of staff assignments.

8:00   The president, emcee, and secondary speaker arrive at the Palace Suite for run-through and rehearsal. Map to Greentree

Hotel attached. Latest drafts of introductions, speech and draft questions, and answers, as well as talking points also attached.

8:15 Final rehearsal of the introductions and speeches. Even if the emcee, president, and secondary speakers are experienced appearing in public, it is important for them to practice in the room. The more equipment involved—teleprompter, projectors, computers, coordinated power points or slides—the more extensive the time needed for rehearsal. Using a laptop and printer, or plugging directly into the teleprompter, the speechwriter works with them to make minor last-minute changes and additions. Nothing drastic can be changed without necessitating switching out the text in the press kits. Some people prefer to wait until the end of the event to provide copies of speeches that are quickly copied in the hotel business center—necessitating lots of last-minute rushing.

9:00 Prepare for arrivals: Check-in staff ready at the check-in table.

Staff members assigned to monitor arrivals at the front door and those who will escort guests, print, and broadcast crews are at their stations (at the front door or the direct entrance from the media parking) ready to personally guide arrivals to the event room or the Green Room.

Each special guest who will be speaking to the press should have a personal escort from your public relations staff throughout the event. If any are bringing their own press officer, prior discussions need to lay the ground rules for the order of the individual interviews and the expectation that they will speak on topic about their connection to Cool Tech's announcement, at least at the beginning of each interview.

As guests arrive, table staff greet them, check them in, give them their badges, distribute press kits, point out the nearest telephones and restrooms, and invite them to enjoy the refreshments.

All staff members also facilitate introductions throughout the event.

9:15   As the speakers are escorted to the Green Room, the speechwriter continues to review quotable talking points to be used especially as sound-bites with the electronic press. If there are revisions or additions, the writer makes the changes and quickly provides copies.

Speakers relax, enjoy refreshments, and greet special guests in the Green Room. Staff members facilitate introductions and serving refreshments.

9:30   Staff members assigned to broadcast media and photographers monitor setup and mediate and solve problems about space, sight lines, electrical, sound, and so forth.

9:55   Or as soon thereafter as the important electronic crews are set up and ready, speakers and special guests are escorted from Green Room to the wings and/or front-row reserved seats.

10:05   Emcee introduces herself or himself and welcomes guests and press.

The emcee introduces the secondary speaker.

10:10   Secondary speaker speaks (no longer than 8–12 minutes). The secondary speaker stays on stage.

10:20	Emcee or secondary speaker introduces the president.
10:24	The president and secondary speaker shake hands and pose for 1 minute for print photographers and video B-roll.
10:25	President speaks (no longer than 15–20 minutes) and unveils the Sextet Communicator.
10:30	Press releases announcing the Sextet Communicator are released through PR Newswire and the Business Wire to comply with Regulation FD [see Chapter Nine].
10:38	President poses for pictures and B-roll and demonstrates that the product is small enough to fit into his shirt pocket.
10:40	Perhaps with the emcee moderating, the president takes questions from the press.
10:55	Emcee intervenes and says, "We'll take two more questions."
11:00	Emcee thanks guests and invites them to continue to enjoy the refreshments.

The head of public relations announces the order in which the president and the secondary speaker, who have sample Communicators in their hands, will give individual three- to five-minute interviews, first to the electronic press and then to print.

Photographers are invited to take "beauty" shots of the Sextet.

The print reporters are invited to speak with the special guests and to have a hands-on experience with the Sextets that each staff member has available before talking to the president and secondary speaker.

Emcee says, "But first I'd like Senator Alice Jones and President George Smith of Titanium Corporation to join us here for photographs and B-roll." A great shot would show the four of them together using the Sextet Communicators, but such product shots should be cleared in advance with the guests.

11:05   The head of PR and a savvy second-in-command escort the speakers first to the electronic crews (remember that broadcast is looking for one good sound-bite, so the speakers should be holding a product sample and using the talking points).

As press prepares to leave, assigned staff members inquire and make notes about their further needs (photos, additional information), their deadlines, and their anticipated coverage.

11:20   Head of PR and second-in-command take the president and secondary speaker to the two separate corners in front of the room, immediately bring the two most important print reporters to them, and offer them beverages. At the five-minute mark, the next reporter is brought close by, and at seven to ten minutes, the interview is cut off and the next person introduced.

11:45   Head of PR and second-in-command and assigned staff extract the president, secondary speaker, and guests from reporters and escort them back to the Green Room. The speakers are reminded to be available from 2:00–4:00 P.M. for phone interviews (phoners).

Staff members facilitate thank-yous and good-byes, as well as movement or transportation to the site of a private luncheon, if one is to follow.

Noon	Other staff members pack and carefully inventory everything they brought with them, especially the number of the sexy, expensive debut product, the Sextet Communicator. The event is officially over.
12:30 and thereafter	From the office or from temporary on-site headquarters, the public relations staffers field calls, set times for phone interviews starting at 2:00 P.M., and arrange for speedy delivery of press kits to important media not in attendance.

An internal time line, such as this one, lets all participants know where they should be and when, as well as how they can locate each other. A time line empowers everyone to take steps to keep the event on schedule.

Emcee Self-Introduction. The press (or any other audience) should never have to wonder who is speaking or why this person is participating in this particular event. Therefore, the person who functions as emcee—for example, the head of public relations or the president of marketing—should at a minimum, and in less than five minutes, set the stage for the event in this way:

- Introduce himself or herself by name and title.
- Welcome the press and other guests.
- Introduce special guests in the audience who will not be speaking.
- Give some background for the day's announcement.
- Mention the order of the program.
- Mention that there will be time for questions, photographs and B-roll, a hands-on experience with the product, and

short individual interviews with the speakers and special guests.

• Introduce the first speaker.

A simple emcee self-introduction for the Sextet Communicator press conference might go like this:

> Welcome. I'm John Doe, head of public relations for Cool Tech. I'm very happy that so many of you are here today for our exciting announcement.
>
> Before we start, I'd like to introduce two special guests who are in the audience—if you'd please stand up: First, President George Smith of Titanium Corporation, whose proprietary bonded, Ultrathin product you'll see put to beautiful use today. Thank you, George.
>
> And second, Senator Alice Jones, who has been an outstanding advocate in helping innovative companies like Cool Tech protect our intellectual property. Thank you, Senator Jones.
>
> Cool Tech is known for its cutting-edge technology and exciting styling. Today you'll be the first to see a new product that combines incredible engineering and breath-taking design.
>
> Two of the people responsible for today's product will speak. There will be plenty of time for questions and photo ops. Afterward, there will also be time for some hands-on with the product and some short individual interviews with the speakers and our special guests. We'll start with the electronic press, followed by print for our Cool Tech speakers and vice versa for Senator Jones and Titanium's President Smith.
>
> Now, it's my pleasure to introduce Dave Douglas, chief technology officer of Cool Tech. Dave is the tech mind

behind everything Cool Tech. As you may know, Dave and Larry started this entire enterprise, which now has thirty-five hundred employees, in Dave's parents' garage back in 2000. Dave's technology has been setting the standard ever since.

Bios of Dave and Larry, as well as a Cool Tech backgrounder and new product fact sheet, are included in your media kits. So with no further ado, here's the tech mind that thinks small: Dave Douglas.

Notice how clearly this emcee self-introduction lets the press know how much access they will have and to whom, including the special guests. Laying out elements of the schedule allows a reporter to decide whether to ask a question during the general press conference or hold it for a chance of an exclusive answer during an individual exchange. "The tech mind that thinks small" is a turn of phrase from Cool Tech's talking points for its new product and helps build anticipation for the unveiling.

Introductions. After the self-introduction, the emcee introduces the secondary speaker. This introduction can be a graceful condensation of the person's biography and should highlight the person's special relationship to the announcement at hand.

A brief example of a speaker introduction is included in the emcee self-introduction. Remember that the higher the rank of the person being introduced, the longer and more elaborate the introduction should be. If you are introducing two people who are truly of equal rank, which may be the case of the two guys who started the company in a garage, the two introductions should be equivalent in length and detail.

Talking Points. Talking points are your two to three main points in their most concise and catchy phrasing. They are for internal distribution only for use when talking to the media. In some cases, they may be printed on palm-sized cards for easy reference or so they can easily be carried in a pocket. (See Chapter Thirteen for further discussion and examples of talking points.)

Possible Questions from the Media and Draft of Answers

An important exercise in preparing for a news conference is to develop a list of questions that might come from the media. This list should be submitted to the people who will be speaking at the news conference so that they can prepare themselves for the questions.

To develop this list, research the subject of your announcement. Ask any questions that are unanswered, or not completely answered, by the news release and speeches. And at every news conference you attend, take notes on the questions reporters ask. This information will help you anticipate questions in the future.

For the Sextet Communicator news conference, executives might expect the following questions:

- When will the device be available to consumers?
- Which retail stores will carry it?
- What is the battery life?
- What is the retail price structure for the product?
- Will it be available in markets outside the United States?
- Are you aware of any other companies that might be introducing a similar product?
- What are your expected first-year sales for the product?
- How long did it take to develop this product?

These questions are typical of those asked during many product announcements.

As the public relations writer, you will also often be expected to develop the answers to these questions. In drafting your answers, follow the same procedures for research, writing, and approval outlined in Chapter Five.

Staffing Assignments

The final draft of the event time line should mention staff members by name. In addition, you should prepare a list of duties organized under such logical categories as supplies, escorts, sign-in, and so forth, annotated with the name of the assigned staff members.

Rehearsal

It's a good idea to hold a dress rehearsal of any presentation or event enough in advance to make necessary refinements or changes. This means having the featured speakers actually deliver their speeches, testing out the teleprompter and all of the other audiovisual equipment, staging a mock question-and-answer session, and generally going over all the details of the upcoming event. Often a rehearsal uncovers details overlooked during planning. Attending to them now will help ensure smooth sailing during the actual event.

In practical terms, on-site rehearsal is usually possible only an hour or so before the event, leading to the sample day-of-event script or time line above that provides for last-minute changes. The time line for the day before the event should include a meeting with the client or senior management reviewing the event script, making any modifications, and also having the speakers rehearse their speeches out loud for feedback from a trusted inner circle.

When you write speeches, you will find that senior executives tend to be both busy and either overly confident or embarrassed by the prospect of rehearsal. Many program participants initially resist full-out participation in a rehearsal, but later may be dissatisfied with you for writing or orchestrating an event that makes them feel awkward or, even worse, leads to sound-bites that are ineffective or embarrassing. Therefore, insist on a complete run-through to the full extent of your personal influence or of the influence you can leverage from others within the organization.

The PR Newswire and the Business Wire

The PR Newswire and the Business Wire are wire services that run public relations announcements for a fee. Most major broadcast and print media assign someone to monitor them.

In many cases, you will want to remind editors about your event by sending a message across these newswires on the morning of the event. For public companies, your wide release of the press announcement should be timed to coincide with the announcement at the press conference. Nonpublic companies may wish to hold the release of the announcement until the end of the news conference.

Often you will want to follow up an event by issuing a release summarizing it. This release will be in the past tense and include such information as the names of any notable individuals who attended; for large events, how many people attended in total; and for charitable events, how much money was raised.

Follow-Up

After the event is over, you will need to conduct a great deal of quick follow-up work with the media. This may include posting event photographs and B-roll shots by your contracted photographer and videographer on a media-accessible Web site or sending them by e-mail; setting up interviews; answering questions; and sending out media kits to those who could not attend. Always have extra press kits for purposes such as this. In addition, monitor the media coverage resulting from the event both personally and through your media monitoring service.

Postmortem

Each event you write or produce can be better than the previous one if you are willing to learn from your experience. As soon as the follow-up activity dies down, but certainly within the week while everything is still fresh in people's minds, have a staff review to discuss what went right and what could be improved:

- What can be done the next time to make an event more successful in relation to the clients and executives? Program guests and VIPs? Broadcast and print media? And the staff members themselves?
- Does the checklist need to be revised?
- Does the time line need to be more detailed or more general?
- Do the participants need more briefing or more rehearsal?
- Most important, if you did not receive the coverage you wanted, why not? What can you do differently next time?

Press Junket

A press junket is a special tour for reporters and editors with transportation and accommodations provided so that the journalists can view or experience a product, service, or a particular event. In return, media coverage is expected (but, naturally, no attempt is made to influence the coverage one way or another). For example, travel writers are often sent on press junkets to the opening of a new resort or to visit a tourist attraction. Many publications have ethics policies that forbid accepting paid travel and accommodations. If your event is newsworthy and they want to cover it, they will pay their own reporter's expenses. They have such ethics policies because the value and lavishness of the gift of travel and entertainment could be seen as compromising a journalist's objectivity and impartiality. Many freelance writers, however, do accept junkets for access to particular stories.

One regular junket to Los Angeles is organized by the Television Critics' Association (TCA) and the major television networks and cable channels, each of which has specified days to present new television shows and interact with the media. A typical day of the TCA press tour (with the public relations writer's responsibilities in parentheses) might include these possibilities:

- Media kits are available (press release, backgrounders and bios for each show, executive bios).
- The CEO speaks on the issues facing the industry and his own company's actions and leadership (CEO speech).
- The president of programming gives a multimedia presentation introducing the network's new shows, presenting exciting video clips and introducing main cast members, and announcing who will be available a bit later for interviews (multimedia presentation).
- The CEO and the president take questions from the press (draft possible questions and answers).
- The stars and producers are available for round-robin interviews (talking points for each show and each person). A round robin can be viewed as speed dating with the media. The TCA press tour is the debut for many aspiring TV stars who may not yet be media savvy or have their own publicists. Major celebrity-oriented broadcast media are given the first shots at the most important interviews; other important reporters or groups of less important reporters are stationed in specified areas or rooms. The interview subjects are escorted from one to the next at specified intervals, and typically the escort will review important talking points or give subtle hints or helpful tips between interviews.

The network picks up the tab for the day's breakfast, sit-down lunch, and an elaborate evening party with entertainment, as well as a proportionate share of the hotel and travel costs for all of those whose organizations allow such costs to be paid.

Pitches are the main vehicle used for inviting press members on junkets. Planning junkets is similar to planning other special events, though there are also many minute travel details to coordinate. For example, executives' contracts and actors' Screen Actors Guild contracts often specify a specific class of airline travel and level of hotel accommodation (such as "best available") and ground transportation (limousine or town car, for example).

Publicity Tour

A publicity tour consists of scheduled publicity appearances in a series of cities. Publicity tours are most often used to publicize books, concert tours, or the introduction of a new product or service into local markets. They are also set up to take advantage of a celebrity or top executive's travel schedule. The planning and writing involved in a publicity tour are essentially the same as those in setting up interviews for print media or in booking broadcast appearances. (See Chapters Three and Seven.)

Chapter Recap

Special events are time-consuming, highly detailed activities that require a great deal of planning and organization. The most important part of a successful event is the planning. Always try to anticipate possible disasters so that you can avoid them or respond effectively. Murphy's law, which states that anything that can go wrong will go wrong, aptly applies to special events.

In review, your checklist when preparing a special event should look like this:

✓ Invitation list—press, celebrities, politicians, and others
✓ Time and date: possible conflicts

- ✓ On-site arrangements
  - ✓ Venue rental
  - ✓ Parking location and validation
  - ✓ Security
  - ✓ Menu
  - ✓ Green Room location and refreshments
  - ✓ Stage: Company logo, dais, podium, microphones, teleprompter, ice water
  - ✓ Press needs: Sight lines, sound plug-ins, electrical, Internet
  - ✓ Audiovisual, computer, Internet hookup, duplicate program media, and other electronic equipment
  - ✓ Signage
  - ✓ Staff communication devices
  - ✓ Sign-in book
  - ✓ Name badges
- ✓ Invitations
- ✓ Media alert
- ✓ Photo opportunity alert
- ✓ Book your own photographer and videographer
- ✓ Hire a media monitoring service
- ✓ Callbacks to invited press members to firm up attendance
- ✓ Associated Press Daybook
- ✓ Media kit
  - ✓ Speeches
  - ✓ Main announcement release
  - ✓ Technology release
  - ✓ Executive bios
  - ✓ Company backgrounder/fact sheet
- ✓ Photos and captions

✓ Event time line, emcee self-introduction, speaker introductions and talking points

✓ Possible questions from the media and drafted answers

✓ Staffing assignments

✓ Rehearsal

✓ PR Newswire and the Business Wire

✓ Follow-up

✓ Postmortem

9

FINANCIAL WRITING

Financial writing is a separate branch of public relations. Master it, and you will have access to a new realm of challenging, and often better-paying, jobs. The reason is that countless public relations people—able professionals in many cases—cannot get the hang of the business side of corporate communications. If you can, your career opportunities are broadened considerably into the areas of corporate communications and investor relations.

Business writing also brings you a whole new and avid readership: the business media and, through them, the investor community. Business audiences are less interested in being entertained than in being informed. They want timely, accurate information about your company, information that will guide their investments. What you write can influence the value of your company's stock, the way the outside world judges your company's management, and possibly the perceived value of your company.

Financial writing also brings you yet another group of interested readers: the U.S. Securities and Exchange Commission (SEC), the federal agency that regulates the world of Wall Street. Most publicly owned companies must file a series of documents with the SEC each year and send to the commission copies of public reports and news releases that relate to the company's financial affairs. Since the 1990s, as part of an ongoing effort to protect investors from fraud, the SEC has required companies to present these documents "in plain English," meaning clear, concrete everyday words in straightforward sentences with active-voice verbs, instead of legal and business jargon in convoluted sentences with passive-voice verbs, as discussed later in this chapter.

Under these conditions, you have little room for embellishment and no room for mistakes. If what you write is inaccurate or misleading, your company may be liable for civil lawsuits. In other words, the creative liberties that might be acceptable in publicizing a rock star or a gallery opening are unacceptable in announcing your company's financial performance.

Learn the Basics of Business

If you plan to make a career in corporate communications of any kind—and especially in the investor relations area—you need to learn at least the basic elements of business and develop a working knowledge of the field or industry in which you have chosen to apply your craft. This may be self-taught (it *can* be done) or acquired on the job (if you're lucky). But if you are still in school or thinking about going back, give some thought to at least a semester or two of business courses. The knowledge has a way of coming in handy. Even if you already understand basic business principles, it may help to review the definitions of the basic vocabulary used in financial writing, some of which are italicized in the following sections.

Let's say you work for a medium-size corporation, MSC, Inc. MSC is a *publicly held* company, meaning it sells shares of itself—stock—to the public through a stock exchange or market. (*Private* companies—sole proprietorships and partnerships—are not as legally obligated to announce their activities. They rarely issue public financial statements.)

MSC takes in money (in the form of *income*, *revenues*, or *sales*) by selling its products or services. It deducts expenses of various kinds. Income minus expenses equals *profits* (*earnings*, or *net income*), which may be computed *pre-* or *post-tax*. Many companies pay a certain amount of post-tax profits to shareholders in the form of *dividends*. Dividends should not be confused with *earnings per share* or *EPS*, which are simply profits divided by the total number of shares outstanding. Some companies use a portion of their profits for *share buybacks*, the repurchase on the open market of shares that are then removed from the market. After each buyback, the earnings-per-share number is computed by using the same profits, but now dividing them by a smaller number of shares. The result is a higher earnings-per-share number, which may lead to a rising stock price, benefiting current stockholders who sell stock.

MSC is governed by a *board of directors*, whose members are elected by shareholders at MSC's *annual meeting* of stockholders (which the company is legally bound to hold). Under the leadership of a board chairperson, the directors appoint the corporation's president and officers.

Follow SEC Reporting Requirements

Because it is regulated by the SEC, MSC must make regular financial reports to the commission and the public: quarterly reports and an annual report to the SEC (Form 10-K Filing) and an annual report to shareholders. Also, it must generally announce any change or event within the corporation that might influence investors.

Enter the financial writer. Your responsibility is to convey the facts and MSC's point of view about the facts as clearly and concisely as possible for the press releases, quarterly earnings announcements and annual reports, and also draft answers to questions that analysts are likely to ask during quarterly conference calls. You may also write press announcements about acquisitions, sales of subsidiaries, and other major business agreements.

Confidentiality and Insider Trading

MSC's obligation to make periodic public disclosures of its financial performance does not mean that every financial fact about your company must be made public. It is crucial, therefore, that you have a clear understanding of what your company wants to disclose and what it wants to keep confidential. For example, MSC may announce revenues and profits for each of its major operating areas but choose not to break out detailed numbers for each subsidiary unit within those areas. The key for you and your department is to adopt a well-defined policy and stick to it.

Everyone in a company who is privy to financial, research, and business information—any kind of information known to an "insider" that could affect decisions of an "outsider" about buying or selling stock—must be very careful about how and when to disclose it. Wall Street has been rocked in recent years by a series of prosecutions for what is called *insider trading*—the use of information that has not been publicly disclosed to trade stocks that are about to skyrocket or plummet. In one of the most publicized cases, Martha Stewart served prison time after being found guilty of insider trading for selling shares of a stock on the basis of an indirect tip from a pharmaceutical company insider. That insider may literally have discovered a cure for cancer, but he is spending years in jail for his own insider trading.

As a corporate business writer, you meet the definition of an insider. Whatever you disclose must be made available to everyone—wire services, the public, financial analysts, large investors—at the same time. If you give an advance look at a particular release to a favored reporter, broker, or investment analyst, you could be liable for a lawsuit or criminal charge.

Until 2000, what was confusing about the interpretation of insider rules was the simultaneous existence of a business custom in which investor relations or senior management would take individual telephone calls or hold private or very selective meetings with analysts or *institutional investors* (large pension funds or mutual funds, for example). Company management would disclose new guidance about upcoming earnings or in some other way tip their favored analysts, brokers, or press about significant upcoming deals or events.

In its background on the new fair disclosure rules, the SEC wrote of concern about

> the selective disclosure of material information by issuers. As reflected in recent publicized reports, many issuers are disclosing important nonpublic information, such as advance warnings of earnings results, to securities analysts or selected institutional investors or both, before making full disclosure of the same information to the general public. Where this has happened, those who were privy to the information beforehand were able to make a profit or avoid a loss at the expense of those kept in the dark . . . .
>
> Issuer selective disclosure bears a close resemblance in this regard to ordinary "tipping" and insider trading. In both cases, a privileged few gain an informational edge—and the ability to use that edge to profit—from their superior access to corporate insiders, rather than from their skill, acumen, or diligence . . . .
>
> Regulation FD is also designed to address another threat to the integrity of our markets: the potential for corporate management to treat material information as a commodity to be used to gain or maintain favor with particular analysts or investors [U.S. Securities and Exchange Commission, 2000].

In response to potential damage "to the integrity of our markets," the SEC issued the new rules to level the investment playing field.

Regulation FD (Fair Disclosure)

Effective October 23, 2000, Regulation FD (Fair Disclosure) puts new restrictions on the timing and the ways a public company can disclose material information, meaning any information that—if known—could move the price of the stock or affect people's decisions about buying and selling a stock. The SEC breaks down the elements of the rule as follows:

> The regulation requires that when an issuer makes an intentional disclosure of material nonpublic information to a person covered by the regulation, it must do so in a manner that provides general public disclosure, rather than through a selective disclosure. For a selective disclosure that is non-intentional, the issuer must publicly disclose the information promptly after it knows (or is reckless in not knowing) that the information selectively disclosed was both material and nonpublic [U.S. Securities and Exchange Commission, 2000].

In practice, what Regulation FD means for companies is this:

- Issue press releases for the disclosure of all information that can affect the price or desirability of stock; do not "tip" privately.
- Distribute press releases widely and simultaneously using a service such as the PR Wire or the Business Wire.
- If information is disclosed inadvertently, issue a press release as soon as possible, within twenty-four hours or for accidental disclosures on weekends and holidays the later of twenty-four hours or before the markets next open.
- Harness digital communications technologies to achieve wide distribution instantaneously. Waste no time at stuffing envelopes with press releases to send out by U.S. mail or faxing them one by one over the course of hours or days.

In fact, the availability of new technologies for distributing business information is at the heart of Reg FD, and although the SEC falls short of specifying which media or combination of media to use, it does give the following model for satisfying requirements:

- First, issue a press release, distributed through regular channels, containing the information;
- Second, provide adequate notice, by a press release and/or website posting, of a scheduled conference call to discuss the announced results, giving investors both the time and date of the conference call, and instructions on how to access the call; and
- Third, hold the conference call in an open manner, permitting investors to listen in either by telephonic means or through Internet webcasting [U.S. Securities and Exchange Commission, 2000].

At the time Regulation FD went into effect, the SEC specifically stated that a posting on the company Web site by itself was not sufficient to meet its fair disclosure requirements, but as technology advances, this may change. The best course is to know and follow the company's established practice and process. Meanwhile, you should let your company know about useful new means of mass communication and news distribution, such as China's recent use of systemwide text messaging to issue a flood warning.

Investor Relations Department

Like most other corporations, MSC maintains a separate department, investor relations, for communicating with Wall Street and with the national and global financial communities. For news releases and other announcements, those in investor relations may work closely with the corporate communications department.

To comply with Regulation FD, most investor relations officers of public companies are unlikely to respond to an individual or institutional investor's query with a tip about undisclosed information; instead, they refer investors with questions to the company's Web site. Such sites typically allow access to archives of press releases, quarterly reports, and the most recent annual report. The Web site can also offer live audio access to a quarterly conference call with financial analysts while it is in progress and to an archived recording for subsequent listening.

Plain English: The Official Style of the SEC

Business writing has a well-deserved reputation for being pompous and boring. From convoluted syntax to clichéd football metaphors, the prose that comes out of some of corporate America often reads like a "don't" list for aspiring writers. If you have only recently encountered your first mutual fund prospectus or your first annual report, you may be surprised to learn that SEC-mandated documents used to be even harder to understand.

In 1998, as part on its new rules to protect investors from fraud, the SEC published A *Plain English Handbook: How to Create Clear SEC Disclosure Documents*. Much of this very useful seventy-seven-page writing guide is devoted to "before" and "after" examples of obscure, legalistic prose and "translations" into plain English more acceptable to the SEC. The rules require that fair disclosure documents actually disclose—not obscure—a company's financial condition.

The handbook, which in now available online for easy access, summarizes the elements of the official style of the SEC:

- Short sentences
- Definite, concrete, everyday words
- Active voice
- Tables and bullet lists

- No legal jargon or highly technical business terms
- No multiple negatives such as, "Don't not use the SEC guidelines" [U.S. Securities and Exchange Commission, 1998, p. 65].

The handbook also asks the writer to avoid:

- Legalistic, overly complex presentations
- Vague boilerplate
- Excerpts from legal documents
- Repetition [U.S. Securities and Exchange Commission, 1998, p. 65].

The SEC's "plain English" rule extends beyond language choice to require that the overall design of documents be visually inviting, logically organized, and understandable on the first reading.

The handbook contains an excellent reading list that includes our personal favorite, and possibly the model for all modern writing guides, Strunk and White's *Elements of Style* (1999). Studying any good style guide will demonstrate that a clear, lean prose style can make your writing—and by extension, your company—look more astute and more professional than the competition's. It will also help your company comply with SEC rules. As the head of the SEC testified before Congress in 2006, the requirements, for example, that sentences be written in the active voice, not the passive voice, is so "investors will be able to figure out who did what to whom" (Cox, 2006).

Business and financial writing assignments offer far fewer opportunities for prose experiments than most other public relations writing assignments do. Don't waste time and energy looking for some offbeat approach; just get the facts down as clearly and understandably as you can. Write in plain English.

Business Release

When something big happens—when your company buys or sells a major segment of its business, when it issues new shares of stock or buys back old ones, when it introduces a new product line—you are likely to issue a release. Here, your headline and approach will be dictated by the event:

"MSC Acquires Nanotechnology Company"

"MSC Wins Government Contract"

"MSC Declares $.17 Dividend"

The form of the release should be crisp and factual, with *what* followed by *why*. The explanation—the why—may come in the way of a quotation from your company president. A paragraph or two of background, perhaps on the company or on the industry as a whole, can then follow.

Quarterly Earnings Release

As a public relations business writer, the most common writing assignment you will encounter is the news release announcing the corporation's performance at the end of each quarter (a three-month period in either the calendar or the fiscal year). These releases begin with a brief statement of the company's revenues and pretax profits, with comparisons with the same period in the prior year. Similar breakdowns by operating division may follow.

Next, usually, come comments about the figures by the president or chairperson. Finally, the release details any noteworthy events from the quarter just completed. The news release also typically contains a chart or table of the financial results in numerical form.

Assuming that the fictional MSC, Inc. has three divisions—MSC/USA, MSC/International, and MSC Ventures—a sample quarterly release might look like this:

FOR IMMEDIATE RELEASE: April 5, 2007
CONTACT: Jane Smith, Vice-President
Corporate Information
202/555-1212
jsmith@msc.com

MSC FIRST-QUARTER EARNINGS PER SHARE
UP 45%

MSC, Inc.'s revenues, net income, and earnings per share for the first quarter of 2007 were all ahead of the record totals for the same period last year, the company announced today. Results for the quarter just completed are as follows:

First Quarter	2007	2006	Change
Revenues	$379 million	$284 million	+33%
Net income	$ 25 million	$ 18 million	+39%
Net income per share	$1.42	$0.98	+45%

"Our first-quarter performance reflects the sharp improvement in domestic and international markets we've been experiencing since the third quarter of last year," said Joseph A. Medium, Chairman and Chief Executive Officer. "We are also seeing positive results from the cost-cutting programs we've implemented at all three of our operating divisions, and we expect to make further progress in this area as the year goes on."

For the three-month period that ended March 31, MSC/USA revenues rose 33 percent over 2006 first-quarter levels, while net income increased 49 percent. MSC/International's revenues and net income improved by 25 percent and 19 percent, respectively, in part because of the weakening of the U.S. dollar as measured against foreign currencies. Revenues for MSC Ventures rose by 18 percent, but net income declined 7 percent, primarily due to start-up costs for the division's new nanotechnology manufacturing operation.

The MSC Board of Directors today also announced a quarterly dividend of $0.17 per fully diluted share of common stock.

As the year goes on, columns of figures comparing six-month, nine-month, and year-to-year totals will be added as well. The year-end summary, as you might expect, is the most detailed, and it serves as a basis for the annual report.

The numbers for financial reports are derived and reported in terms of GAAP (generally accepted accounting principles). Some companies with special financial circumstances also announce *pro forma results,* which say how the results would differ if certain one-time charges or one-time expenses were considered. Pro forma results require special attention from the company and the financial writer, because the SEC scrutinizes them carefully to make sure that the financial picture they present is accurate. In 2002, for example, Trump Hotels and Casino Resorts (THCR) settled a case with the SEC that its

> Earnings Release was materially misleading because it created the false and misleading impression that the Company had exceeded earnings expectations primarily through operational improvements, when in fact it had not. The Release expressly stated that the net income figure excluded a one-time charge. The statement that this one-time charge was excluded implied that no other significant one time items were included in THCR's stated net income. Contrary to that implication, however, the stated net income included an undisclosed one-time gain of $17.2 million
> . . . .
>
> The misleading impression . . . was reinforced by the comparison of the stated earnings-per-share figure with analysts' earnings estimates and by statement in the Release that the Company had been successful in improving its operating performance [U.S. Securities and Exchange Commission, 2002].

The bottom line on bottom lines is that earnings releases must present an accurate picture of the company's financial condition.

Headlines and lead sentences in quarterly reports should meet the same journalistic standards as those in other kinds of news releases. They should always be clear and concise. If there is something to emphasize, highlight it: "MSC Posts Best-Ever First-Quarter Results," "Sales, Earnings Up at MSC," "MSC Revenues Rise for Ninth Consecutive Quarter." If the news is not so good, you are under no obligation to trumpet it. A common approach—and a perfectly acceptable one—is this: "MSC Reports First-Quarter Results." Some companies use that form even when the news is good. But always avoid a headline like this: "MSC Year-End Totals Announced." Using the passive voice (totals were announced by whom?) sounds like the news is being dragged out of you. Stick to active voice verbs ("MSC Announces").

You should expect to draft the quotation from your chief executive as well. This should be basic, straightforward, and explanatory. Stick with simple sentences and active verbs.

After you've written a draft, your most important job begins: fact checking. You could send out the most boring, hackneyed quarterly report in the history of finance, and probably not one investor or financial reporter would complain. But misstate a fact or calculate the numbers incorrectly, and e-mail will pour in as though *New York Times* language columnist William Safire had made a grammatical error.

So add the numbers correctly. Use a calculator. Make sure the statements in the release have been cleared by the financial department or the legal department, or both. Remember that you are writing for highly skeptical readers. You want to present your corporation as the sound, savvy, responsible business it is. You have the ability—a much greater ability than you might suspect—to influence how Wall Street sees your company. Strict factual accuracy at all times is paramount.

Quarterly Conference Call

A quarterly conference call is scheduled and announced in advance to take place within hours of the release of an earnings report. The calls take the place of formerly exclusive tips to big investors or analysts' meetings. They fulfill fair disclosure requirements because anyone can listen in by signing up with the company or listening to a Webcast. On the call, the CEO and one or more others such as the chief financial officer or the chief operating officer make short opening statements about the past quarter's financial results and perhaps offer *company guidance* about the upcoming quarter and the prospective year-end results. During the call, active participants such as stock analysts who cover the company or the industry, business reporters, and large investors ask questions that may bring out further information about the company's financial position and prospects.

A financial writer may draft opening statements, Q&As, and talking points for the quarterly conference call. The opening statements of the senior managers are short, informally phrased speeches. These statements should be researched and drafted following the principles outlined in Chapter Five.

To draft answers to anticipated questions from the securities analysts on the conference call, follow the suggestions for drafting Q&As in Chapters Five and Eight.

Talking points are your company's two or three strongest messages in their strongest phrasing, the sound-bites most likely to be quoted in the press. (See Chapters Seven and Thirteen.)

Annual Report

Delivering an annual report to stockholders is an SEC requirement. Preparing the report offers the company a controlled and expansive way to deliver its message to its current and potential stockholders. The finished product inevitably says a lot, in words, and in pictures, about the company that creates it. For example, Google projects a creative, playful image, ExxonMobil promotes a scientific look, and Gap Inc. presents youth and excitement while featuring its clothing lines. The look and presentation of a company are the topics of discussions at the highest levels of the company from early in the fiscal year.

Some shareholders complain that the money spent on these expensive productions would be better put into their dividends. Many companies would also like to save the expenses of the massive printing and mailings. For a number of years, corporations have been posting PDF versions of their annual reports on their Web sites for easy referral or downloading by potential investors. Corporations are now in the process of asking their shareholders to opt in to an electronic solution to the problems of too much money spent, too much paper used, and too many trees destroyed. Nevertheless, most shareholders still prefer to receive a beautifully designed, four-color report printed on high-quality, glossy paper. For most investors, annual reports are a form of entertainment and a tangible symbol of the pride they feel in owning a piece of corporate America.

Your job, as the writer of your company's annual report, is to reinforce that pride. The report should project as positive and upbeat a picture as possible without straying past the boundaries of accuracy and clarity as set forth by the SEC.

Setting a Timetable

Annual reports must be published on a strict schedule. By law, your company must hold an annual meeting that must be preceded (by more than a month) by the issuing of a proxy statement and a report to shareholders. If you are responsible for turning out your company's report, you must meet that deadline in delivering an accurate, attractive, and traditionally printed and bound report.

Your work starts with the creation of a schedule that will ensure the report's timely release. Begin with that date and work backward, figuring in how long it will take your printer to print and bind the report, how long for your art director to assemble photos and illustrations and lay out the report, and how long for you to research and write the text. Build in lots of time—several weeks, at least—for securing approvals from management and making corrections and changes. No matter how brilliant and appropriate your prose, changes will be made. Count on them, and budget for them. If your company operates on a calendar year and you want to issue your annual report in March, the planning should begin in late summer or early fall, and the actual gathering of art materials should follow soon after. The writing itself and the approval process should be well under way by December. (For more information on publications and printing, see Chapter Ten.)

Design and Production

The look of the report represents the company to current stockholders, prospective stockholders, and the business press. Design decisions such as color, weight of paper, typeface, number and size of photographs, and the charts to be used all contribute to the effectiveness of the final product. The graphic designer selected should have experience with annual reports and other corporate publications and work well with experienced professional photographers and freelance writers, so that the written material and the visual elements fit together and enhance the company's brand image. A professional designer shepherds the report through design, prepress, printing, and binding in a timely and cost-effective manner.

What Is in the Report

By law, an annual report must contain a variety of financial statements (the preparation of which will probably be the responsibility of the financial department); a discussion of the state of your industry, the financial condition of your business, and the results of its operations in the past year; and a description of your company's structure and the businesses in which the company is engaged.

From a writer's standpoint, annual reports offer a chance not only for a longer, more developed piece of work but also for a more flexible and interesting approach to style. Boring annual reports make a company look stodgy. Good annual reports should read like a good business magazine, while projecting a confident, dynamic image for the company. You are writing for intelligent, knowledgeable readers. Don't insult them, and don't kid yourself into believing you can hide your company's problems (if there are any) behind verbal fluff.

A Sample Framework

In most cases, you'll want to put the numbers at the back. Many shareholders won't read the financial statements, and in any case, it is the words and pictures, not the numbers, that generate the pride and positive feeling you are trying to foster. A page of financial headlines at the beginning makes a good introduction. These are often printed on the inside front cover and perhaps the facing page, complete with brightly-colored, eye-catching graphs and pie charts.

Here's a sample framework, with elaboration on items 2 and 3 given in the following sections:

1. Financial highlights (inside front cover)
2. Chairperson's letter to shareholders (introduction)
3. Description of the business
4. Detailed look at operating areas
5. Introduction to the financial section
6. Financial statements

Think of your annual report as a long news article. Each of your readers is interested in the article to some degree. Some will read every word; some will look only at the pictures. To please and inform as many of these people as possible, organize the report so that it moves from the general to the particular; the more the shareholder reads, the more he or she will find out about the company's year. The ultimate details—the financial breakdowns—come last. Sometimes it seems that the most useful and revealing information is buried in the footnotes to the financials, a possibly deceptive practice that the SEC's "plain English" and "fair disclosure" rules have tried to eliminate.

Chairperson's Letter. In the general framework outlined, the chairperson's letter makes an ideal introduction. It should include an overview of each major area of business and commentary on the year just concluded. A shareholder who reads no further will have a general understanding of what is going on at the company.

Unless your chairperson takes pride in an especially eccentric style (and there are more than a few such executives), the tone of the letter will be clear and businesslike. Since your readership includes the SEC, what you write about your business must accurately reflect what the numbers at the back of the report say.

Here's an example of a letter to the shareholders:

TO OUR SHAREHOLDERS

We remain extremely pleased with our company's continued strong performance in 2007. MSC's financial results—income from continued operations, net income, and revenues—were at the highest levels in the company's history. Our sales of new and expanded lines of handheld devices were also at an all-time high. We achieved this success by paying close attention to our customers, controlling our costs, and improving the quality of our products and customer service.

Our largest business, MSC/USA, completed a year of substantial growth and greatly improved profitability. At a time when the domestic market for handhelds was experiencing little or no growth, MSC's long-time commitment to research, development, and now manufacturing of nanotechnology proved extremely fortuitous, and we continue to invest heavily in this area, including making significant acquisitions.

MSC/International enjoyed another year of significant expansion in an ever-lengthening list of foreign territories. During the past twelve months, the division has opened subsidiaries in Brazil, Russia, and India. Discussions are under way to create a cooperative venture between MSC and the People's Republic of China.

During the past year, MSC continued expanding into new business areas through the MSC Ventures division. Our miniaturized products remain our fastest-growing business, and we look forward to continued steady growth in this area. Through MSC Ventures, the company has also entered the field of nanotechnology manufacturing. In the fourth quarter, we broke ground on a nanotech factory adjacent to our existing handheld plant in Indianapolis, and we expect the new facility to be online by the first quarter of next year.

In closing, we want to share our feelings of pride and gratitude with all the MSC employees around the world who have contributed so much to our success. They deserve all our thanks, not only for what they have achieved, but also for the promise those achievements hold for our future.

[Signature]

Joseph A. Medium
Chairman and Chief Executive Officer

Description of the Business. By law, the annual report must include a description of the business, a concise summary of your corporation's structure (often illustrated by a chart), and the businesses in which the company is engaged. Keep it simple, direct, and factual. If you're writing more than, say, three hundred words, either you work for a very large, very diversified company or you're overwriting. For MSC, the description could read like this:

THE MSC ORGANIZATION

MSC, Inc. is a diversified handheld device and nano-technology company with more than 10,000 employees worldwide. Its principal businesses are designing, manufacturing, and marketing handheld devices and software; and the research, development, and manufacturing of nanotechnology applications. The company consists of three divisions: MSC/USA, MSC/International, and MSC Ventures. MSC is a leading designer of handheld communication and computing devices domestically and around the world, as well as one of the top five U.S. designers and manufacturers of software applications for the handheld marketplace. MSC Ventures operates a world-class research and development program in nanotechnology with partnerships and joint ventures with a number of leading international companies in the areas of hardware, consumer products, and medical devices. MSC also operates a new state-of-the-art manufacturing facility in Indianapolis, with others to open in the next two years in Brazil, Russia, and India through MSC/International.

Annual Meeting

Under SEC rules, an annual meeting open to all stockholders is required for all public companies. A month in advance of the meeting, stockholders must receive notice of the meeting's time and location, a ballot for voting on important issues to be decided at the meeting (the *proxy statement*), and an annual report and financial statements.

Annual meetings can be planned following the general process suggested for press conferences in Chapter Eight, keeping some special considerations in mind.

Location

The SEC doesn't say where the meeting must be held, only that stockholders must be notified and invited. Some companies, such as Warren Buffett's Berkshire/Hathaway, customarily hold annual meetings that are rousing celebrations of the company and its culture at company headquarters or in the city where the headquarters are located. Some companies prefer to rotate the meeting among various large cities (in theory making the meeting accessible over a number of years to more stockholders). Coincidentally, when the year's results have been particularly dismal, the occasional company may schedule the annual meeting in an obscure backwater with limited public transportation and hotel accommodations on the pretext that the location is the site of a subsidiary's manufacturing plant or the birthplace of the folksy CEO. With live Webcasting of the annual meeting and the availability of replay on the Internet now fairly standard, companies may become more straightforward in their choice of a site, perhaps even choosing the area where the largest number of their stockholders live.

Executive Presentations

The program of the annual meeting is a live, in-person version of the annual report. That printed material needs to be reformulated, however, into speeches and multimedia presentations written in a more conversational style.

Q&A

The Q&A from stockholders is the part of the program most anticipated by stockholders. Usually any stockholder in attendance (even the owner of one share) can speak, harangue the management, or ask a perceptive or stupid question. This is the part of the annual ritual most dreaded by some senior managers and boards of directors. They have to endure the podium year after year while stockholder gadflies, as they are pejoratively called, berate them about CEO overcompensation or shareholder rights or the environmental damage caused by the company's manufacturing operations. Management and their speechwriters need to be prepared with draft responses and talking points for the Q&A sessions that are thoughtful, respectful, and concise, never arrogant, dismissive, or bullying. Most important, managements under fire for hot-button issues might want to remember the media and shareholder outcry in May 2006 when Home Depot limited the Q&A at its annual meeting, even cutting off power to the audience's microphone. The company later had to issue a public apology and announce a return to its traditional annual meeting format for the next year (Harris, 2006).

Press Release

Most companies issue a press release immediately after the annual meeting to announce the results of the shareholder votes on the election of directors, company initiatives, and shareholder initiatives, as well as any other material matters, such as share buybacks that are announced during the meeting.

Chapter Recap

In review, the steps for creating effective business and financial news releases are these:

- Follow the steps for producing media releases as outlined in Chapter Two.
- Learn basic financial vocabulary, and use it correctly.
- Research thoroughly, and recheck all figures for accuracy.

- Write in a clear, direct style.
- Maintain confidentiality.
- Fulfill the requirements of Regulation Fair Disclosure (Reg FD).
- Meet all SEC timing and reporting requirements.
- Write in plain English.

In addition, when writing annual reports and presentations and Q&As for annual meetings, do the following:

- Set a timetable that will ensure meeting the deadline set by the SEC.
- Create a framework or outline that covers all the information required by the SEC and goes from an overview, to sections about the business, to the specifics of the financial results—for instance:
  - Financial highlights
  - Chairperson's letter to shareholders (introduction)
  - Description of the business
  - Detailed look at operating areas
  - Introduction to the financial section
  - Financial statements
- Choose a design professional to oversee design and production. Work closely with the graphic designer to fit copy and to ensure that the text and the visuals work together to enhance the company image.
- Allow ample time for several rounds of approvals and changes.
- Recast the annual report material in a more conversational style for annual meeting presentations.
- Draft Q&As that are thoughtful, respectful, and concise.

10

PUBLICATIONS

The Editorial Stage

The public relations agency, marketing and publicity, and corporate communications departments are typically responsible for creating a varied spectrum of literature about the organization or client. Unlike a commercial publication that lists numerous people on its masthead, indicating a division of labor among many, a corporate publication is usually supervised at all stages of planning and execution by one editor-writer.

In-house publications (those written and published by the company itself) may include product or promotional publications, often referred to as collateral advertising, as well as annual and quarterly reports and other publications aimed at employees, distributors, and key market and customer segments. Companies that sell services such as management consulting sometimes commission research projects on topics of interest to their customers and publish the results in the form of simply designed "white papers" as a service to current and potential customers.

In-house publications can range from a one-page newsletter to, say, a sixty-four-page, four-color magazine. A company's marketing goals may call for promotional brochures explaining how the company functions, the services it offers, or the products it manufactures. Or a client may require an annual report to shareholders, material for fundraising, program guides, or direct mail solicitations. In-house publications are also used for internal purposes; an example is an employee newsletter that informs employees about projects and activities within the company.

The task of publication falls into two distinct categories: editorial and production. This chapter offers an overview of the specialized vocabulary and procedures involved in planning, writing, compiling images, and editing sponsored publications—the editorial part of publishing.

In the digital age, many periodic publications are designed only the first time they appear. After that, the writer-editor simply transfers the edited stories, photographs, and graphics into the publication's template. The production process or "publishing" can then mean pushing the Print button for a few copies, sending the publication as an attachment to an e-mail list, posting it on a Web site, and perhaps sending out an e–mail alert with a link to the new issue. Some company publications, such as annual reports and brochures, are still designed and printed on glossy paper using the more traditional prepress and printing press production process, following the specifications of a designated printing company.

Since this is a book on writing, this chapter focuses on the editorial side of publication.

Editorial Considerations

Begin the editorial process by asking yourself these general questions:

- What overall message do I want to communicate, and to whom? (It's important to know, and never lose sight of, this audience.)
- What information do I want to convey? What do I want to exclude? (Publications that try to cover too much ground are usually ineffective.)
- What image do I want to project?
- How do I combine these factors?

Then ask yourself these more specific questions:

- What kind of editorial treatment will meet these goals? What are the features to be communicated (for example, a new product or process or a merger or expansion), and, more important, what are the potential benefits to the target audience?

- How many pages should the publication run, and what size format should it have? Most publications are designed as multiples of four pages, because the majority of printing presses work most efficiently on that basis. Mailing considerations may influence your decision on the size and dimensions of the publication: the more the publication weighs, the costlier it is to mail, and an odd size or shape may not fit into any standard-size envelopes and thus require expensive, custom-made envelopes.

- Should this be a one-time publication, a series, or a regularly issued newsletter?

- How much of the copy can I write, and how much should be assigned to others (freelance writers or staff members)?

- How will my editorial content be different from that of my competitors' publications and commercial publications? What is the environment in which this piece must be positioned? Are there too many newsletters reaching this target audience already? Is this a me-too product, even though it is new for this company or client? If it is, what's better or distinctive about it?

- What is the shelf-life of the publication, and how soon will it be outdated?

- Who needs to approve the editorial plan before I begin implementing it?

By now, the theme of getting approvals before you proceed on projects should be familiar. Find out who must review your ideas, and present them clearly and concisely. It's advisable to offer editorial proposals (in writing or at meetings) with more ideas than one publication can actually contain. That way, you are prepared with alternatives to ideas that are rejected. Most people like choices, and the more you give them, the better the chance is for speedy approval. If and when your idea is rejected, don't be defensive or take the rejection personally. Be professional and eager to please. Remember, it's your client's publication, and your client has to be happy with it. Your role is to suggest ideas and formats and oversee them to completion.

To help decide on the specific editorial content of your publication, always put yourself in the role of the typical reader you are addressing. Ask yourself: "If I were a member of this organization (or an employee of this corporation, a customer of this business, or a constituent of this official), what would I want and need to know? What would be helpful and informative to me? What would convince me to think (or plan, buy, or vote) a certain way?" Your answers to these questions will lead you to useful editorial ideas.

Often you will be able to draw on existing material from your public relations files and use it as background for your publications. For instance, a speech given by your client could, with a little alteration, become an editorial column in a magazine. A series of advertisements could provide a basis for a sales promotion brochure or a persuasive article. A series of press releases could be adapted as newsletter items. Be aware of all of your client's activities and the resources available. Good research is an essential prerequisite to writing and producing effective publications.

Newsletters

The content, style and design of newsletters should be geared toward the specific group of readers you want to reach and influence.

Internal Newsletters

Larger companies often circulate newsletters internally to employees on both the management and lower staff levels. A 2005 study revealed that "48 percent of 472 organizations surveyed worldwide said their management has not effectively communicated their business strategies to employees and engaged them in living it in their daily jobs. As a result, only about one-third—37 percent—of organizations reported that their employees are effectively aligned to the missions and visions of their businesses" (International Association of Business Communicators, 2005).

Internal newsletters often carry messages from the president. They can apprise the rank and file about how the company puts its mission and philosophy into action, as well as about policy changes, the company's outlook, different departments' priorities, company benefits, and so forth. They are an excellent way to let employees know what is going on in areas outside their immediate sphere—how the different pieces of the organization fit together.

The challenge for editors of in-house publications, as for all other publications, is to tailor them to the interests of the readers. Employees will probably not read a newsletter that they perceive as one more list of benefits from human resources or the same old clichés from the CEO. The articles and features have to be new, interesting, and important to the individual employee's work life or personal life.

As incentives for employees to read newsletters, many include personal items such as promotions, department changes, retiree news, informational quizzes, department features, marriages, births, and the results of company sports team competitions. People like to see their names in print, even in a company publication, and such items can give a company of any size a personal touch.

In large corporations with locations throughout the country or world, it is becoming increasingly common to produce employee newsletters in video form. Essentially, the editorial challenge remains unchanged, and the copy becomes a series of scripts. Some companies may also deliver internal news by e-mail or post it online on a special employee-accessible page of the Web site.

When writing for any internal publication, keep in mind that it might also be read by people external to the company, including members of the media.

External Newsletters

Newsletters can also be used to inform audiences outside the company, such as the media, members of a particular industry, dealers, distributors, suppliers, and securities analysts, to name just a few. The editorial content of a newsletter varies with each client. If you are writing one for a hypothetical company, Cool Tech, for example, you might focus on new products or sales of existing lines. You might also report on interesting trends in a certain division, new technology applications, or significant research results.

If you're producing a newsletter for a prominent rap artist, you will craft the newsletter in an entirely different way, including a different visual style. You might report on new recordings due for release, itineraries of upcoming concert tours, or recent awards received or distinctions achieved. In many cases, topics of general interest to the industry are discussed, with a slant toward how your client is involved or affected.

For every client, you must analyze the composition of your audience and decide what information will both fulfill your client's objectives and interest your readers.

Corporate Brochures

Corporate brochures are key items in sales, promotion, and media kits. The brochure is normally a presentation of the company's distinctive capabilities as they apply to the corporation as a whole, an operating division, or a single product line. The form—four-color or black-and-white design and photography, art, or illustrations, or choice of design or paper stock—is dictated by the content. A style appropriate to consumer products, for example, might appear too frivolous for financial products, which require a straightforward style.

The corporate brochure presents information about a client and usually covers these areas:

- Who we are.
- Where we come from (that is, background on the company).
- What we offer (the service or product).
- How or where we are available.
- Why we're special.

From the outset, it's critical to identify the key messages in terms of features and benefits. Features are the nuts-and-bolts of a company or product; benefits describe what's in it for the reader.

The length of the corporate brochure is determined by the messages the client wants to communicate, the budget, and how often the brochure will be updated. Brevity is unfailingly a virtue. The most effective brochures are almost invariably those that succeed in communicating their key messages with the greatest economy of words. The life expectancy of a brochure—or its shelf life—is an important planning consideration, particularly in deciding if a large enough quantity is needed to justify the cost of four-color commercial printing, as opposed to printing a limited number of copies on a laser printer. Another economical approach is to design the brochure electronically or design and then scan it and post it on the Web site as a PDF file to be read or downloaded. In this case, the quality of the printing and photographs will be reduced by the use of plain white paper, and the potential client may not be thrilled by using his or her expensive time and ink to print your brochure.

Assigning Stories

When developing a publication or a new issue of a periodical, you may need to assign some of the copy tasks to other members of the public relations team or to outside writers. For a variety of reasons (discussed in other chapters), it is always important to know which reporters cover your industry. For your in-house publication, you may want to solicit copy contributions from reporters at trade and consumer publications that cover your field. Some reporters are allowed to accept outside assignments.

It's wise to build contacts with several competent freelance writers and to use good ones regularly. Such practices enable writers to learn how best to work with you and gain some knowledge of the operations and communications needs of the clients you serve. List your choices of two or three writers for each article to be assigned. Call your first choice, and ask if he or she is interested in a freelance assignment, and briefly describe the nature of the article, the fee, and the deadline.

Establishing Editorial Guidelines

Whether you plan to write copy yourself or assign it to another writer, the first task is to compile a body of source material that can be used as a starting point in developing the piece. The second task is to frame a general outline to serve as an editorial guideline for the writing. The more specific your plans are at the outset, the more likely it is that the resulting draft will be on target. It is easier to write a first draft in a disciplined manner than to rewrite an unsuccessful effort. Here are the key elements in an outline (or treatment):

- A statement of the nature and focus of the article. Never be vague. When appropriate, suggest people to be interviewed.
- A statement of the article's length and deadline.
- A sampler of similar articles that serve as good models of what you are seeking.

If you are assigning the piece to an outside writer, you'll also want to compose a letter commissioning the assignment. Also enclose background information about the company, background information you have about the topic, and sample articles of the kind you expect from the commissioned writer. Following is a sample letter of commission:

Dear [writer's name],

This letter confirms our conversation commissioning you to write an article for [title of publication]. Your article should cover [subject] with particular attention devoted to [focus].

The article should run between [number] and [number] of words, or approximately [number] double-spaced pages in 12 point Courier or Courier New type. I'd like you to interview the following people for the article: [names, titles, phone numbers, and e-mail addresses]

The deadline for the piece is [date], and on acceptance we will pay you $[amount].

I've attached a few samples of similar articles we've published that might be helpful to you. Also attached is background information about our company and some material related to your topic.

Please feel free to call me for any reason. I'll be happy to answer any questions you might have or assist you in any way. I'm delighted you are available to contribute to our publication, and I look forward to working with you.

Sincerely,

Name
[title]

Letters of commission vary according to the writers and the assignments. If you are working with an experienced writer, you may want to leave out the rejection clause ("on acceptance"). Most of the time, it's a good idea to build into your editorial deadlines room for rewriting the piece or for reassigning it should the writer not deliver what you need. In other words, don't assume the article will be submitted in perfect shape. You must allow adequate time for editing.

Other Concerns: Format, Timeliness, Style, Approvals, and Copyright

Creating publications is a complex process that requires many skills, and often within the corporate world requires one person or a tiny staff to accomplish many disparate tasks and fulfill many roles, such as writer, editor, designer, production manager, and record keeper. This section covers some of these additional concerns.

Format

You will have many editorial formats to choose among for your publication. Familiarize yourself with what your client has published before and liked or disliked. Always be aware of what your competitors produce, and take notes on what you may want to imitate. For a professional-looking final product, you may want to work with a design professional. Decide whether your final product will be distributed digitally or be printed traditionally on paper, or both, and work with your Web master or your printer from the beginning of the editorial process.

Timeliness

Copy should usually be written in a way that does not make it time-bound. You may be writing copy that will not be published for several months or that must remain accurate for months or years to come. Production is a major expense, and brochures, in particular, may require a fairly long shelf life to be cost-effective.

Here's an example of how to free copy from a time frame. Instead of writing, "Six years ago, Larry Davidson was named president of Cool Tech," you could write, "In 2004, Larry Davidson was named president of Cool Tech." Or if you're writing about a company's product line, you might write, "The company's products *include* X, Y, and Z," instead of "The company's products *are* X, Y, and Z." That way, the copy will be accurate even if new products are added after your publication is printed.

Style

Use a style sheet or a stylebook to ensure consistency in spelling, abbreviation, punctuation, and other editorial matters. Some editors create their own style sheets, but most use *The Associated Press Stylebook and Briefing on Media Law* (Associated Press, 2004) or *The New York Times Manual of Style and Usage* (Siegal and Connolly, 1999).

Approvals

When your copy is written, edited, and corrected, do a round of approvals so that everyone concerned is still informed before you go to the expense of layout and design. Keep a record of all approvals in case questions arise later.

Copyrights

Be sure that you publish only original or company-owned material, which is material for which your company has a written document of release or sale for this particular purpose. Photographs in company files can be particularly troublesome, because use depends on the original agreement with the individual photographer and whether one-time use or a full buyout of all rights was purchased. As mentioned in Chapter Two, each photograph should be printed with a copyright designation, date of creation, and the name of the photographer or other copyright holder, such as a photo agency.

Each of your publications should be published with the copyright symbol, the date, and the full name of your company—for example, "©2007, Your Company's Name, Inc."

Production

When all your copy has been written, edited, and approved, you are ready to move into production, the second phase of an-house publication. Many newsletters and other kinds of publications now exist only digitally. News of their "publication" may be sent by an e-mail alert to the list of subscribers, who then access them using a link to the Web site, where they can be read or downloaded as a PDF file.

If you will be publishing on paper, choose a designer and a printing company early in the process, so you can create the right quantity of material for the intended layout and design and so that you know the printing company's prepress requirements for such elements as black and white photography and color images and design elements.

Files and File Copies

Keep complete files, including files of extra copies and not-to-be-touched files of permanent "File Copies," along with a file of "Rights Agreements" for each publication or separate issue.

Also keep "Editorial Files," "Approval Files," and "Production Files" of materials at all the stages of the publications development. A record of approvals is extremely important.

Your files will serve as a record of the process for you, a pattern for your successor to follow, and a source of answers to questions about rights that may arise many years down the line.

Chapter Recap

Here are some guidelines for the editorial stage of in-house publications:

- In planning a publication, decide what you want to communicate, identify your audience or audiences, consider what image you want to convey, and determine what kind of editorial treatment will achieve your goals. Also decide what size the publication will be, how often it will appear, how it will be different from your competitors' publications, and who needs to approve your editorial plan before you begin implementing it.

- Decide if you need to produce actual physical copies printed on paper. If not, work with the company's Web site supervisor to determine where on the site the newsletter can be located for maximum accessibility and impact.

- When you have decided on your editorial guidelines, make writing assignments that state the nature and focus of the article, the people to be interviewed, the article's length, and the deadline. If you're using an outside writer, send him or her a letter of commission, attaching background material about the company and the topic, as well as samples of the kind of article you expect.

- Check everything twice—you can never be too careful. Verify information in a manuscript; whenever possible, have professional copyeditors check the manuscript before it is typeset. Verify photo captions. Assume nothing is correct until you get corroboration from reliable sources.

- Get approvals for everything. That applies to copy, art, and layout.

- Be sure your company has clear rights to any material you publish, paying particular attention to photo copyright designations. Also put a copyright designation, date, and the legal name of your company on each publication.

- Keep organized files. Save the original of copy that has initials of approval on it and research files that have sources for information cited.

- Plan an editorial and production schedule that allows adequate time for each stage to be completed properly.

11

WRITING FOR THE INTERNET

The digital age and the Internet present public relations writers with a number of challenges and opportunities. Clarity, brevity, and correctness become more important than ever before as the public relations writer uses digital communications tools and technologies. E-mail, Web sites, and blogs make communications fast, visible and essentially immortal.

E-Mail, Instant Messaging, Paging, and Wireless Internet

Speed and twenty-four-hour access to people and information are the boon and the bane of the public relations profession in the digital age. In the past, communications professionals might have provided their home telephone number to their immediate superior and one or two of their most important media contacts. Now almost everyone, including PR professionals of all levels, can be contacted almost any time of the day or night and on weekends and vacation. Telephone and cell phone caller ID, callback, and paging functions, as well as wireless text messaging and e-mail, have erased the distinction between work and private time. The pressure is on to respond fast and by writing words that are transmitted digitally into cyberspace.

The Immortality of Errors and Indiscretions

E-mail and instant messaging allow for communications that are speedy but not necessarily deep. Their speed and the ease of pressing the Send button make it highly tempting to "save time" by skipping proofreading and reviewing the list of recipients. Don't!

One experience trying to correct an error that you have sent into cyberspace will use up all the time you could have "saved" during an entire career as a public relations writer. And your career—or at least your current job—can be cut abruptly short if a financial document is distributed containing a stock-moving error or an internal draft of an important press release is inadvertently disclosed to a member of the press or the financial community before it is fairly disclosed to everyone. (See Chapter Nine.)

Always remember that an e-mail message lives on even after you delete it. Digital communications can be retrieved from hard drives, servers, Internet service providers, or recipients, among other places. Companies such as Enron learned this to their regret during the course of lawsuits. Lawsuits have revealed e-mail messages that expressed doubts about the safety of a company's new drugs, reservations about the legality of accounting practices, and indications that executives' private thoughts about the company's financial soundness differ from their public statements. These "private" communications, used as evidence of who knew what when, have brought down entire companies, convicted executives, and led to adverse judgments in cases about a hostile work environment, sexual harassment, and discrimination. For anything truly confidential, pick up the telephone, walk down the hall, or arrange to talk face-to-face.

Compelling E-Mail Subject Lines

Getting your e-mail read by the recipient depends on your subject line. E-mail subject lines serve as headlines to what follows, so take time to craft good ones that succinctly billboard the content. When appropriate, especially when pitching a story, write them as teasers. (See Chapter Three for examples of good subject lines.)

Web Sites

A well-designed Web site that allows easy archiving and retrieval of written material such as press releases and annual reports can enhance a company's relationships with the media, customers, stockholders, and job seekers.

Although it is relatively easy and inexpensive to start a simple Web site, professional support is always recommended. Numerous Web providers do the following essential services:

- Register domain names (.com, .net, .org, .info, .biz).

- Offer templates and services for designing Web sites—even online stores with secure, encrypted financial transactions.

- Provide Web hosting, including registering the site with search engines such as ask.com, go.com, google.com, msn.com, technorati.com, and yahoo.com, among many others.

- Provide services that may be too complex or too expensive to do in-house. For example, first-page results—the chances that a Web site will be among the ten on the first page of search engine results—can be enhanced with a design that considers search engine optimization. This is especially important for sites that sell ads at a rate based on page clicks or page "hits," meaning the number of times people click on a page and click from page to page of an interesting site.

Web service providers charge yearly and monthly fees based on the level and complexity of service.

By now, most organizations and companies recognize the importance of owning the domain name or names by which they are best known, as well as common misspellings of their name. Some companies have learned to their great regret and expense that entrepreneurs have bought up these household names for themselves in order eventually to extract money (sell the domain back) or to lure unsuspecting visitors to a porn site. So even if a company does not yet have an up-and-running Web site, the public relations office should make sure the organization's most commonly used names are purchased as domain names and renewed yearly.

An individual with a basic knowledge of computers can launch a simple Web site using a Web provider's tools or other inexpensive services or software such as Dreamweaver. By now, most companies have some sort of a Web presence, often one that was designed several years ago. Make sure it looks up to date and has the capabilities now needed for efficient public relations activities, customer relations management, and audio, video, and downloading capabilities. In fact, most companies recognize the need for a sophisticated Web design with a unique look and intuitive functionality that enhance their image and branding.

In addition, the Securities and Exchange Commission's Reg FD (discussed at length in Chapter Nine) means that a public company's PR and Web functions must be well coordinated. Press releases and financial communications need to appear on the Web site simultaneously with their release to the press and financial community. The Web site should also have a provision to allow access to financial conference calls; simulcasts of annual meetings are also becoming more common.

For the Media

For the media, the company Web site can offer a "For Journalists," "For the Media," or "Pressroom" area that includes this information:

- The names, titles, telephone numbers, e-mail addresses and contact information, and areas of responsibility of various corporate, divisional, regional, and subsidiary public relations officers
- Press releases, which also serve as a history of significant events when they are archived in reverse chronological order
- Biographies of senior management

- Company backgrounder, time line, and fact sheet
- Information about the company's citizenship, environmental concern, nonprofit activities, and awards
- Links to the customer areas of the site that post positive print and broadcast coverage of products, services, and community service
- Links to the archive of business articles in the "Investors" area of the site
- An opt-in function to allow the journalist to be added to your distribution lists to receive your future press releases and newsletter alerts

A special password-protected area of the Web site can be used to restrict access to print- and broadcast-quality photographs, video, and broadcast scripts, or these can be sent electronically as requested by reputable media outlets. The "For the Press" area of the Web site may provide summaries of video or thumbnails (small, relatively low-resolution pictures) of high-quality photographs suitable for use in print, B-roll that can be edited into news reports, or any video news release created by the company in two versions—one with a narrator (not to be identified as a "reporter" because of ethical concerns) and one without the voice-over narration but with a suggested script (see Chapter Seven). In other words, the section of the Web site designated "Pressroom" can include or provide access to everything usually found in traditional printed press kits and electronic press kits discussed in earlier chapters.

In addition, a journalist interested in doing a story on a company will certainly browse throughout the site to get a sense of the company's scope—and to look for contradictions, omissions, and story ideas. Although their own company's ethics policies *should* prohibit them from making anonymous posts or provocative comments, members of the media will most certainly check out any blog, live chat, or open forum the site offers.

Because thorough journalists do comprehensive Web searches for prior stories and material about the company, these guidelines are important:

- The material you write and post on the Internet is accurate, up-to-date, and clearly and correctly written.
- You immediately ask for deletions or corrections of inaccurate information posted by others to head off the sorts of viral rumors that can quickly damage a company's reputation (see Chapters Twelve and Thirteen).
- You and the people you work for keep a sense of humor about Web posts that poke fun at the company or client in ways that do no real damage. Be aware that satire is protected as free speech in the United States.

For Customers

A company's Web site can function in these ways for customers and potential customers:

- A telephone book listing, so visitors should be able to find addresses and local telephone numbers of headquarters, branches, and regional offices easily
- An introduction to the company through "About Us" and "FAQ" functions
- A sales brochure for products, services, and capabilities
- A source of audio downloads and Podcasting
- A way to access video for downloading
- A retail store for ordering products and accessories
- An archive of prior positive stories about the company's products, services, and community service or links to the stories
- An archive of prior positive television and radio coverage

- A gateway to technical support for products through e-mail questions or a live-help function
- Access to ongoing information by offering sign-ups for newsletters or e-mail alerts
- A clubhouse via a blog or live-chat function
- An extension of the brand experience.

A company Web site, opt-in e-mail distribution lists, and live online help cannot entirely replace sales, marketing, and customer support functions previously handled by telephone; nevertheless, these and other digital options can augment, enhance, and accelerate the ways customers communicate with the company.

For the Financial Community

For stockholders and potential stockholders, the Web site can provide a number of services:

- A snapshot of the current state of the company by having a stock ticker or a stock price chart on the site (of course, such a function graphically illustrates when the stock price is going down as well as when it is going up)
- Access to the latest news affecting the stock, with links to the press release archive
- An archive of business stories in opinion-maker publications or links to them
- Access to public financial information in an archive of annual and quarterly reports and perhaps other Securities and Exchange Commission information filings
- Access to live audio of the company's quarterly conference calls with stock analysts and continued posting of a recording of the call

- The street address (so visitors can find the building), the mailing address (if it is different from the street address), and the main telephone number of company headquarters and any regional branches
- Names, telephone numbers, and e-mail addresses of investor relations officers of the company;
- An opt-in function to sign up for automatic receipt of future press releases, financial communications, and newsletters or to be notified about them
- Access to live audio or video of the annual meeting and posting of excerpts or highlights, including the CEO's and other executives' speeches

Before adding an e-mail address to a distribution list, the current best practice is to require an opt-in or double opt-in (meaning that the person has to opt-in again in response to the first e-mail message). E-mail alerts should then include an option to be removed from the list. This list removal function gives you quick feedback on whether your written communications are helpful and informative or nuisances. In sum, a Web site can provide easy digital access to the various kinds of financial communications discussed in Chapter Nine.

Customer Feedback, Acquisition, and Loyalty

Companies are finding that a Web site can offer real-time tracking of customer behavior, preferences, and opinions. Carefully written online opinion and preference polls can supplement focus group testing of marketing materials such as promos, ads, and movie trailers. Since online testing can garner a large number of responses for a low cost, it may soon usurp focus groups and other traditional testing techniques.

On the Internet, customer response to an open-ended question is likely to demonstrate that people typing in the privacy of their online worlds are less hesitant than in a face-to-face group to express their opinions, particularly negative opinions. In groups, even positive opinions might make them look "uncool" to their peers. Online, people are less inhibited, for better or for worse.

Because e-mail promotes a personal, one-to-one interaction, some companies find an e-mail link for visitor feedback is effective for gaining new customers and promoting customer loyalty. E-mail works, however, only if someone answers it quickly. Even a small company may need someone to spend several hours a day answering e-mail.

Blogs and the Blogosphere

The online world has magnified the importance of peer opinions, whether in the form of peer reviews or rants and raves on various social network sites or blogs. People value the opinions of people like themselves and those with real-life experiences with a product over the judgments of so-called experts or critics.

The field of peer-to-peer, social network, or viral marketing used to be confined to chain letters, illegal pyramid schemes, and a few multilevel marketing companies such as Avon. Now a vast world of products and experiences is touted by "real" people and not-so-real peers—those hired strictly by marketing companies to pretend to be teens enamored by a new garage band, for example.

Ethics and Regulations

Ethical standards in the blogosphere may seem somewhat fuzzy; the Word of Mouth Marketing Association's draft code of ethics (2005), however, among other things, calls for "honesty of relationship":

- We encourage word of mouth advocates to disclose their relationship with marketers in their communications with other consumers. We don't tell them what to say, but we do instruct them to be open and honest about any relationship with a marketer and about any products or incentives that they may have received.

- We stand against shill and undercover marketing, whereby people are paid to make recommendations without disclosing their relationship with the marketer.

Under "Honesty of Identity," the code states:

- Explicit disclosure is not required for an obviously fictional character, but would be required for an artificial identity or corporate representative that could be mistaken for an average consumer.

For example, while it is obvious that "The Burger King" is fictional, although he has his own MySpace account, "Crissie," a thirteen-year-old girl who loves Burger King burgers and talks about them on her MySpace site, would require disclosure if she were fictional and her posts were really being written by twenty-year-old interns or vice presidents at a marketing company. The Word of Mouth Marketing Association (2005) summarizes its word-of-mouth marketing ethics code:

1. Consumer protection and respect are paramount.
2. The Honesty ROI: Honesty of Relationship, Opinion, and Identity.
3. We respect the rules of the venue.
4. We manage relationships with minors responsibly.
5. We promote honest downstream communications.
6. We protect privacy and permission.

In addition, the Children's Online Privacy Protection Act of 1998 (COPPA) specifically regulates the collection of personal information from children under age thirteen. For example, it requires not just verifiable parental consent to collect information but also a notice of what kind of information is collected and how it is used. Perhaps, most important for those in marketing, COPPA:

> prohibit[s] conditioning a child's participation in a game, the offering of a prize, or another activity on the child disclosing more personal information than is reasonably necessary to participate in such activity; and
>
> ... require[s] the operator of such a website or online service to establish and maintain reasonable procedures to protect the confidentiality, security, and integrity of personal information collected from children.

And for those in public relations, any violation of Children's Online Privacy Protection Act of 1998 would surely bring on a media crisis requiring all of the skills discussed in Chapter Thirteen.

Monitoring Blogs and Viral E-Mail

It is essential for the public relations department or firm to be continuously aware of what is being said about a company or client over the airwaves, in print, and on the Web.

Now, in addition to its long-established roles of monitoring and clipping opinion maker and trade publications daily and tracking story placements, the public relations function has to monitor "the buzz"—what is being posted on social Web sites and blogs, said in chatrooms, and forwarded to friends and contacts through viral e-mail. Viral e-mail is a message or an attachment that is repeatedly forwarded by one recipient to many others, usually because of its humor, outrageousness, or inflammatory content.

Nothing substitutes for personal sampling and direct experience of postings to keep an executive or writer in touch with the public mood. Because of the mind-boggling size and complexity of the Internet, however, and the speed of response necessary to squelch rumors and respond to complaints about product flaws before they are read by millions, many companies now contract with Web-monitoring firms to perform this function.

The problems of the Kryptonite lock company are an eye-opening case study in the viral communications power of the Internet. In September 2004, one customer complained on a cycling site that a model of the company's U-shaped bike locks could be picked with a common pen. Within two days, someone posted a video how-to. By day five, approximately 1.5 million blog readers had seen the sites. The company issued a public reassurance, which was covered by the traditional media over the next couple of days, causing blog readership to soar. Then days after the first posting, the company offered to exchange the locks at a cost estimated at $10 million (Rubel, 2005). The exchange offer lasted for a year.

But the crisis was not yet over, and the company's reputation was not yet restored. Subsequently Kryptonite made an antitheft protection offer to pay the cost of a stolen bike. And two years after the first blog posting, the lock-picking video was still the number three Google search result for the term "Kryptonite lock." Consumers' doubts lingered, and the video lived on in cyberspace.

It is essential that those in public relations monitor the Internet and the blogosphere. They must also keep a sense of humor, differentiate between posts and videos that are fun and those that are damaging, and respond quickly and truthfully to serious allegations. (See Chapter Thirteen for approaches to crisis situations.)

Corporate Blogging Policies

By now, most companies are aware that their employees may be involved in Internet social networks. Every company should have a written policy about personal blogging for various categories of employees:

- Is blogging permissible on company time?
- Is blogging permissible on a company-provided Web site?
- Is blogging permissible using the company's PC, server, or Internet connection?
- Is blogging about the company permissible?
- May employees write negative comments about the company or other employees, even during private time? If not, does this policy violate constitutional protections of free speech?
- The policy should also outline expected standards of language and etiquette—no profanity and no personal attacks, for example. At Sun Microsystems, the corporate council "gave a one-time briefing about the relevant securities laws to all Sun employees—about 3,000 of them are blogging—and then trusted them to stay out of trouble" (Stross, 2006).

Both insiders and outsiders are likely to perceive employees as company spokespeople, even in their private lives and during their personal musings on blogs. So all employees, and especially those in public relations functions, including PR writers, need to be aware of their company's blogging policy.

Corporate Blogs

More and more companies are establishing corporate blogs in connection with their Web sites and trying to determine the role of public relations writers in corporate blogging. Both internal and external blogs have their uses and their drawbacks.

Internal blogs are limited to postings and readers from inside the company or even limited to those within a specific department or project team. Some companies may use the excuse of the possibility of rude or inappropriate posts to veto setting up an internal blog. An unspoken concern for a traditional corporation, however, is that internal blogs level traditional management hierarchies: a post can be as easily read by the person at the top as by the blogger's immediate boss. Such a leveling tends to be refreshing and energizing to those on the bottom and on the top but frightening or challenging to those in the middle. Many companies have discovered the usefulness of getting wide feedback on difficult technical problems from all their best minds. A study by Forrester Research (Charron and others, 2006) concluded that social computing means that "innovation will shift from top-down to bottom-up" and that "creating value means relinquishing control." Internal blogs foster communication within a company but don't allow feedback from the customers who are the end users of the product.

External blogs are open to readership and postings from the world at large, including customers and the media. External blogs are time intensive, risky in terms of public image, and potentially rewarding in terms of customer engagement, loyalty, and product improvement.

Press coverage can be positive, praising the company for being open, forthcoming, and transparent. Of course, after reading customer complaints, a journalist could also write a negative product story. Companies always have to weigh that risk. Some start an external blog only when they believe that "the bad news is all out there"; others start a blog when the buzz is overwhelmingly positive.

When starting a blog, companies need to consider that those in the blogosphere expect authentic communications and would like at least some posts to come from the very top. In summer 2006, during a particularly challenging time in Dell's company history (its stock price was down, and competitor Hewlett-Packard was gaining market share), the company initiated an external blog. The second response posted on Dell's blog (2006) read: "This is great. But where's Michael Dell? I don't see the point in blogging if the big guy isn't posting."

Before a blog is started, internal questions might include these:

- Does the big guy want to post?
- Who has the time to keep the blog fresh and interesting?
- What about writing ability and social skill?
- Should the public relations writer act as an editor or as a ghostwriter?

Using a ghostwriter for a blog is risky for a CEO because of the danger that the deception will be unmasked. Unlike speeches, which are seen as public communications, a blog post presupposes personal communication in the person's own voice. A blog post is not one-to-one communication like a telephone call; it is probably more like a quarterly conference call, where the executive answers questions extemporaneously—perhaps working from answers and suggestions drafted by a public relations writer (see Chapter Nine). One option is for the executive to acknowledge in a post that he or she runs posts by a trusted editor, writer, or colleague, a process recommended by one blogger, who also works as an editor, writer, and ghostwriter and may therefore be biased (Gahran, 2006).

Since blogging is a time-consuming social medium that works best when communication is open and honest, any company initiating a blog needs to know how much time people at various levels can devote to both original posts and responses and what their writing, social, and blogging skills are.

The blog site needs to manage expectations about which executives will and will not be posting. Most CEOs do not. In July 2006, Jonathan I. Schwartz of Sun Microsystems was cited as the only CEO of a Fortune 500 company who actively blogs (as opposed to posting an occasional reprint of a speech). Schwartz laid out the challenge: "My No. 1 job is to be a communicator. . . . I don't understand how a C.E.O. would not blog if committed to open communication" (Stross, 2006). He has predicted that CEO blogging would become as common as using e-mail. Unlike e-mail, blogs are public from the start, so most CEOs will be using some editorial advice and input.

The biggest advantage of having an external blog is direct customer feedback. Before the Internet, salespeople were the most likely executives to hear what customers really thought, but maybe only when they said, "Your last product stank, and I'll never buy another one." Customers never really knew if their comments were conveyed to the product teams working on the next model or generation. Now, external blog postings serve as a written record of what works and what needs improvement in the company's products or services or customer service. Blogs also allow customer input and innovation, which means harnessing the brain power of all those people who were smart enough to buy the product in the first place. These are the people who can think of even more uses and refinements for it. So in addition to leveling internal hierarchies, blogs also bring customers into the development process. Then why wouldn't they buy the next generation? Their own ideas are already integrated into the product. Blogs have an important social function in creating a community ranging from customers, engineers, and marketers to the CEO, if he or she is ready to participate in the conversation.

Chapter Recap

Skilled public relations writers are discovering new opportunities within the growing digital world. For these communications, remember the following tips:

- Clarity, brevity, and correctness are essential.
- E-mail messages and instant messages cannot be deleted from cyberspace.
- E-mail subject lines should be tantalizing.

- Web visitors need to opt in or double-opt-in before receiving e-mail or newsletter alerts.
- Web sites need to be updated frequently with fresh content.
- Site updates should incorporate new technology and a contemporary look.
- Company Web sites should have complete, correct contact information, including the headquarters street address and mailing address.
- Special areas can be provided for the media, customers, and the financial community.
- Word-of-mouth marketing or collecting information, especially from children, demand a heightened awareness of ethics and special regulations.
- Your company's blogging policies should be known and observed.
- Internal blogs cut across corporate hierarchies.
- External blogs raise expectations of high-level executive participation and response.
- Any public relations writer involved in editing an executive blog will need a light touch, and "editing" should probably be acknowledged.
- Disclosure and transparency are important.
- Blogs allow you to listen to the customer.
- Blogs allow you to integrate customer feedback to create a better product.
- Blogs create social communities around products, experiences, and ideas.
- Blogs can attract new customers, strengthen customer loyalty, and turn customers into product evangelists who rave about a product or service to their friends.

12

RESPONSIVE WRITING

Setting the Record Straight

Most writing for public relations concentrates on positive news, such as product introductions, concert tours, factory openings, increased sales, and countless other items that serve as focal points for press releases and pitch letters. But what happens when negative information about your client appears in the media or on the Internet or if your company or client is overlooked or ignored? Do the same writing rules apply? Is the writing style different?

There are various forms of responsive writing for problematic situations. Problems can range from an executive being misquoted in a newspaper article to a potentially damaging allegation, criticism, or unsubstantiated rumor posted on a Web site or Internet discussion board that begins spreading like a virus. Before a situation becomes a crisis, a timely letter to the editor, a Web response, or a guest editorial (op-ed piece) can correct a mistake, misconception, or criticism and can often also simultaneously present the company's position from a positive point of view. (Crisis communications in response to a large-scale disaster and official statements or talking points are detailed in Chapter Thirteen.)

Letters to the Editor

The letter to the editor of a newspaper or magazine is probably the most frequently used form of responsive writing. In many cases, these letters are simple notes of praise for a story well done or a congratulatory note on an interesting article—both of which can serve to bring a positive issue back into the spotlight.

In addition, there are letters written in response to a negative or inaccurate statement about your client.

Letters to the editor should be timely responses to an article or letter previously printed or present a point of view about an issue of ongoing debate and interest within the pages of the publication itself or among the publication's target readers. Instructions and restrictions for submissions are posted on the letters page. To be considered for publication, a letter must not be anonymous or written under a false name. Include a company or organization title only when the letter is being written in an official capacity. Always include the writer's name, address, and daytime telephone number. Most publications now request that letters be submitted by e-mail or fax.

When a negative, incorrect, or unbalanced article about your client is published, you, as a public relations writer, are often asked to draft a letter to the editor that either corrects inaccuracies in the article or points out positive elements that were omitted from the story. In this chapter, we review several types of responsive letters, as well as discuss situations in which making no response is the best course of action.

Letters Correcting Mistakes

News articles are occasionally published with incorrect facts. Sometimes the mistakes are minor, but they can be damaging nonetheless. When this happens to a client of yours, you should request a correction by telephone or send a letter or e-mail of correction to the editor, or do both. (The broadcast equivalent of a letter to the editor is an editorial reply, wherein local stations invite listeners or viewers to respond to issues discussed on the air. Guidelines for broadcast writing can be found in Chapter Seven.)

The usual letter of correction to the editor responds to an error in the article. Imagine that a newspaper prints a story on your client, Sweet Gear, Inc., and reports that the company's margins fell by 50 percent in the third quarter instead of the correct margin change of a drop of 5 percent.

Clearly a 45 percent mistake needs correcting. First, you should find out whether the paper prints a regular corrections column, and if so, the name of the editor to whom you should address your submission. If a corrections column is not published, you should write a letter to the editor for the regular letters column. In many cases, you will be drafting the letter for your client, your supervisor, or the appropriate senior executive to sign.

Your letter of correction should usually include the following elements:

- The date and page on which the incorrect article appeared
- The incorrect information that was printed
- The correct information that should have been stated
- The name and title of the author of the letter

Thus, your letter on behalf of Sweet Gear, Inc. might look like this:

Your recent article on falling margins in the clothing industry ("Bottoms Are Falling in Jeans," April 1, 2007, p. C20) incorrectly stated that Q3 margins at Sweet Gear decreased by 50 percent. The correct figure is a mere 5 percent decline, in contrast to severe problems at many of our competitors.

Sweet Gear's fashion-forward product mix and innovative marketing under visionary CEO Nikki Johnson have resulted in gains in market share, particularly in the highly profitable $150+ jeans segment, almost offsetting higher costs due to the recent short-term spike in the price of denim fabric.

Today, if you see an eye-catching woman in exquisite jeans intently sending a text message, she may well be alerting her friends to the arrival of the latest Sweet

Gear collection, and at the same time participating in our innovative customer rewards program.

Jane Doe
Chief Financial Officer
Sweet Gear, Inc.

To avoid confusion, it is sometimes more prudent not to mention the incorrect information that was originally printed. Your decision on whether to include these errors will depend on the severity of the situation and how it affects your client, as well as publication policy. Some media outlets print only the corrected figures, without mentioning the original error.

Letters of Correction as Publicity Tools

Notice that Sweet Gear used its letter of correction to present a positive positioning statement about the company's strengths versus its competitors. Letters to the editor often present excellent opportunities for positive publicity, whatever the initiating context or pretext.

The following letter to the editor carried by the *Los Angeles Times* not only corrects misinformation but generates positive publicity for the company's product ("Airbus Says Its Design Cuts Room for Error," 2005):

> Allow me to provide our point of view for readers of *The Times* regarding "A Skeptic Under Pressure" (Sept. 27), which stated "there is no manual override system" for the Airbus A380 cabin pressurization system. The new A380 aircraft does feature a highly advanced manual override system—one that is different from and represents an improvement over previous designs.
>
> Traditional aircraft typically have two pressurization valves with automated controls to achieve correct cabin pressure. In an emergency, a pilot can turn off the automated system and manually switch on another

motor to directly regulate cabin pressure. However, this system leaves some room for error. If a pilot switches on the manual override system by mistake, it could produce a dangerously low amount of oxygen in the passenger cabin.

By comparison, the A380 has four pressurization valves. Our override system allows the pilot to control the valves through a separate computer system in case the automated pressurization system fails. This backup system prevents the accidental creation of a dangerously low oxygen level because it will allow a pilot to select only a safe aircraft cabin pressure.

The differences between older override systems and the A380 are akin to those between a manual typewriter and a computer-based word processor. Both systems effectively transfer a user's desired keystrokes to a printed page, but the computer-based method includes safeguards that reduce chances of a spelling error.

Clay McConnell
Vice President
Communications
Airbus North America [McConnell, 2005]

As in the two examples above, a convincing response to a critical or erroneous business or product article may require a certain number of technical terms and details. Always keep your style simple, clear, and concise, and calibrate your language not just to the expert but to the informed general reader. Notice how effectively the final image of the Airbus letter reinforces and clarifies the point for the general reader: the new Airbus system is a leap forward, equivalent to the difference between a high-tech computer and the competition's outdated typewriter.

Each of these letters is short, clear, and unemotional, and each contains the full name and title of the author, who is writing as a company spokesperson.

Letters Criticizing a Reporter's Conclusions

More complex and challenging to draft are letters that take exception to a reporter's conclusions or implications about a client's personality, integrity, or professional standing. For example, an article that reports on the mismanagement of a company or a personal scandal often angers a client to the degree that he or she demands a scorching response be submitted for publication.

When drafting such response letters, keep in mind the following guidelines:

- Support your points of contention with facts. Do not use emotional responses to defend your position.
- Keep your letter brief.
- Try not to bring in lawyers or threaten to pull advertising from the publication.
- Make your opinion clear and easily understood.
- State your case professionally and tactfully. There is no need for the tone of your letter to be accusatory, derogatory, or in any other way inflammatory.
- Maintain good relations with the media. Don't anger or alienate reporters with vitriolic and overly critical letters.

The last point—the necessity not to alienate—often seems less important to the angry, egotistical executive or celebrity client than it is to the public relations writer. The seasoned public relations person knows that even if an error is egregious and even if the reporter is eventually fired (which seldom happens), the reporter will most likely resurface at another similar publication on a similar beat, taking his anger at the letter of response (and the PR person) with him.

Using degrading, belittling, or mocking language in a letter to the editor will make both the public relations officer and the company lasting enemies, no matter who signs the letter. Effective public relations work depends on mediating between the press and the client and maintaining cooperative and professional relationships with both.

Following is an example of a letter to the editor that takes exception to a published article. Such letters should be short, emphasize one or two very strong points, and use hard facts to back up claims:

> ### Regarding "Executives' Pensions Are the Deal of a Lifetime," Jan. 29:
>
> I was disappointed in the article about the discontinuance of pension plans.
>
> Our company, First American Corp., was prominently mentioned, citing the discontinuance of our pension plan.
>
> We replaced our pension plan with an excellent 401(k) matching plan that was not mentioned in the article.
>
> Our 401(k) plan matches up to $2 for every $1 of employee savings, so long as First American profits meet a certain level. In 2005 alone, First American's contribution to our employees' 401(k) plan was more than $60 million.
>
> The real story here Is the grievous reserving regulations and reporting requirements imposed by the federal government in recent years. Because the management of a few companies misused their pension reserves and understated their liabilities, the pension rules were changed and it became nearly impossible for companies to comply with these new rules.
>
> The act of a few hurt us all. First American responded by adopting a better 401(k) plan that allows us to channel more money to our employees and less into the useless costs of complying with these rules.
>
> Parker S. Kennedy
> Chairman and chief executive
> First American Corp.
> Santa Ana [Kennedy, 2005]

The letter refers directly to the original article and states its point clearly. Rather than berating the writer, editor, or publication, the letter describes positive company information that was overlooked: its excellent new 401(k) plan. Rather than ending on this positive note, however, the letter goes on to blame others for the current situation: government overregulation of pension funds in response to problems at other companies. This lobbying effort might have been better addressed in a separate guest editorial, where there would have been space to support the assertions about "the real story" with detailed examples, facts, and figures.

When Not to Respond to a Critical Article

Writing a critical letter to the editor is a delicate matter. There are times when it is in your best interest not to respond to a negative article with a letter to the editor. For example, if a particularly unpleasant incident is accurately reported about your client in an article, a letter to the editor would serve only to generate additional negative publicity about the incident.

You should be very careful when responding to negative news with a letter to the editor, particularly when criticizing a long-lead publication that takes pride in the accuracy of its in-depth investigative reporting or independent research. In many cases, a publication will print the critical letter, followed by a response from the editor or writer that refutes the points in the letter one by one, to devastating effect.

The publication's defense of its article extends the damage caused by the original article. Customers are again warned of the dangers the original article described, such as lack of testing, suppressing data, or the CEO's alleged personal misdeed. Thus, in letters of response, as in other public relations writing, it is essential to know your audience and not respond at all in some cases. In others, choose the right respondent and an appropriate tone for your factual, very specific criticisms.

Letters Pointing Out Omissions

In addition to correcting and responding to negative articles, letters to the editors are written when mention of a company, product, client, or point of view on an issue is left out of an article in which it might have been included, especially if its peers have been featured. This type of letter is frequently used as a publicity tool, as in this example:

> I read with interest your recent article, "Restaurants In the Arts District," and I agree that there are now a lot of dining choices in the area. In fact, I am the owner and executive chef of the club Delights, which is now also a fine restaurant. Delights offers an extensive menu from noon until nine. Then we turn down the lights, crank up the music, and become the hip club that was the first sign of night life in the Arts District when we opened three years ago.
>
> In fact, we have long been recognized as pioneers in reviving the area at night, and now we are pleased to be joined by the newer places your article mentioned in bringing wonderful dining to the district during the day and early evening.
>
> Sincerely,
>
> JayJ DeeDoe
> Executive Chef and Owner
> Delights

Without directly criticizing anything specific in the original article, a skillful letter writer can achieve some publicity and recognition for a company, product, or point of view that might also have been included in the original article.

Congratulatory Letters

Finally, there are simple congratulatory letters to the editor that can be used as vehicles for promoting yourself, your client, or your organization's position on an issue, as in the following letter to *Vanity Fair*:

> Thank you for bringing us to the front lines of the recruiters' war ("The Recruiters' War," September). Michael Bronner did an extremely sensitive job of conveying the systemic problems in military-recruitment programs and their heartbreaking effects on the lives of both young people and recruiters.
>
> As a staff member of an organization that has spent 88 years working for truth in recruiting and providing alternative service for young people, I applaud *Vanity Fair*'s excellent coverage of the Iraq war's impact on all levels of our society.
>
> Mary Lord
> Assistant General Secretary for Peace and Conflict Resolution
> American Friends Service Committee
> Philadelphia, Pennsylvania [Lord, 2005]

Such congratulatory letters serve to keep an issue in the public eye and publicize the writer's organization.

Web Responses

Internet content ranges from legitimate newspaper Web sites to blogs and discussion boards that post personal rants. Even the most obscure blog may be linked to hundreds or thousands of other sites and may receive thousands of Web views daily. On the positive side, this phenomenon has led to viral marketing and using the Web to create word-of mouth recommendations for a product or service. The downside of this development is the way that a single negative comment can become an epidemic of misinformation that is destructive to a client's carefully created brand image. As a result, just as the publicity or corporate communications department has long read, clipped, and circulated newspaper clippings, the PR function must now monitor the Web and quickly rebut any negative postings. (See Chapter Eleven.)

Web responses generally follow the format of letters to the editor, with two modifications: they should be short, in conformity with Web style, and they should contain a Web link to the client's site, especially to the most relevant page, if it is directly accessible.

Guest Editorials

Almost all major newspapers and magazines have an editorial page devoted to articles and letters expressing personal viewpoints on a wide variety of issues. These editorial pages usually contain one section in which the opinions of the publication are printed and another in which readers express their views.

These sections, frequently called op-ed pages, for "opposite editorials," are often seen by public relations executives as valuable and influential publicity opportunities. These pages may accept letters to the editor, articles with bylines, or editorial statements, all referred to as editorials.

Getting your editorials published is difficult, particularly in large newspapers and magazines. Competition is stiff: the *New York Times* receives twelve hundred submissions for its op-ed page each week but has room for only twelve hundred words a day—which translates to one or two essays. *Newsweek* receives 150 or more submissions per week for the one opportunity to be published in its "My Turn" column, although it now also publishes a few more in "My Turn Online." For both the magazine and the Web version, *Newsweek*'s Web site states that it wants an original essay that is "personal in tone" and "not framed as a response to a *Newsweek* story or another 'My Turn' essay."

There is no strict method for writing an editorial. Writing styles vary, from colloquial to academic. There are, however, some general guidelines to follow when preparing an editorial:

- Submit a brief essay. The average length of an editorial is three to five double-spaced, typewritten pages, or approximately five hundred to eight hundred words.

- Choose a timely topic. The essay must be newsworthy and of current interest. Typical subjects are pending legislation; political, social, or economic controversy; recent disasters; changes in government; and new ordinances.

- Present a strong point of view. Because space is limited, your point must be made clearly and emphatically. Your opinion should be crystal-clear to the reader.

- Offer a prestigious authority. Being famous or being a leader in your field helps. For example, it would be much easier for Steve Jobs, the chief executive officer of Apple, to have his article accepted by a technology publication than for an average citizen. For the op-ed page of the *New York Times*, however, its editor is on the record as saying, "The bar of acceptance gets nudged higher for people who have the means to get their message out in other ways—elected officials, heads of state, corporate titans. It's incumbent on them to say something forthright and unexpected. Op-Ed real estate is too valuable to be taken up with press releases" (Shipley, 2004).

An editorial usually requires an in-depth and passionate viewpoint on a particular subject. In most cases, you will be ghostwriting for a top executive, and it is essential to interview that executive before drafting the editorial.

Never plagiarize. Your job and the executive's reputation are on the line. The ease of copying wholesale from the Internet and the pressures to perform every task quickly keep growing.

And thanks to the Internet and its search functions, so do the public discoveries and shaming. For example, in April 2005, it was revealed that the CEO of Raytheon had cribbed someone else's "rules of management" and built on them in his speeches until years later, he stopped attributing his original source. The board of directors docked his pay $1 million. In another example, a college student was first exalted for having published a novel about getting into an Ivy League college and then unmasked as having plagiarized from a similar book published by her own "book packaging" company. Her rising star plummeted.

As with feature-style press releases discussed in Chapter Two, essays can have a direct or a delayed lead. Following is a guest editorial with what amounts to a five-paragraph-long delayed lead in which the author, Andy Heyward, chairman and chief executive of DIC Entertainment, details his and his company's expertise and process:

AIRTIME: Guest Commentary

Yes, They *Do* Call This Educational

DIC Entertainment has produced over 3,000 episodes of children's programming, with emphasis on shows for the 6- to 11-year-old audience that meet the requirements of the FCC's Children's Television Act. Among them are *Where on Earth Is Carmen Sandiego?*, *Madeline* and *Captain Planet.* We have won not only numerous Emmys but Humanitas, NEA, and Environmental Media Awards.

We work with the most gifted academics and recognized medical professionals from top universities. They are prominent researchers and publishers in the fields of education, child development, communications and pediatric public health.

Their input and guidance have been at the core of our programming. Notable among them are Dr. Don Roberts of Stanford University and Dr. Gordon Berry from the UCLA Graduate School of Education, as well as others from the USC School of Communication and the Department of Pediatrics of the Mayo Clinic.

We have convened industry seminars under the auspices of the PTA and the National Education Association from which to determine responsible content guidelines for children's programs.

Our head of creative affairs, Robby London, is a long-standing advocate of positive children's programming and is a former chair of Mediascope. The producers of DIC Entertainment take the counsel of our advisers with the utmost seriousness.

Having said the above, we find the University of Arizona's Dale Kunkel's recent criticism of two of our shows superficial, uninformed and irresponsible. *(B&C,* "They Call This Educational?" 9/13, page 36.)

The programs he criticized target 6- to 11-year-olds, not preschoolers. These older kids crave drama, conflict and jeopardy in the stories they watch. "Job one" of any educational program *must* be to attract an audience, a reality acknowledged by the FCC itself.

Nothing in the Children's Television Act or any other FCC edict suggests that conflict, action and jeopardy (often put under the pejorative term "violence") preclude a show from being educational.

Kunkel fails to acknowledge a difference between action that is portrayed responsibly, appropriately for children, and in service of a valuable lesson and violence that is gratuitous, graphic or inappropriate. In fact, two of DIC's proudest moments were our series *Liberty's Kids* on PBS, which told accurate stories of the American Revolution, and *Our Friend Martin,* in which kids time-traveled to the time of Dr. Martin Luther King Jr. and experienced the horrors of racial discrimination. These shows were informed by child-development experts. If one were to accept the position of Kunkel and his cohorts, these shows are not educational.

The presumptive overall objective of the Children's Television Act was to make TV a positive tool for kids in support of their development. The "child advocates" seem to have lost sight of that goal. If stations can air programs that draw kids to the television and keep them there and those programs have been informed and approved by the participation of academicians and educators, the Children's Television Act itself has been a wonderful success story.

We strive for that in every DIC program submitted in fulfillment of the Children's Television Act. We question those who make specious comparisons of today's legitimate children's educational television with claims of 15 years ago regarding *The Flintstones* and *The Jetsons* [Heyward, 2004].

As the chairman and chief executive of the company, the author, Andy Heyward, presents a logical, thorough defense of the ways his company conforms to both the letter and the spirit of the FCC regulations regarding children's programming. He focuses on a central stand and backs up his claims with a variety of facts and insights. Although its style and content are suitable for the trade magazine in which it appears, the editorial is uncomplicated and easy to read. A good editorial leaves a reader more knowledgeable and understanding about a particular issue than he or she was prior to reading it.

The following example is a guest editorial with a fresh perspective on a topic of general interest: the progress of the rebuilding efforts after 2005's Hurricane Katrina devastated New Orleans, written by Susan Howell, a political science professor at the University of New Orleans, and John Vinturella, a business consultant:

> No discussion of New Orleans after Hurricane Katrina fails to focus on the stark class and racial differences that supposedly determined its residents' fates. The city's Lower Ninth Ward has become an international symbol of the neglect suffered by low-income African-Americans, while the white middle- and upper-class neighborhoods on higher ground are portrayed as having hardly been affected. But as gripping as that story may be, it's an oversimplification.
>
> New Orleans was also home to a large black middle class, which is now in a quandary. Although we are white, we know this first hand. Along with tens of thousands of black middle-class families, we lost our homes and our belongings in the low-lying section of the city called New Orleans East, the northern part of the Ninth Ward.
>
> For more than 30 years, New Orleans East was a haven for the emerging black middle class. It was the suburban "black flight" neighborhood: as the central city and inner suburbs deteriorated, middle-class and educated black citizens went there seeking safer suburban lives, with better schools and houses with lawns. The relatively low housing prices in New Orleans East made this ideal affordable, and black families in this neighborhood did not face the racism they might have in the white suburbs.
>
> Many of the neighborhood's residents were the first homeowners or college graduates in their families. Households commonly included two wage earners, often stretched to the limit to pay mortgages and

provide for their children. Many were also supplying financial aid to relatives in the central city.

Now the Bring New Orleans Back Commission has designated parts of New Orleans East "delayed recovery," meaning that residents can rebuild only at their own risk, without any guarantee that there will be basic services, like working sewers or police protection, in the near future.

The two of us can feel comfortable resettling anywhere in the metropolitan area. But for black families, the decision is not so simple. Many would rather not deal with racism in the white suburbs, some of which are also unaffordable for these displaced families. But how do we ask them to return to the central city areas that many worked so hard to leave?

These are people who overcame the odds, played by the rules, broke out of the infamous "cycle of poverty," bought homes, built families and enjoyed a taste of what Americans define as success. And they are being told that their community is not on the immediate recovery list.

It should come as no surprise that these residents are fighting the commission and the planners to save their neighborhood. Unlike many of their black brothers and sisters, they had a piece of the American pie [Howell and Vinturella, 2006].

While the regular middle-class blacks who have been displaced might not see the importance of getting their message to mainstream newspaper readers, these writers know the importance of opinion-maker publications in influencing public perception and the political process. Although they are writing about a situation that affects them personally, they make their argument in terms of the more severe difficulties affecting a large group: their black, middle-class neighbors. Their writing is specific, factual, and unemotional, as befits people of their occupational backgrounds—professor and business consultant—demonstrating again that a prestigious by-line can add weight to a guest editorial.

Chapter Recap

Responsive writing presents a company or client's point of view about a journalist's or newspaper's point of view, about an issue, or about a crisis (discussed extensively in the next chapter).

Letters to the Editor

Letters to the editor can bring a client or point of view positive recognition. Do *not*, however, respond to a critical article that is accurate. Your response may bring new attention to the negative publicity.

Letters correcting mistakes and inaccuracies should include the following:

- The date and page on which the incorrect article appeared
- The incorrect information that was printed
- The correct information that should have been stated
- The name and title of the author of the letter

In letters criticizing a reporter's conclusions, you should adhere to these guidelines:

- Do not use emotional responses to defend your position.
- Support your points of contention with facts.
- Keep your letter brief.
- Try not to bring in lawyers or threaten to pull advertising from the publication.
- Make your opinion clear and easily understood.

- State your case professionally and tactfully. There is no need for the tone of your letter to be accusatory, derogatory, or in any other way inflammatory.
- Maintain good relations with the media. Don't anger or alienate reporters with vitriolic and overly critical letters.

Letters serve as publicity tools by explaining why a company, product, client, or point of view should not have been left out of the article.

Guest Editorials

Op-ed pieces should be:

- Brief
- Original
- Personal
- Passionate but carefully argued
- Timely

Web Responses

Similar to letters of correction, Web responses are concise rebuttals to untrue negative comments on the Internet with prominent links to the positive information available on your company's Web site.

Timely Response Essential

A timely official response is essential to avert the possibility of a much larger, more-difficult-to-manage crisis. Because of the viral nature of material that can be transmitted digitally on the Web, through e-mail, and by various handheld communication devices, it is important to quash untrue negative information quickly and definitively.

13

CRISIS COMMUNICATIONS AND OFFICIAL STATEMENTS

Preparing for a Crisis

Poor, slow, late, incomplete or dishonest communication during a crisis creates additional risk. Early, open, and honest communication decreases risk. To ensure that your organization is ready to make things better during a crisis, it makes sense to prepare emergency communications plans and materials.

In the past, most companies dealt with day-to-day business and did little crisis planning. Preparing for a natural disaster meant that a California company should think about the possibility of an earthquake. Contingency planning meant that a company using hazardous materials would have some idea of what to do if there was a spill or explosion. Most businesses, however, were more focused on this quarter's earnings than protecting their brand during a crisis. They gave little thought to the long-term damage to the company's reputation and the lost business that could result from bungling the public handling of a minor issue, a major crisis, or a minor issue that soon burgeoned into a public relations disaster because it was badly handled. Now, companies must be aware of the negative consequences—even the possibility of bankruptcy—that can result from an accident, malicious mischief, or the company's failure to squelch an untrue rumor quickly.

A wide range of real and perceived crises can destroy a company's reputation or damage a valuable brand—for example:

- A rumor that a high-level executive is leaving the company
- A terrorist attack

- A business setback such as the Federal Food and Drug Administration's failing to approve a developmental drug for next-stage testing
- A reported death from the use of a product
- A video on the Internet purporting to demonstrate a product malfunction
- Public outrage caused by the organization's perceived mishandling of hazardous materials
- Shareholder outrage because of poor stock performance
- Electronic fraud, such as the release of a fake press release or Web distribution of false information about a stock or a company's financial position
- A law enforcement inquiry or a Securities and Exchange Commission inquiry into insider trading
- An accident or crime involving an official
- The arrest of a senior executive or celebrity client for drunken driving, drugs, or sexual misconduct
- An executive's messy divorce, especially if another employee is involved or if the divorce papers reveal details of an unusual company compensation package

Official Statements

An official statement is developed for a crisis situation or controversy. Your client's views must be summarized and presented clearly in one standard or official comment. There are several reasons for developing an official statement. For example, if a company or an individual is involved in a lawsuit, it is important to keep control of what is said to the press. Speaking with a single voice is particularly important in large organizations with hundreds of employees, any of whom the media can identify as "an employee," implying that this person represents the official company stance. Official statements should be factual. They should state what is known at the time and not speculate about what might be the cause or what might happen next if the cause or the outcome is unknown.

Official statements are often sent to all top executives involved in the issue at hand. They can also be posted on employee Web sites or circulated to employees by e-mail to make sure the company viewpoint is understood and adhered to by everyone. For example, if twenty-five people were killed in an explosion at one of the factories of X&Z Industries, an official statement from X&Z should be drafted to explain the company's perspective on the tragedy and express compassion for the victims. That statement would then be used in these ways:

- Company spokespeople would use it in radio and television interviews.
- News releases issued on the explosion would be written using the official statement as a guideline.
- Company editorials or letters to the editor about the incident would stick to the points outlined in the official statement.
- Employee briefing materials would be created for use by first-line supervisors. Employees should not speak to the media but will likely talk to friends and family and can be good ambassadors during a crisis.
- Official statements would be used by customer support or other staff responding to telephone, e-mail, or Web inquiries.

Official statements should be developed by top management and public relations executives in cooperation with legal counsel. In addition to minimizing confusion, these statements are often used to protect a company or individual from saying the wrong thing or straying from the issues at hand.

Let's assume you are the public relations representative for Johnny Amp, a rock star who has just been arrested for cocaine possession. Your official statement to the press might look like this:

> I can confirm that Johnny Amp was arrested by local police at 3 A.M. this morning at a private party in Culver City. I do not yet know the full details of the arrest or the scope of the allegations. Johnny deeply regrets this incident and has asked me to express his most sincere apology to everyone involved. I have a background bio and B-roll available for news use. I have nothing to add now, but I will provide an update at an appropriate time. Meanwhile, I hope the media will respect the privacy of Johnny and his family. And on his behalf, I want to extend his thanks to his fans for their ongoing support.

This is an example of a very short, simple official statement in response to questions about a matter that your client would prefer not to comment on.

The spokesperson's presentation of the statement to the media serves several purposes. First, it expresses openness, not a cover-up. Second, it makes a public apology, which Johnny can reiterate and expand on in the future. Third, it provides electronic media with several options for visuals beyond just focusing on Amp's mug shot for the minute-and-a-half length of the report and all press with positive copy about him:

- Footage of the spokesperson
- Concert footage
- Interview footage showing Amp in better days looking clear-eyed and concerned and talking intelligently about his music or his passionate dedication to a good cause
- Amp's history of charitable work from his bio.
- Amp's bio could include a reference to past "personal" problems, implying that this morning's incident is "not news"

In addition to satisfying the electronic media's need for video footage, this statement lets all members of the Johnny Amp entourage know that they should not comment, thus feeding the media frenzy and extending the life of the story.

There seems to be no limit to the public's interest and "need to know" about the private doings of public figures, so much so that those involved in "reporting," and especially the aggressive paparazzi trying to photograph celebrities, can actually instigate incidents that make news, as illustrated by the following Los Angeles report of a minor incident half a world away:

> Dame Edna Everage's alter ego, Barry Humphries, punched a photographer who pursued him outside a restaurant in Sydney, Australia, on Wednesday, his publicist said.
>
> The 72-year-old Australian actor, who plays the purple-haired character with oversized rhinestone eyeglasses, struck celebrity freelance photographer Malcolm Ladd, 54, publicist Suzie Howie said.
>
> "I can confirm to you that Barry did hit him," Howie said. "He was obviously very upset."
>
> "But at least he didn't throw a phone," added Howie, referring to Australia-based actor Russell Crowe, who was given a conditional discharge by a New York court last year after pleading guilty to throwing a phone at a hotel receptionist ["Dame Edna Actor Hits Photog," 2006].

If the publicist had limited the statement to confirming the incident, the story might have been only two paragraphs long. In this coverage, however, the incident is leveraged for publicity purposes, demonstrating the often ambivalent relationships between celebrity public relations practitioners and the press or paparazzi. The angle and lead of the actual press statement released to the media by the publicist encouraged humorous expanded coverage by saying: "Veteran funnyman Barry Humphries' alter-ego Dame Edna Everage has issued a comedy statement on his behalf." This approach harkens back to the old-time press agent's motto: "Any coverage is good coverage. Just spell my client's name right." Only rarely, and in fairly innocuous crises, do publicists still take this approach. More often, the goal today is to release all known relevant information so that the public has the news and there is nothing for the press to add during subsequent news cycles.

Official statements can range from simple acknowledgments to complex dissertations, but there are some common elements to keep in mind:

- Official statements are used to control the message your client is communicating on sensitive or complicated issues.
- Statements should be drafted, approved, and released as soon as possible following an incident. This early, open, and honest communication creates a positive, proactive posture for your organization.
- Statements should always be approved by top management and legal counsel.
- Statements should be distributed internally to anyone who might be contacted by the media, public, or other stakeholders.
- Statements can name the designated spokespeople for the benefit of journalists, industry analysts, and insiders.
- To help the executives who have company clearance to speak to the media, talking points or a Q&A can also be circulated, listing probable specific questions and suggested or approved answers. (See Chapter Two for guidelines on constructing a Q&A.)
- There can be an internal distribution of both the statement and talking points.

Talking Points

Talking points are bulleted points of the two to four key messages to be presented to the media by any insider giving interviews and speeches or answering questions on a crisis or issue. In connection with the Johnny Amp statement given above, talking points distributed to his family, friends, and entourage might read:

- Johnny is "talented" or "a great friend" or "a wonderful human being."
- I feel for him and his family.
- Mr. P. Relations is handling updates.
- I hope you'll respect our privacy.

Talking points were used effectively to control the administration's message during George W. Bush's campaign and early in his presidency. *The Daily Show with Jon Stewart* often edited together clips of numerous members of the administration repeatedly using the same three set phrases when speaking on an issue, thus revealing the widespread dissemination of the talking point.

Drafting, getting approvals, and issuing official statements and talking points can be complicated and time-consuming. The only way to do them well is to be prepared in advance.

Crisis Media Plan

Companies, prominent individuals, and organizations—and especially the public relations writers who develop their brand and guard their reputations—need to be prepared in advance. They need to foresee the unforeseeable or anticipate unintended consequences and have a crisis media plan in place.

Communicate Early, Openly, and Honestly

The plan for a crisis should be disclosure to the media, not a cover-up. People want news immediately, and reporters see it as their job to get the full story, which means answering three basic questions:

"What's going on?"

"How long have you known about it?"

"What are you doing about it?"

Your responses to these three questions should contain the answers to the five W's: Who? What? Where? When? Why? Anything less than immediate and full disclosure of all facts known at the time, including a time line of who did and knew what and when, will most likely backfire.

Any pertinent information you omit will result in a follow-up story, thus extending the time the issue is at the center of public attention and intensifying the damage to your client. If you inadvertently omit an important fact, you and your client will be seen as inept or unresponsive.

If you intentionally omit a germane fact, three things are likely to occur. First, the fact will come out sooner or later in a media, governmental, or legal investigation or from an "unnamed source," such as an insider getting off his chest "what really happened and when." Second, the press and the public will become angry, and the new upsurge in stories will become ever more negative. Third, the story—and your client's negative role in it—will continue to be thrust before the public eye, extending the story through news cycle after news cycle.

So when a crisis occurs, be prepared to get out the full story, including a time line, as quickly, simply, and accurately as possible, being consistent with your client's crisis plan and emergency approval process.

Act Quickly

Do not allow foot dragging. In the abstract, the need to disclose seems fairly obvious and straightforward. During an actual crisis, however, human nature (especially group or committee decision-making behavior) tends toward inaction or paralysis. In a real crisis, someone is sure to advocate waiting "to see how the situation plays itself out," which is another way of saying, "Let's play ostrich and hope the whole mess will go away." It won't.

In an open and democratic society, an individual or a company, no matter how important, cannot entirely control the press, much less the burgeoning blogosphere, which is rife with self-proclaimed vigilantes and conspiracy theorists. A "story," that is, an incident that is news, will not go away until all of the press's and public's questions are answered. And if they aren't answered, the story will live on.

When questions are never answered to the public's satisfaction, an event can live on as a conspiracy theory or urban myth, as has happened with the assassination of President John F. Kennedy (How many shooters were there, and who were they working for?) and the rumor that the Procter & Gamble "moon and stars" logo implies that the company donated some of its profit to the Church of Satan. Although Procter & Gamble has changed its logo, the rumor lives on.

Accept Responsibility from the Start

Don't try to shift blame. Don't delay. Have the highest-ranking company executive available state that she or he is taking responsibility and acting quickly to disclose what is known and to make changes to prevent further damage. For example, say that in the interests of public safety, the company is recalling its product from the shelves or closing all restaurants in the chain until the source of the problem can be pinpointed. This is known as "controlling the symbols" of a crisis. Any waffling or finger pointing now will most likely keep the issue in the news, as demonstrated by this article from the *New York Times:*

> BP has revised its statement that workers were primarily to blame for a refinery explosion that killed

15 people and injured 170 others in Texas City. Now, company officials are saying worker error was a critical factor in the March 23 blast but not the deeper cause. "We simply used the wrong language to describe the report's findings," Hugh Depland, a company spokesman, said of the interim report released last week. The true causes have not yet been identified, Mr. Depland said. Since the report, BP has been criticized by union leaders and victims, who said the company was ignoring management responsibility ["National Briefing Southwest," 2005].

The inadequate statement of responsibility in the follow-up report thrusts the controversy into the news again two months after the accident. Blaming the workers in this case is blaming the victims, which will always cause outrage.

Express Compassion for Victims

Express *regret*, as opposed to *accepting responsibility* (what legal counsel wants to avoid), for whatever disruption, damage, or bodily harm has occurred. Then *act* compassionately. Talk with individual family members. Visit victims in hospitals. Attend services. In other words, talk and act like a neighbor or friend.

Offer Immediate Financial and Psychological Assistance

Keep in mind that people do not choose to become victims of an industrial accident. Offering to cover the costs of additional expenses incurred for medical help and emergency housing and supplies is the right thing to do. Bringing in professionals trained in crisis and post-traumatic stress psychology will also be appreciated. Compassionate action now may also head off future lawsuits. The cost of responding responsibly now will pale in comparison to the cost of doing nothing.

Meet the Red Face Test

Make sure that official statements express compassion and humanity. If the statement would or should cause a reasonable person to blush with embarrassment because it blames the victims or contradicts well-known facts, it does not meet the "red face" test. Revise it.

Anticipating Needs in a Crisis

All companies face the possibility of a crisis, so anticipate your needs before a disaster strikes by trying to answer the following questions:

- Does your company have a crisis response plan?
- Does the plan have clear guidance from company executives and legal counsel?
- Are the company's vulnerabilities outlined?
- Do you have all available background information on hand?
- Does the plan provide for a crisis management team?
- Does the crisis management team fully accept in advance that accurate and timely disclosure is the best way to control negative coverage?
- Does the plan provide for rumor control?
- Does the company have a designated crisis information center, complete with a rumor control function, interview areas, and information management teams?
- Have you prepared preapproved, fill-in-the-blank news releases for the employees, the media, your stockholders, and the public?
- What is your planned method for distributing information to each of these constituencies? Such methods might include live news feeds, press conferences, newswire distribution of bulletins, e-mail lists, conference calls with stock analysts, and special Web sites for employees and media.

- Do you have a list of all personal telephone numbers, e-mail addresses, and other private contact information for all key people, plus companywide telephone and e-mail lists?

- Have plans been made to address media access to company property, and have provisions been made for buses, security badges, and escorts for media, and amenities, including Internet access?

- Have you established a private area for victims and their families with acceptable amenities (such as hosting staff, water, food, bathroom facilities, and security) away from the eyes of the media?

Disclosure

Disclosure is central to handling a crisis effectively and ethically. When a crisis as dramatic as an airline crash, a product defect causing a death, or a mining accident occurs, getting information to the media swiftly is essential. Timely and frequent status reports help control false rumors and ensure an accurate flow of facts as they become available. Such reports also help officials avoid having to respond to questions with a "No comment," which will look like stonewalling and lack of compassion for victims when it is played repeatedly on the local news and twenty-four-hour news channels. It is always advisable to assemble a crisis information team that has direct access to top company officials or the highest authorities involved and to make the most senior executive the designated spokesperson. In some cases of massive media interest, you may want to assign different types of interviews to different designated spokespeople: for example, all television and radio interviews to the CEO, all print to the head of communications, and all financial analyst inquiries to the head of investor relations. In such cases, they should all work from the same official statement, talking points, or drafted Q&As (see Chapter Two).

Crisis Releases

Much of the writing involved in crisis situations conforms to the principles and formats already discussed in previous chapters. These are worth reviewing in this context, and there are some additional points of form and style to keep in mind for crisis releases:

- Gauge the scope of interest your crisis is likely to attract. Is your story local, regional, national, or international? Assessing the range of interest will help you decide how much you will need to explain and to whom. The story will play differently in Shanghai than it will in Iowa.
- Use bullets in writing the facts to make it easy for reporters to extract key information quickly.
- Release all information on official letterhead and on your Web site.
- Have reactive communications available in your e-mail and telephone contact centers.
- Put a date and time on every release.
- Include the name, telephone number, and e-mail address of a person who can be contacted twenty-four hours a day.
- Double-space the information in the release.
- Consult with legal counsel before releasing information.

Here is a statement issued immediately after a 2006 explosion at Ford Motor Company laboratory and posted on the company Web site:

Statement: Emergency Contained at Ford Laboratory

Dearborn, Mich., April 27—A chemical explosion occurred at Ford Motor Company's Research and Innovation Center in Dearborn, Mich., at approximately

2:18 P.M. today. The explosion occurred in a glass laboratory container and was quickly contained. Two people
in the laboratory were injured and transferred to Oak-
wood Hospital for treatment. Three others were taken to
the hospital for observation. Employees in the building
were evacuated until it was safe to re-enter. Employees now have been allowed back in the building and are
being allowed to go home or return to work. The air in
the building has been checked and declared safe.

Note that while the language is straightforward and dispas-
sionate, the statement presents a subtly positive point of view: in
the headline, the emergency is described as "contained," and the
last word of the statement is *safe*.

Minimizing Negative Reports

There are additional ways to minimize damage in public relations
crisis management:

• Television news broadcasts need videotape and/or live
reports from the scene to bring a story to life. If they have
nothing else to broadcast, they will rerun shots of the disaster
over and over each time they update the report. Make sure that
your company's point of view and positive efforts are covered
by providing press opportunities and/or a videotaped statement
by a senior spokesperson, such as the CEO, the head of corporate communications, or the chief safety officer, following the
guidelines given above for Official Statements.

• Executives and spokespersons should not host the media
in a fancy boardroom or conference room. Rather, they should
do their standup interviews with shirtsleeves rolled up, standing
outside, near the story, or in an informal setting.

• Follow your industry's general practices regarding cancel-
ing television and radio advertising and guest appearances. For

example, the airline involved in a crash, as well as all of its competitors, usually cancel major advertising for a period of time following a disaster.

- Fully cooperate with independent and governmental investigations, and make certain to highlight this fact in briefing material.

- Review your company's Web site for potentially inflammatory material. If your company owns the *Titanic*, for example, and it is sinking in the North Atlantic, be aware that your Web site brags, "This ship is unsinkable." Consider removing this claim.

- After reviewing the Web site, provide the Web address or an active link in all written material to provide easy access to positive information, photographs, and B-roll video about the company.

- For radio, release an audiotaped statement by a company spokesperson.

- The general public's appetite for human interest stories, tragedy, and suffering means that the media will be interviewing actual or self-proclaimed victims and their relatives and friends. The company must present a humane and empathetic media presence and must not appear to downplay the suffering of victims. You should also be sure your client supports and thanks those who have acted heroically during the incident.

- Prepare press kits that include background information a reporter can use to put the current incident into context. For example, for an airplane crash, such background material might cite government studies on the low ratio of accidents per passenger-mile compared with that of automobile travel.

- Keep a log of what information was released, when, to whom, and by whom.

- Consider the use of answering machine messages and a priority answering system to handle telephone inquiries.

- Design a standard procedure for quick responses, rumor control, news conferences, and regularly scheduled briefings (see Chapter Eight for information about arranging events such as press conferences).

- During ongoing public relations crises, some companies open "war rooms" staffed with special crisis consultants or in-house issue management teams much like those of political campaigns. These teams respond to criticism using all available tools such as Web postings, e-mail distributions, and barrages of telephone calls to reporters and editors' private numbers to pitch positive story angles and counter disparaging information.

Threatened or Ongoing Litigation

Companies should have a policy for answering queries about threatened lawsuits and ongoing litigation. These statements should be developed in close consultation with company legal counsel or the attorney in charge of the specific case. Usually the company's response will be some version of "no comment," patterned on one of the following models:

- Threatened litigation: "We do not comment on rumors and speculation."

- Newly filed litigation: "Our attorneys have not yet had an opportunity to review the filing. We have no comment at this time."

- Ongoing litigation: "We do not comment on ongoing litigation. John F. Smith of the law firm of Smith Smith and Smith represents us on this matter."

In litigation in the pretrial settlement stage, some companies face a potentially costly class-action suit or a precedent-setting personal injury trial that could be applied to a large class of litigants. In such cases, most likely using a specialty public relations consultant, a company or its legal representatives may launch an aggressive media campaign against the litigant's case while presenting the company's strongest arguments. Used with more or less success in recent years by tobacco, drug, and automotive companies, the strategy is essentially to "try the case in the press" or "win in the court of public opinion," in an attempt to force the claimant to settle before a verdict sets an expensive precedent. This strategy has also been used to influence public opinion in high-profile criminal trials.

A Case Study in How Not to Handle a Crisis

The Vice President Accidentally Shoots a Hunting Companion

The following time line is based on one widely disseminated by the Associated Press three days after the incident.

At approximately 6:30 P.M., Saturday, February 11, 2006, Vice President Dick Cheney accidentally wounds Harry Whittington, a seventy-eight-year-old hunting companion, in the face, neck, and chest. The accident takes place on the vast South Texas ranch owned by Katharine Armstrong. Within the hour, an ambulance transports Whittington to the nearest hospital. The White House is told about an accident but not that Cheney is involved. The Secret Service reports the accident to the local sheriff, who agrees to delay speaking with Cheney until the morning. About twenty minutes after the initial report, President Bush is told that Cheney is the one who shot the gun.

That evening at dinner on the Armstrong ranch, according to reports, no one discusses how, when, or through which spokesperson to make the incident public. At 9:15, Whittington is flown to a larger hospital and put in intensive care.

When informed of Cheney's involvement about 6:00 A.M. Sunday, the White House press secretary urges Cheney's office to disclose the accident quickly. Nothing happens. Around

9:00 A.M., Armstrong begins leaving messages for a reporter for the local Texas paper, but her calls are not returned until noon. It is almost 3:00 P.M. by the time the paper confirms the facts with the Vice President's office and posts a short Web article. About twenty-one hours after the incident, the AP moves the story on its wire. Sunday evening, Cheney sees his friend in the hospital and flies back to Washington to be in meetings on Monday.

Some details trickle out on Monday, including that Cheney does not possess the proper seven-dollar hunting stamp. Meanwhile, with Whittington out of intensive care, comedians and pundits take up the incident and run with it.

It's less funny on Tuesday morning when Whittington has a heart attack, probably caused by some pellets near his heart.

The AP time line and others begin appearing Tuesday evening. The accident is still news, because numerous questions have been left unanswered: Who did what? What happened? When? What did they know? And when did they know it? With these questions left unanswered or having the answers delayed, the press corps is also asking: Why was this national story given to a local reporter? Why weren't we told? Why doesn't Cheney make a statement? What are they hiding? What and how much were they drinking?

By Wednesday morning, the *Washington Post* is reporting that even Republican supporters are urging that Cheney speak publicly:

- The Republicans said Cheney should have immediately disclosed the shooting Saturday night to avoid even the suggestion of a coverup and should have offered a public apology for his role.

- Marlin Fitzwater, a former Republican White House spokesman, told Editor & Publisher

magazine that Cheney "ignored his responsibility to the American people."
- The incident is turning into a defining moment
for Cheney [VandeHei and Barker, 2006].

On Wednesday afternoon, Cheney finally answers questions,
and takes full responsibility. The venue he chooses is a Fox
News interview with Brit Hume. Other media criticize Cheney
for choosing a softball forum instead of submitting to the hard-
ball questioning from the full and furious Washington press
corps.

In the following days, further questions are raised about
why the White House did not take the lead in disclosing and
whether something is being covered up. More than one seasoned
Washington spokesperson criticizes the way the incident has been
handled, and several spokespeople in the mix to be consulted are
quoted as saying that the delay and timing were "not my decision."
Cheney may take responsibility for the accident. No one, however,
takes responsibility for the mishandling of communications during
the growing tumult.

Chapter Recap

Developing a Crisis Plan in Advance

Develop a companywide crisis response plan that has the advance
approval of senior management and legal counsel and that
includes the following:

- An assessment of the company's vulnerabilities
- Company background information to be provided to the press
- Provision for a crisis information and rumor control center,
  interview areas, and information management teams

- Prepared, fill-in-the-blanks news releases for the media, the public, and the employees
- Home telephone numbers for all key people, plus a company-wide telephone list and e-mail addresses
- Provisions for media access and escorts on company property

Crisis Releases

Prepare crisis releases following these guidelines:

- Gauge the scope of interest your crisis is likely to attract.
- Use bulleted points in writing the facts.
- Release all information on official letterhead.
- Put the date and time at the top of every page.
- Include the name, telephone number, and e-mail address of a person who can be contacted twenty-four hours a day.
- Double-space the information on the release.
- Consult with legal counsel before releasing information.

Heading Off Negativity

To minimize negative reports, take these steps:

- Disclose the facts of the story quickly and accurately.
- Provide updates as new information becomes available.
- Accept responsibility, and act ethically.
- Demonstrate compassion for victims.
- Provide television news staff members with B-roll or live reports from the scene, as well as interview opportunities to bring a story to life so they will not continue to rerun shots of the disaster.

- Review your company's Web site, and excise any information that might be inflammatory or inappropriate during the crisis.
- After reviewing the company Web site, include the company Web address on all written material to direct readers to access the positive material available there.
- Prepare press kits that include background information reporters can use to put the current incident into context.
- Keep a log of what information was released, when, and to whom.
- Consider the use of answering machine messages and a priority answering system to handle telephone inquiries.
- Design a standard procedure for quick responses, news conferences, and regularly scheduled briefings. (See Chapter Eight on arranging special events.)
- Review the response for compassion, how will it play in different regions, and whether it passes the "red face test."
- Use a strong lead to capture attention and a compelling follow-on message to maintain momentum and attention for the issue's duration.

14

PROGRAM WRITING

Selling Your Concept to the Client

A program is the blueprint for a public relations campaign. It is what a client buys from a public relations agency or what an in-house department often submits for budget approval within an organization. The program maps out the goals and strategies of a public relations campaign.

One of the more famous public relations programs was devised by Edward L. Bernays, the founding father of public relations. Bernays was asked by the makers of Ivory soap to invent a way to change the negative attitude children had toward soap. His solution? Ivory sponsored a soap-carving contest that ultimately had 22 million kids across America submitting soap sculptures.

Writing a public relations campaign is a challenging and important task. Programs are often written under tight deadlines yet require careful analysis and creative thinking. The secret to writing a good public relations program is to have a solid understanding of a client's needs and goals, coupled with innovative ideas that are put forth in brief, incisive writing.

Traditional campaigns typically include generating press releases; conducting media relations (how you successfully distribute and place the releases) with newspapers, magazines, newsletters, radio news and talk programs, and in some instances television news and entertainment shows; developing press kits, case studies, and feature stories; and appearances at trade shows or major industry-related conferences or events.

The digital age has also introduced emerging media or new media—additional layers of public relations campaign possibilities that include gorilla marketing, also known as PR stunts or viral marketing, and Internet marketing using chatrooms, blogs, UGC (user-generated content) sites, and RSS (Really Simple Syndication or Rich Site Summary) to attempt to initiate viral marketing. Viral marketing is making a campaign element so captivating that it is forwarded repeatedly through e-mail or posted on numerous personal pages on social Web sites such as MySpace.

Also fairly new to the PR campaign plan are product placements, and brand-generated feature films or television programs; street teams, which have been used for a while by record labels; and experiential marketing, which is creating an actual place or total environment in which the consumer can experience the essence of the brand.

Gorilla marketing and PR stunts, along with viral marketing, use clever ways to transmit information or communicate messages without looking as if they came directly from the client. For example, before a popular new kind of pomegranate juice was introduced to the consumer marketplace, the manufacturer of the juice offered upscale trend-setting bars and restaurants in New York and Los Angeles free bottles of the juice for use in martinis. Patrons of the bars were in turn offered free martinis with the new beverage, and positive word-of-mouth started to spread about the new drink. The stunt also helped create a demand for the drink before it was widely available, and today the product has a respectable share of specialty juice sales.

Internet chatrooms, blogs, UGC sites, and RSS offer clients all kinds of options to extend traditional messaging. According to the *New York Sun* (Francis, 2006), Edelman Public Relations, the world's largest independent agency, had nine full-time bloggers who advised clients on how to blog and how to deal with blogs. Certain blogs can stimulate media coverage when they are read by reporters and editors in the mainstream media, who then call the client to pursue a story. A good example is when Microsoft promoted its Xbox using blogs that cover gaming to get traction and create a positive predisposition for consumers and the media.

Two of the largest examples of UGC sites are MySpace.com and YouTube.com. One PR company promoted a new body spray among teens by placing information about the spray on the popular MySpace blog, attracting more than fifty thousand responses to the promotion.

RSS is another means for generating the spread of information using the Internet. The way it works is that a Webmaster creates an RSS file containing specific headlines and information that pops up when consumers search the Web. It is a free and easy way to promote a site.

The widespread use of TiVo and other digital video recorders (DVRs), which allow viewers to fast-forward through television commercials, has led to an increase in product placement. Product placement usually requires significant fees and involves getting your client's product featured in a TV or movie scene or more subtly embedded into the plot of a production.

Brand-generated content or programming goes a step further. Instead of relying solely on traditional advertising or even product placement, the company or client develops and produces its own entertainment feature film or television program around one of its company products or icons—for example, a Burger King character stars in a company-made feature-length film. The client then completely controls the context.

The use of street teams, most common in the music industry, involves just what is sounds like: a team of "brand ambassadors" who hit the streets (or airport bars, beaches, parks, or college campuses, for example) and hand out information, product samples, or gag gifts that get people's attention and get them talking about the product.

Experiential marketing is also what it sounds like: it gives consumers a chance to experience something and can be as simple as when Nescafe distributed samples of coffee to attendees leaving an Olympics event or as elaborate as kiosks set up to promote a new TV beauty show by offering free makeovers to female mall shoppers.

Structure of a Public Relations Program

Written programs can take many forms, depending primarily on the style and format preferred by the organization or individuals who approve them. Some corporations insist that a program be no longer than two typewritten pages. Others prefer a program set forth in large binders containing detailed market research and other supporting data. In this chapter, we review a basic formula for creating a public relations program that can be tailored to different organizational writing requirements. This formula comprises the following categories:

- Introduction or situation analysis
- Objectives
- Target audiences
- Strategies
- Activities
- Management, staffing, administration, tracking, and evaluation
- Budget

Let's assume you have been asked to devise a program to support the sales of a new brand of blue jeans called Pirate Jeans. Following is a step-by-step primer for developing your public relations program.

Introduction or Situation Analysis

The opening section of the program describes the reason the program is being written and raises all the issues the program is designed to answer. This section is usually called the introduction or—because it summarizes the situation necessitating a public relations program—the situation analysis.

Pirate Jeans has come to you because it is introducing a new model of blue jeans into the market. The distinguishing feature of these jeans is their prewashed look with jewels, and they are targeted to the fourteen- to twenty-one-year-old market. The Pirate Jeans people have supplied you with ample background: the principal competitors, the current sales trends for denim, the results of their test marketing, the theme of their advertising campaign, and so on. You must now go one step further and dig up even more information that will help you develop the ideas you need for your program:

- Find out in which media outlets your client wants or thinks it deserves coverage.
- Research the interests and buying habits of fourteen- to twenty-one-year-olds.
- Look up information on programs being used by competitors.

This section should summarize the data you've collected and describe the challenge facing Pirate Jeans blue jeans. Generally introductions should not exceed one to three double-spaced paragraphs in length. Yours might begin like this:

Blue jeans have become the first choice in fashion, and the trend toward wearing faded and ripped jeans with frayed hems answers consumers' demand for imperfection. Shipments of denim are up 30 percent for the first six months of this year, and the trend seems to be continuing.

Pirate Jeans must compete with the most upscale labels selling today, including Paper Denim & Cloth, Citizens of Humanity, and Sacred Blue. Research today shows that teenagers like to consider themselves rebellious but are nevertheless attracted to such traditional values as upward mobility, stability, and fitness.

This public relations program is designed to capitalize on the sexy and rebellious image of Pirate Jeans yet cater to the traditional values of today's teens. The program is intended to build awareness and excitement for Pirates Jeans by drawing widespread attention to the product through a series of teen-geared activities that will generate mass media and viral coverage.

The goals for the introduction of your program are to demonstrate your knowledge and understanding of the client's needs and build excitement and interest in the program that follows. When you write an introduction, make sure you answer the following questions:

- Have I adequately explained the public relations challenge facing the client?
- Have I demonstrated my understanding of the situation with solid facts and figures?
- Is the introduction written in such a way that it compels readers to review the program?
- Is it three pages or shorter?

If the answer to all these questions is yes, then it is time to move on to the objectives section of the program.

Objectives

The objectives of the program should be listed with bullets or numbers rather than written in paragraph form. The objectives for your program might be written as follows:

- Create excitement and national awareness of Pirate Jeans.
- Stimulate nationwide sales of Pirate Jeans.
- Establish Pirate Jeans as the jeans of choice for teenagers.

The objectives are stated clearly and concisely; there is no need to add flowery prose, and you should never obscure the meaning of the sentences. Like all the other parts of a public relations program, the objectives should be straightforward and demonstrate your understanding of the client's needs. Once you have established your objectives, you present the target audiences.

Target Audiences

The target audiences section of the program helps you as well as the client. As you do research to identify the audience your program is trying to reach, you will begin to focus your thoughts on what types of people the program is aimed at. The target audiences section helps define your activities, strategies, and objectives.

When writing the target audiences section, list the various audiences in bullet form. The target audiences section of your program could be written like this:

- MALES AND FEMALES AGES FOURTEEN TO TWENTY-ONE
  - Middle- to high-income families
  - Fashion-minded teenagers
  - Leaders of peer groups
- PARENTS OF TEENAGERS
- OPINION LEADERS FOR TEENS
  - Professional athletes
  - TV/movie personalities
  - Rock stars
- CLOTHING RETAILERS
- MEDIA
  - Fashion writers
  - Entertainment editors

- Tabloid magazine editors
- Photo editors
- NEW MEDIA
  - Fashion bloggers
  - Popular social Web sites
  - Rock music chatrooms

Note that the categories that require elaboration (such as opinion leaders) are broken down into specific subgroups. The target audiences section serves as a guideline for the program's activities. After developing your activities, check them against the target audiences list to make sure they coordinate with and complement one another.

Strategies

The strategies section outlines the methods or vehicles you will use to achieve your objectives and reach your target audiences. It describes in broad terms the channels you will be using to communicate your messages. If your program calls for one-on-one interviews with security analysts, that would be mentioned in the strategies section. If the program is built on word-of-mouth publicity for a product, that would also be described in this section.

As with the objectives and target audiences sections, the strategies section should be in bulleted form and its points stated briefly. The strategies section for your Pirates Jeans program might look like this:

- Generate enthusiasm for Pirate Jeans by associating them with celebrities recognized and admired by teens.
- Create excitement over Pirate Jeans through a national contest for teens.

- Work with retailers to establish Pirate Jeans special events that will bring more teenagers into their stores.

- Establish visibility for Pirate Jeans by having them worn in motion pictures.

- Make Pirate Jeans a "must-have" article of clothing for the target audiences.

- Saturate the appropriate media outlets with information about the new line of jeans.

The strategies should describe—again, in broad terms—how you will achieve your objectives. This is quite different from the activities section, which describes in detail the actual work you'll be performing for the client.

Activities

The activities section requires the most creative thought and is the most important part of any program. It is here that you unveil your specific ideas for promoting Pirate Jeans. It is here that Edward L. Bernays would describe his concept of a national soap-carving contest for kids.

Each of the previous sections has been building toward the activities section. The ideas in this section are what a client will be scrutinizing closely.

When developing the activities section, describe individual activities in paragraph form, keeping in mind these guidelines:

- Demonstrate how the activity is suited to the target audiences for your program.

- Explain why the activity is likely to get media attention.

- Establish why the idea is suited to your client or product. (In other words, *how* will this idea sell more blue jeans?)

- Cover all your bases. Do not leave any glaring unanswered questions. Anticipate all of the possible questions the client might ask about logistics, markets, and other concerns.

- Keep it brief. Get right to the point with your idea, and explain why it will work.

The activities section of your Pirate Jeans program might look like this:

A. JOHNNY DEPP LOOK-ALIKE CONTEST

Johnny Depp, star of the phenomenally popular series of films, *Pirates of the Caribbean,* is an icon among teens. They emulate his ragged style of hair and dress. He represents rebellious youth, yet his wealthy movie star stature makes him an all-American role model for today's youth. We recommend Pirate Jeans sponsor a national Johnny Depp look-alike contest.

All entrants would be required to wear Pirate Jeans during the contest. Entry forms would be picked up at the Pirate Jeans section at retail stores. The grand prize winner would receive a family cruise for four on a private yacht in the Caribbean and become the Pirate Jeans model in an advertising campaign.

There would be five regional winners, each of whom would receive free Pirate Jeans and be entered into the national finals that would be held on the Disney film studio lot in Hollywood.

B. PIRATE JEANS NIGHT AT THE PITTSBURGH PIRATES BALLPARK

To create a "must-have" excitement about Pirate Jeans, we recommend that Pirate Jeans work with stadiums in selected target markets—and kick off at a home game of the Pittsburgh Pirates—to sponsor a Pirate Jeans night at the ballpark. During the event, anyone wearing Pirate

Jeans gets admitted into the ballpark at no cost. This will generate word-of-mouth publicity, visibility for the jeans, and add incentive for kids to purchase them. We will work to publicize the events in local newspapers and other media outlets to gain more awareness for Pirate Jeans.

C. GENERATING MEDIA COVERAGE

A regular stream of announcements to the appropriate media would highlight new styles and celebrity sightings. We would disseminate photos of opinion makers wearing Pirate Jeans to individual editors. Tip sheets to wire services, newspapers, magazine editors, fashion bloggers, and popular social Web sites would establish the Pirate line as the "must-have" brand.

D. RADIO PROMOTION

Most television networks and large television syndicators place promotions on radio stations on a regular basis. Television series that target teens could offer excellent opportunities for offering Pirate Jeans as prize giveaways. Typically the department that handles the promotions are either marketing or advertising and promotion.

Your own goal in writing the activities section is to create enthusiasm for your ideas. You must sell the client on the concept and demonstrate how and why it will work. Above all, you must explain how the specific ideas will help sell more of the client's product.

Although every program is designed differently for each client and there is no set number of activities a program should contain, the number of activities is usually governed by the size of the budget: the bigger the budget is, the more flexibility you have in your activities.

Following is an example of a program that Ketchum Public Relations created for Kodak, one of its clients:

Cutting the Cord: Kodak Leads the Wireless Photography Revolution

Situation Analysis

With its roots dating back 115 years in film photography, Kodak announced in 2003 that it would re-focus its business model on growing its digital products and services at an accelerated rate—a statement met with great skepticism by the photography industry and international business community. Headlines such as "Kodak fades in race to go digital" and "Kodak must change before digital passes it by" screamed from prominent publications worldwide. Kodak was achieving respectable success with its EasyShare line of consumer digital cameras, but the company was still considered a me-too player in the crowded global digital camera space. Fast-forward to 2005, when the company determined the time was right to launch a category breakthrough—the Kodak EasyShare-One (ESO) wireless digital camera. This groundbreaking product features a number of first-time innovations such as wireless picture e-mailing, the industry's largest touch screen display, and the ability to hold 1,500 favorite pictures. Together, Kodak and Ketchum launched this niche but high-profile product with the goal of showcasing the brand's leadership in digital imaging. Kodak planned the launch of ESO in five key "market leader" countries—U.K., U.S., France, Germany and Australia—with the common platform of bringing Kodak's innovation to life through wireless experiences in unexpected places around the globe.

Research

Global Consumer Research: Kodak conducted a Cross Category Brand Equity survey in 2004 to understand its brand positioning across categories and competitors. Ketchum conducted primary research in March 2005 in the U.S. and Germany to determine consumers' opinions of Kodak as a leader in digital photography. Findings pointed to the continued need to position Kodak as an innovator in digital imaging. In addition, Kodak conducted extensive consumer positioning research on ESO in the U.S., Europe, and Asia, the results of which drove PR message prioritization.

Competitive Analysis: Review of competitors' sponsorships pointed to an opportunity for Kodak to break away from the pack and create opportunities for audiences to experience Kodak.

Media/Analyst Analysis: Leading consumer technology coverage revealed that Kodak was not viewed strongly as an innovator. There needed to be a concerted effort to educate specific reporters on Kodak's recent innovations and commitment to digital advancements. Increasing focus on all things wireless pointed to the opportunity to capture media/analyst attention with ESO, which featured wireless picture emailing, an industry innovation for a full-featured camera.

Consumer Segmentation Research: Kodak conducted extensive global research of consumer camera owners to break down their habits and analyze their needs; results then fed into planning to target high priority consumers and influencers.

Partner Programs to Extend Reach: The U.S. team used Intel's "Most Unwired Cities" survey, which ranks the top 100 cities for greatest wireless Internet accessibility, as a way to identify markets for media outreach surrounding a Kodak/T-Mobile partnership. Through a comparison of T-Mobile and Kodak hotel partners, Hyatt was identified as a mutual contact and chosen for VIP product trials.

Planning

Objectives

1. Position Kodak as a leader and contemporized brand in the digital imaging market.

2. Generate widespread awareness for ESO timed for product availability.

3. Increase cross category brand equity innovation score by five points.

Strategies

1. Pre-availability: Start 2005 with a bang by unveiling ESO at the international consumer electronics show, ensuring that it emerges as one of the most innovative and memorable products at the show for both media and attendees without sacrificing coverage down the road when the product hits the shelf.

2. Launch: Bring the brand to life in new and unexpected environments for media and consumers in five countries. The U.K., U.S., Germany, France and Australia PR teams developed programs with a common planning platform of "wireless experience, unexpected locations—a window into Kodak's innovation." The team determined that personally *experiencing* Kodak would translate into support for Kodak's digital products and services as a pre-availability influencer.

Targets: Primary—Tier A consumer and technology media as conduit to consumers, including international technology media who cover CES [Consumer

Electronics Show] announcements and retailers. Secondary—CES show attendees as "buzz reporters" to attract additional media on site.

Consumer targets (as defined by proprietary Kodak research): *proactive sharer, digital control* and *leading edge.*

Media (upon availability): (MRI and Roper Reports helped identify media outlets most widely used by consumer targets.) Tier A consumer and technology media as conduit to proactive sharer and digital control segments; alternative media as conduit to non-traditional consumers.

Challenges: PR had to execute the majority of the 2005 program in Q4 due to product development delays. Announced in January 2005, and originally slated to hit shelves in June, ESO did not make it to market until October 2005. By product launch time, Nikon had developed its own wireless camera. Without a strong media relations plan, ESO could have easily fallen off of editors' radars—with the potential of leaving the door open for Nikon to reap the benefits. Instead, the PR team developed a plan to ensure the media continually stayed apprised of ESO product availability so coverage would remain strong. The team was able to turn this challenge around to be a benefit by owning top media markets around the world during *both Q1 and Q4.*

Messaging: The first-of-its-kind Kodak Easyshare-One digital camera is designed as much for sharing pictures as for taking them [Ketchum, 2006].

Management, Staffing, Administration, Tracking, and Evaluation

Now that you have laid out the creative portion of the program, it's time to explain who will implement the campaign and how much it will cost. If you're submitting the program as an independent consultant or on behalf of a public relations agency, you'll need to include a section on management, staffing, and administration. This section typically answers the following questions:

Management. Who from your agency will oversee the program? Why is he or she particularly well suited to the task? What relevant experience does this manager have?

Staffing. Who is responsible for day-to-day implementation? How many staffers will work on this account? What are their roles? Why are they qualified for those roles?

Administration. Who are the primary contacts for the client? What is the timetable for implementing the program? What subcontractors or consultants will be used?

Tracking. Which media monitoring service will you use to track coverage of your program activities in the print and broadcast media?

Evaluation. Will you use qualitative tools such as before and after customer perception surveys to evaluate how your program has changed perceptions about your brand? Will you use quantitative tools such as tracking increases in sales in the local market immediately before and after the ballgame promotion, versus sales in an unaffected baseball city? Or changes in sales in markets running radio promotions? Or by tracking online sales by zip code and correlating increases in sales with media used in that market?

The goal of this section of the program is to convince your client or management that you have a competent team and adequate resources to meet the stated objectives. Typically this section contains brief biographies of the members of the account team who will be implementing the program. (For guidance on how to structure a biography, see Chapter Four.) This section should also show that the tracking and evaluation will adequately demonstrate the value received for dollars spent on public relations.

Budget

After laying out the mechanics of how your program can be implemented, you must now explain the true bottom line: the budget.

Budgets can be presented in many formats, but one practical method is to attach a cost to each of the activities you are proposing. This allows your client or management to take a menu approach to selecting activities when budgets are limited.

If you are submitting a program on behalf of a public relations agency, you must also include a budget for the staff time your agency will expend on the client's behalf. Agencies and consultants typically bill their time based on an hourly rate.

One way to lay out the budget is to provide a brief summary of costs that includes a line item for each activity. Attached to the summary would be a more detailed look at how you arrived at your cost estimates. Thus, the summary of your budget for the Pirate Jeans program might look like this:

Activity	Cost
A. Look-alike contest	$ 454,000
B. Night at the ballpark	$ 300,000
C. Media initiative	$ 75,000
D. Product placement/radio promotion	$ 150,000
E. Tracking and evaluation	$ 50,000
Total program cost	$ 1,029,000

For the detailed estimate, it is helpful to provide as accurate a breakdown as possible of the costs involved in the activities.

A detailed estimate of activity A, for example, might look like this:

A. Johnny Depp Look-Alike Contest	Cost
Collateral materials (Entry forms, point-of-purchase displays, posters for 1,000 retail outlets)	$100,000
Press kits (Photographs, news releases, fact sheets, backgrounders; 2,000 kits)	$ 25,000
Prizes (10,000 key chains, 5 regional cash awards, 1 grand prize)	$ 75,000
Press conferences (5 regional conferences and 1 national conference; facility, catering, AV)	$100,000
Travel and entertainment (Media lunches, agency travel, general expenses)	$ 50,000
Agency fee	$104,000
Vice president 120 hours at $200/hour	
Account supervisor 200 hours at $150/hour	
Account executive 250 hours at $100/hour	
Account executive 250 hours at $100/hour	
TOTAL	$454,000

Similarly, you would next lay out a detailed breakdown of costs for implementing the other three activities.

Be aware that the budget items do not reflect the actual amount per hour paid by the agency to the public relations executive or the actual cost of each activity to the agency. Each item here includes the agency markup according to formulas the agency has established to cover overhead, benefits, expenses, new business development, and, it is hoped, a profit.

The level of detail in the budget will vary according to client or organizational demand, but suffice it to say that you should not submit a price estimate without thoroughly researching the true cost of implementing a program. Your company's profit, and ultimately your job, will depend on the viability of your budget and your ability to manage your projects so that you bring your activities in on budget.

Chapter Recap

Public relations programs can take many written forms, but all should be written with the needs of the client in mind. Some people prefer one- or two-page documents with bulleted points, while others want to see reams of data. Regardless of the format, all should strive to include the following salient information:

- An introduction or situation analysis
- Clearly stated objectives
- An explanation of the target audiences
- Strategies to achieve your objectives
- Activities that follow the strategies
- An outline of the management, staffing, and administration needed for implementation
- A realistic and detailed budget or cost estimate

Appendix A

RESEARCH AND INTERVIEW TECHNIQUES

Research is the key to all informed and effective writing, and the digital age has made most kinds of background research easier and faster than in the past. As applied to public relations writing, research is essentially a fact-finding process that enables you to evaluate information in terms of ideas and distinctions.

Internet search engines and digital databases provide access to articles from thousands of newspapers, magazines, and scholarly journals and to Web sites ranging from the frivolous and fake to those maintained by subject experts and college professors that present the latest theories, reliable information, and current research results. Digital technology also provides access to original documents in archives that were previously accessible only at a remote location and only to those with an academic affiliation and letters of introduction. In addition, large-scale projects are underway to scan the contents of millions of books, all to be available from your desk or wireless device.

Digital research requires you to:

- Try a variety of search terms and combinations of terms until the results are both highly relevant and limited to a few pages of entries.
- Quickly sort out and discard unreliable sources and duplicate or derivative articles.
- Carefully analyze the quality of each source.
- Document the source URL and the date the page was accessed.

- Save any material that you will be citing, because links change constantly as companies, particularly media companies such as newspapers, update their Web sites.

The key to Internet research is to judge the quality and the reliability of the source. It is usually better to inform yourself about the subject through written sources before doing interviews. Do an Internet search. If you work in a public relations office, check the files related to your subject matter, and call any place that might supply relevant literature, or visit relevant Web sites.

Whether or not your company or agency subscribes to an electronic clipping or information service, you can search online by topic, company, or product or by the name of a person, such as an interview subject or a journalist. Some databases have better internal search engines than the sites of publications themselves. You may need to try multiple approaches until you find the information you want or until you can refine your search terms enough to receive meaningful, focused results.

Before you interview a knowledgeable person in the field, become familiar with the person's background and accomplishments by obtaining a bio. Talk with people in the field you are researching before you schedule any formal interviews. Collect background tidbits and impressions, and pay attention to the adjectives people use in describing your interview candidates. You may discover information unavailable from published sources and gain hints that will prove valuable when you conduct interviews.

When setting up interviews, keep in mind the hierarchy of interview situations:

- Best is in person, which fosters a lively give-and-take, while providing numerous details not available otherwise, ranging from facial expressions and body language to style of dress and office decor.

- Second best is by telephone, which at least gives you the person's natural speech patterns and allows you to ask follow-up questions when an answer is incomplete or provocative.

- The last resort is e-mail. E-mail gives no physical clues, allows no flexibility in questioning and no follow-up questions, and it often elicits only short, stock answers and clichéd or pompous phrasing. It is also easy to misinterpret the tone of statements in e-mail, and it is inappropriate to use emoticons (such as smiley faces) in professional e-mail.

Unless distant travel is required, always try to schedule in-person interviews with your most important subjects and sources.

Decide if you want to tape-record the interview or write notes by hand. Some interviewers do both. Because it is too time-consuming to type complete transcripts of taped interviews, they write from their notes and then use the tape to confirm the quotes and figures.

Make sure that the tape recorder is working, that you have enough blank tapes, that the sound level is adequate for the distance between the person and the microphone, and that you set the recorder so that you can tell when the tape runs out. At the start of the interview, you might say, "I'd like to tape-record this, if you don't mind, so I can double-check quotes and figures." If you are conducting the interview by telephone, be aware that in some states, it is illegal to record a telephone call without the other person's express consent.

Since you are interviewing for public relations writing, not journalism, you may or may not decide to offer to let the person check the quotes. In any case, the people you are interviewing within the company or the client's company may be given approval over your writing. Since quotes and information given to you by less senior staffers may be attributed to their boss or to the CEO in the final version of your piece, those lower in the hierarchy should probably be told who in their area will be giving final approval over what you write and that you are interviewing them for background information, not necessarily to quote them.

Because improvisation rarely works well, never go into an interview unprepared. You should be equipped with a list of specific questions that were not answered by your other research. Know the person's biography and areas of expertise. Instead of wasting time on commonplace information, good preparatory research allows you to use the expert's time in an efficient, enlightening, and engaging manner. Of course, you want to confirm a documented fact or two, but let the subject know that you are doing just that and move through it quickly. Nothing disenchants an interviewee faster than an interviewer who is not prepared. Conversely, asking intelligent, informed questions will keep your interviewee engaged by demonstrating that you are informed about both the subject matter and the expert's interests.

Listen carefully during the interview. Don't be so fixated on your prepared questions that you can't respond naturally to what is being said or pick up on an interesting angle you hadn't anticipated. Establishing rapport with your interviewee will yield better, more complete, and more honest responses.

Ask qualitative questions. You are seeking the most illuminating, descriptive answers possible. Rarely do you want a simple yes or no response. For example, if you are interviewing a novice diver who accompanied Philippe Cousteau on a scuba expedition, you do not want to ask, "Did you have difficulties as a novice diver?" Rather, ask, "What were your difficulties as a novice diver?" It's a subtle difference, but one that will help elicit the kinds of responses you can better use to let quotations tell the story.

Finally, when interviewing, never hesitate to ask your subject to explain something if you are not absolutely certain what he or she is saying. If you are unsure about a word or a reference, always ask, "What do you mean by that?" or "Do you mean. . .?" and summarize what you think the interviewee is saying. Those who are afraid to ask will never know. Certainly you should be well informed from all the research you've done, but communication is a delicate process, and you should, as much as possible, confirm that you understand what is being said.

As soon as possible after the interview, thank the person in writing. A handwritten note is always appropriate and will be much appreciated. Within a company, an e-mailed thanks is probably acceptable.

In summary, doing research, including interviewing, before you start to write is key to effective writing. Your sources, which you carefully evaluate for quality and authority, may include these:

- Material on file
- Internet publications and Web sites
- Electronic databases
- Books
- Magazines
- Newspapers
- People in the field
- Interviews—preferably in person, or by telephone, if necessary; avoid e-mail interviews

When interviewing someone, follow these guidelines:

- Research thoroughly.
- Prepare specific questions that are not already answered by your research.
- Tape-record the interview or write out notes (or both).
- Listen carefully.
- Ask qualitative questions.
- Ask follow-up questions.
- If you don't understand something, ask for clarification.
- Send a handwritten or e-mailed thank-you note soon after the interview.

Appendix B

GRAMMAR REFERENCE

Most people today are much more *used to* (not "use to") hearing English than to reading—much less writing—it themselves. And when they do write, they often write quickly and carelessly using abbreviations to speed along *their* (not "there" or "they're") instant messaging or casual e-mails.

When it comes to media and public relations writing, however, only correct English usage is appropriate. Whether you are writing a formal white paper or a quick e-mail note, never forget to use the spelling and *grammar* (not "grammer") functions of your program. Then proofread again, perhaps more than once, because those programs won't catch homonyms (sound-alike words that are spelled differently) or words that are spelled correctly but chosen incorrectly for your context. Your supervisors, clients, and members of the media are all in professions that value language. Your supervisors will be embarrassed if you send out anything that is written incorrectly, because they know that outsiders will be judging your organization (and them) on the *basis* (not "bases") of how well you communicate.

The grammar challenges that follow have been collected from the recent writing of college students. While no list could capture all the ways that English can be mangled, this alphabetical reference should be useful to those who want to improve or double-check when they are uncertain. For advice on improving clarity and polishing writing style, we suggest referring to the classic book, *The Elements of Style,* by William Strunk Jr. and E. B. White.

Abbreviations Guide

n. = noun; *sing.* = singular; *pl.* = plural: a person, place, or thing.

Pron. = pronoun: a word that substitutes for a noun (*he, she, it*).

adj. = adjective: describes a noun or pronoun.

v. = verb; *v.trans.* = transitive verb, which requires a direct object or an implied direct object to receive the action (He *threw* the ball); *v.intrans.* = intransitive verb, which does not requires an object (She *runs*).

adv. = adverb: modifies a verb (ran *quickly*); modifies an adverb (ran *very* quickly); or modifies an adjective (a *really* big house).

prep. = preposition: part of a phrase followed by an object that is either a noun or pronoun (I travel *from* home *to* work *by* car).

conj. = conjunction: joins words or clauses: *and, or, but, since, because*. Coordinate conjunctions join equal clauses, each of which could stand alone as a sentence (She visited the store, *and* then she did other errands). Subordinate conjunctions introduce clauses that cannot stand alone as sentences (*When* she went to the store, she forgot to buy milk).

Usage Guide

A Indefinite article modifying a noun and meaning no particular one, used before words that begin with a consonant sound. A *boy* walks on the sidewalk.

An Same as "a" but used before words that begin with a vowel sound. Half *an* hour.

The Definite article modifying a noun and pointing to a specific one. *The boy* in blue walks on the sidewalk. (There are other possible boys but you are answering the question "Which boy?") The distinction between *a* and *the* is particularly difficult for those whose first language does not use articles.

Accept (v.), acceptance (n.) Include, agree with. I *accept* your edits. Your *acceptance* to graduate school is on the way.

Except (prep.), exception (n.) An exclusion. I *accept* every charge *except* that one. That is the *exception* to the rule.

Across (prep.) *Across* the street is the store.
A cross (n.) A *cross* marks the grave.

Ad (n.) Short for *advertisement*. I saw the *ad* on television.
Add (v.) Just *add* water. *Add* the numbers.

Advice (n.) Rhymes with "ice." Words of wisdom. Your advice helped me.
Advise (v.) Rhymes with *wise*. If you *advise* me, I promise to take your *advice*.

Affect (n.) The physical expression of an emotion. He had a bored *affect*.
Affect (v.) Influence. Can your argument *affect* the outcome?
Effect (n.) Result. What is the *effect* of the new law?
Effect (v.) Bring about. Use as a verb only in the phrase *"effect a change."* It is time to *effect a change* in their behavior.

A lot Two words. I had *a lot* of fun.
A little Two words, not *alittle*. I'd like *a little*, please.

All ready (pron. and adj.) "Ready" meaning prepared. Referring to the whole group of people or actions. I was *all ready* (bathed, dressed).
Already (adv.) Time word. *Already* at six in the morning, they were *all ready* for the trip.

All together (adj. phrase) Considered as a whole. *All together*, the total is $98.65.
Altogether (adv.) Intensifier. It is *altogether* too cold today.

A lone (article and adj.) A single one. A *lone* gunman committed the crime.
Alone (adv. or adj.) Without aid. He acted *alone*. He *alone* knows the truth.
A loan (article and n.) Borrowed money. He needed *a loan*.

Along (prep. or adv.) We saw our friends *along* the way. We went along.
A long (article and adj.) Distance, length. We went *a long* way to see our friends.

Altogether See all together; altogether.

Any one (adj. and pron.) Considers each of a group separately. *Any one* of them could do the job.
Anyone (pron.) Any person at all. *Anyone* could answer that question.

Apart (adv.) Separation. Don't keep them *apart*.
A part (article and n.) A role or a portion of the whole. The actor played *a part*. That is *a part* of the picture.

Are (pl. v.) We *are* here.
Our (possessive pron.) *Our* places *are* here.

Assay (v.) To try. He *assayed* the test but failed.
Essay (n.) Written prose nonfiction. He wrote a long *essay* to answer the question on the test.

Aspect (n.) Point of view or side.
Expect (v.) Hope or wait for. I *expect* to study the problem from every *aspect*.

Base (sing. n.); bases (pl. n.) The bottom; the four corners of the diamond in baseball.
Basis (sing. n.), bases (pl. n., pronounced base-ees) There is no *basis* for your accusation.

Barren (adj.) Not fruitful.

Baron (n.) An aristocratic title. The *baron* was left with only *barren* land.

Board (n.) A piece of wood; a group of officials.

Bored (adj.) Not interested. The *board* of directors appeared *bored* by the long speech.

Brake (n. or v.) You push on the *brake* to *brake* the car and slow it down.

Break (v. or n.) Damage, put into pieces, or a gap. Don't *break* the dishes when you wash them. I can't wait for spring *break*.

Caller (n.) A visitor or one who uses the telephone. The *caller* hung up.

Collar (n.) The neck piece of a garment. He hung up his jacket by the *collar*.

Cite (v.) Make a reference to. *Cite* your sources.

Sight (n.) Vision or view. With his *sight* restored, the formerly blind man saw the *sights*.

Site (n.) Place, venue. The arena is the *site* of the ceremony.

Collar *See* caller/collar.

Conscience (n.) Inner voice. His *conscience* bothered him.

Conscious (adj.) Aware. He was *conscious* of making a mistake.

Decent (adj.) Fair, modest, or acceptable. Rhymes with "recent." "He is a *decent* boss.

Descent (n.) Heritage; going lower. His line of *descent* went back to royalty. The *descent* into the mine is dangerous.

Dissent (n. or v.) Differing opinion. We have the right of *dissent* if we disagree.

Dew (n.) Moisture that condenses from the air. The *dew* sparkled in the grass this morning.

Do (v.) *Do* the work.

Due (adj.) A deadline, amount owed, or reason. The *due* date was yesterday for the money *due* the gas company.

Due to The reason or excuse. *Due to* bad weather, we rescheduled.

Each (sing. pron.) Always takes a singular verb. *Each* of them *is* an individual.

Some (pl. pron.) Always takes a plural verb. *Some* of them *are* similar.

Effect *See* affect/effect.

Elicit (v.) Bring forth. Try *to elicit* a response.

Illicit (adj.) Illegal. An *illicit* drug.

Essay *See* assay/essay.

Except *See* accept/except.

Expect *See* aspect/expect.

Fair (adj.) Just, pale, or average; (n.) carnival. The judge made a *fair* ruling about the tall, *fair* man's negligence, which contributed to the death of a boy at the *fair*.

Fare (n.) Ticket price or food. How much is the *fare* to Chicago? What kind of *fare* does the restaurant serve? (v.) result. Did you *fare* badly in the elections?

Fast-paced *See* pace/fast-paced.

Foreword (n.) A statement at the beginning. He wrote a new *foreword* for the second edition of the book.

Forward (adv. or adj.) In front, aggressive. The plan went *forward*. The most *forward* sales representative was the most successful.

Forth (adv.)   Away. Go *forth* and multiply.

Fourth (n.)   He finished *fourth* in the race.

Heroin   An illegal drug.

Heroine   A female hero.

Hole (n.)   A gap.

Holistic (adj.)   An approach to healing that considers both the physical and psychological conditions. The East-West Medical Center specializes in *holistic* medicine.

Whole (n. or adj.)   Entire. I can't believe I ate the *whole* thing.

Hour (n.)   Sixty minutes

Our (possessive pron.)   *Our hour* of class is over.

However   Introduces an exception or a contrast and is set apart with two commas. Should not be used at the beginning of a sentence or clause. Correct: The other men, *however,* were different. Correct: Three of them were from Mexico and spoke Spanish; the rest, *however,* were from Brazil and spoke Portuguese.

I (pron.)   Used as the subject of a clause. When paired with other subjects, "I" goes in last position. My friend and *I* went to the movies.

Me (objective case pron.)   Never used as a subject, as in "Me and my brother." When paired with another object, "me" goes in last position: The gift was addressed to him and *me.*

Its (possessive pron.)   *Its* door was broken. (No apostrophe is used.)

It's   Contraction for *it is*. *It's* time to go = *It is* time to go.

Knew (v.)   Past tense of *know.* He *knew* the truth.

New (adj.)   Recent. That drug is a *new* discovery.

Know (v.)   Grasp mentally. I *know* the answer.

No (adj.)   Negative adjective. *No* answer is complete.

Knows (v.)   Grasps mentally. He *knows* the latest news.

Nose (n.)   Part of a face. He has a *nose* for news.

Lay/lie   *See* lie/lay.

Led (v.)   Rhymes with "ed." Past tense of "to lead." He *led* the orchestra last night.

Lead (n.)   Also rhymes with "ed." A metal; part of a pencil.

Lead (v.)   Present tense. Rhymes with "seed." Please *lead* the way.

Let's   Contraction for "let us." *Let's* talk tomorrow.

Lets (present tense v.)   Allows. The cell phone *lets us* talk daily.

Lie/lay/have or had lain (intrans v.)   To change position. I *lay* down yesterday. The injured man *had lain* in a coma for three days.

Lay/laid/have or had laid (trans. v.)   Requires an object. Right now, I *lay* the book on the table. (v.) What a bird does; to set out. The chicken *laid* an egg. I thought I had *laid* the ground rules.

Life (n.)   Existence, spirit. Rhymes with "wife." (Pl.) lives. Rhymes with "wives."

Live (adj.)   Not dead; not inanimate. Rhymes with "dive."

Live (v.)   Pronounced with a short "I," as in "kid." To *live* a long, happy life is his goal.

Loose (adj.)   Not tight. Rhymes with "moose." The *loose* moose was recaptured by the zoo.

Lose (v.)   Negative outcome; rhymes with "ooze." If you *lose* this match, you're out of the tournament.

Loss (n.)   Not a win. Rhymes with "toss." The *loss* was sad.

Manner (n.)   Style or politeness.

Manor (n.)   Big house. Being born in a *manor* doesn't necessarily mean having good *manners*.

May be (v.)   That *may be* the answer.

Maybe (adv.)   *Maybe* I'll go.

Me   *See* I/me.

Medal (n.)   An award.

Metal (n.)   A hard substance.

Mettle (n.)   Strong spirit. The athlete proved his *mettle* by winning a *medal* made of bronze *metal*.

Might (helping v.)   Expressing uncertain action or (n.) strength. I *might* go. Does *might* make right?

Mite (n.)   A tiny insect; (adj.) small. He was a *mite* of a boy but strong.

Moral (n.)   Lesson.

Morale (n.)   State of mind. The *moral* of the story is that a coach needs to keep the team's *morale* high.

New   *See* knew/new.

No   *See* know/no.

Our   *See* are/our.

Our   *See* hour/our.

Pace (n. or v.)   Speed, step. His *pace* was two miles per hour. He *paced* toward me. (The past tense *must* end in -d, even before a -d/t sound.)

Fast-paced (compound adj.)   Must end with -d. The *fast-paced* tempo made people want to dance.

Packed   Past tense of verb *to pack*. He *packed* his suitcase.

Pact (n.)   An agreement. They made an official *pact* to help each other.

Pass (n. or present tense v.)   Toss or move something; an adequate grade. Please *pass* to the right. She received a *pass* in the course.

Passed (v.)   Past tense of *pass*. He *passed* the course. He *passed* to the other player.

Past (n. or adj.)   A time before now. The *past* is our history. *Past* days will never be forgotten.

Peek (v. or n.)   To look. Please *peek* at this.

Peak (n. or adj.)   The top. The mountain *peak* was beautiful. *Peak* performance is the goal.

Pick up (v.)   *Pick up* the guest at the station.

Pickup (n.)   A small truck. He drove a *pickup* to the station.

Picture (n.)   A drawing or photograph

Pitcher (n.)   A vessel with a pour spout; the baseball player who throws the ball to the batter.

Presence (n.)   Opposite of *absence*. Your *presence* is expected at the meeting.

Presents (pl. n.)   Gifts. The *presence* of stacks of *presents* brings holiday cheer.

Profit (n. or v.)   Money remaining after expenses.

Prophet (n.)   Person who foretells the future.

Rain (n. or v.)   Drops of water from the sky.

Reign (n. or v.)   Period of rule. The king's *reign* lasted two years.

Rein (n. or v.)   Used to guide, as a horse. He *reins* in the horse and rides home ahead of the *rain*.

Role (n.)   A duty or a part played by an actor.

Roll (n.)   A small, round bread item.

Roll (v.)   What a ball does.

Roll (n.)   A list of group members. The coach's *role* was to take attendance, serve a snack of *rolls* and butter, and then *roll* the ball into the court.

Sale (n.)   Transaction for money or a price reduction.

Sell (v.)   Exchange for a price. The coat was *for sale*, but did not *sell*, so the store put it *on sale* for 25 percent off the regular price.

Sense (n.)   Perception, (v.), perceive. Use your *sense* of history to *sense* the changes.

Since (prep. or conj.)   Time word. *Since* the beginning, we've been ready. *Since* you are all here, we will start.

Set (trans. v.)   A person *sets* an object on a table. A person *sets* the table. (A person does not "set down" in a chair.)

Sit (v.)   A person *sits* in a chair. An object *sits* on a table.

Shone (v.)   Past tense of *shine*. The sun *shone* yesterday.

Shown (v.)   Past tense of *show*. The film was *shown* last night.

Sole (adj.)   Meaning "only." He was the *sole* survivor. (n.) The bottom of a shoe.

Soul (n.)   Meaning "spirit." The *sole* representative of *soul* music had holes in the *soles* of his shoes.

Some   *See* each/some.

Sum (n.)   Total. Answer to an addition problem. The *sum* of two plus two is four.

Steal (v.)   To take illegally. To sneak.

Steel (n.)   A metal alloy. Superman, the man of *steel*, would never *steal* into a bank and *steal* something that did not belong to him.

Sum. *See* some/sum.

Suit (n.)   Pieces of clothing that go together; the cards in a deck that have the same symbol.

Suit (n.)   A legal action. He filed a *suit* in civil court.

Suite (n.)   A group of rooms. Pronounced "sweet."

Suppose to (present tense v. and prep.)   The combination is correct only with an object. I *suppose it to* be time to go.

Supposed to   Action required in the past but not done. We were *supposed to* get ready by eight o'clock, but we didn't have time. Note that you do not *hear* both the -ed in "supposed" and the t- in "to."

Is supposed to (not "is suppose to")   An action that is required or expected. He *is supposed to* finish by two o'clock.

Tail (n.)   The dog wagged his *tail*.

Tale (n.)   Story; sometimes a lie. This is the *tale* of a boy born in poverty. Don't tell *tales*.

Than   Denotes a comparison. This one is better *than* that one is.

Then   Denotes a past time or sequence. That was *then*; this is now. He called and *then* waited for an answer.

That (subordinate conj.)   Introduces a dependent clause defining a noun and not set off by commas. The bicycle *that was stolen* was my favorite. (Which bicycle? The lost bicycle.)

Which (subordinate conj.)   Introduces a dependent clause not defining the noun and set off by two commas. The action, *which I regret*, could not be changed. (Which action? We don't know.)

Who Refers to a person. Used in the same way as *that* or *which*, depending on whether it answers the question, "Which one?" The man *who* came to dinner was a stranger. ("Who came to dinner" is necessary to the sense of the sentence, so there are no commas.) Joe Doe, *who* happens to be my brother, is a famous engineer. ("Who happens to be my brother" interrupts the main sense of the sentence, so it is set off with two commas.)

The *See* a/an/the.

Their (n., pl. possessive pronoun.) *Their* money was *theirs* alone.
There Place. Answers the question, "Where?" Don't go *there*.
There're Contraction of "there are." Avoid this awkward use.
They're Contraction of "they are" *They're* on *their* way *there*.

To (prep.) Denotes direction (*to* the store) or part of the infinitive of a verb (*To be* or not *to be*).
Too Also. I want to go to the store *too*.
Two Number.

Track (v.) Follow. **(n.)** Path. Try *to track* the changes in the data. The monorail runs on a single *track*.
Tract (n.) A negative term for a position paper. His dogmatic *tract* was pure propaganda.

Use to (present tense of transitive v. and prep.) Combination; correct only with an object. I *use it to* type.
Used to (past tense v.) Action done in the past but no longer. I *used to* type, but now my computer uses voice recognition. Always requires the -ed ending.

Vary (v.) Change. Try to *vary* your sentence structure.

Very (adv. that intensifies an adj. or adv.) *Very* big or *very* fast.

Verse, verses (n.) Poetry or a song lyric.
Versus (prep.) Comparison of one item to another; denoting a contest. Bears *versus* Raiders.
v. Abbreviation for *versus* used in cases of law. *Roe* v. *Wade*.

Waist (n.) The middle of the body.
Waste (n. or v.) Unused or left-over material.

Ware (n., usually pl.) Products. (The company's *wares* were clothes that *wear* well.
Wear (v. or n.) To put on one's body. He *wears* baseball caps.
We're Contraction of "we are."
Where (adv.) Place or question. *Where* is it?
Where're Awkward contraction of "where are." Avoid using it.

Wave (v. or n.) Motion. She *waved* to her friend. He caught a big *wave*.
Waive (v.) Release from a requirement. The clerk *waived* the fee. He received a fee *waiver*.

Wear *See* ware/wear/where/where're.

Weather (n.) Climate.
Whether (conj.) *Whether* to buy is always a difficult decision. *Whether* the *weather* is warm or cold, I'm taking my vacation.

Were (v.) Past tense of *are*.
Where Place or a question about place. *Where were* they going?

Where *See* ware/wear/where.

Which (relative pron.) *Which* one is she?
Witch (n.) A female who is believed to have and to use magical powers. *Which witch* is the wicked *witch*?

Which   *See* that/which.

Who (pron.)   Question. *Who* did it? Used as the subject of a dependent clause. The man *who came to dinner* was funny.

Whom (pron.)   Used as the object in a phrase or dependent clause. *To whom* it may concern. The man *to whom I gave my ticket* punched it. In the second example, *I* is the subject of the clause and *whom* is the object of the preposition *to*.

Whose (relative pron.)   *Whose* is it? No apostrophe is used.

Who's   Contraction for *who is. Who's* that?

Whole   *See* hole/holistic/whole.

Sentence Structure and Punctuation

Sentence Structure

In addition to applying your knowledge of sentence structure, there are three tests of proper end punctuation. (1) Figure out why your grammar-check program is highlighting lengthy passages. (2) Read your draft aloud and listen for a natural pause where your voice falls, which may indicate the need for a period. (3) Have someone else read your writing aloud to you; the places where the reader stumbles may require end punctuation.

Clauses   Independent clause—can stand alone as a sentence. I went to the store. Dependent clause—cannot stand alone as a sentence. Incorrect: After I finished my work. Even short sentences must have an end punctuation mark such as a period, an exclamation mark, or a question mark. Correct: I finished. Correct: Go! (This command has an implied subject "you.")

Comma splices or run-on sentences   Sentences cannot be joined together with just a comma and no conjunction. Incorrect: I went to the store, I bought a lot of groceries. Correct: I went to the store, and I bought a lot of groceries. (*And* is a coordinating conjunction used to join equal terms, such as two independent clauses, two nouns (Joe and Susan), or two verbs (ran and played).

Dangling modifier, dangling participle, or misplaced modifier   Descriptive modifiers (also called adjectival phrases) usually attach themselves the closest noun or pronoun. Correct: Relieved of my duties, I went home with my friend. (I was relieved of my duties. We are told nothing here about my friend's duties.) Incorrect: Singing in the rain, the day was memorable. (Here the day is singing.) Correct: Singing in the rain, Gene Kelly danced happily along the street. (Here Gene Kelly is singing.) *Hint:* Often an edit or revision that changes a passive voice verb to an active verb will correct a dangling modifier. Incorrect: Ignoring the consequences, homework wasn't done by the student. ("Homework" cannot "ignore consequences.") Correct: Ignoring the consequences, the student decided to skip doing homework. (Here "the student" is "ignoring the consequences.")

Semicolon to join independent clauses Two closely related independent clauses may be joined by a semicolon (;) without using a coordinating conjunction. Correct: I went to the store; then I went home. (Note that *then* is an adverb indicating sequence, not a conjunction. Incorrect: I went to the store, then I went home.)

Punctuation

Correct punctuation clarifies meaning. Overly complicated sentences with multiple commas, semicolons, and parenthetical phrases should be rewritten as two or more shorter, clearer sentences.

Apostrophe Used to indicate possessive case of:

> **Singular nouns** Spell the singular word, and add apostrophe and *s*: The *boy's* hat.
>
> **Plural nouns** Spell the plural word. If the plural ends in *s*, add an apostrophe: The two *boys'* hats. If the word does not end in *s*, add an apostrophe and *s*: The *children's* hats.
>
> **Pronouns** My hat, your hat, his hat, her hat, *its* hat (no apostrophe), our hat, both your hats, their hats. No apostrophe is used.
>
> **Pronouns** That is *mine*; that is *yours*; that is *his*; that is *hers*; that is *ours*; that is *yours*; that is *theirs*. No apostrophe is used.
>
> **Indefinite pronoun** *Whose* is it? No apostrophe is used. *See* whose/who's.

Colon (:) Punctuation mark that introduces a list or a subtitle. *See also* semicolon.

Quotation marks Double quotation marks are used with quoted words; single marks indicate quoted words within other quoted words. In American English, most punctuation marks go inside the end quotes (." and,") except colons and semicolons (word"; and word":). When deciding on the placement of a question mark, ask yourself whether it is part of the quotation (He asked, "Are you ready?"). If it is part of the main sentence, it goes outside the end quote (When did he say, "I'm ready to go"?)

Semicolon (;) A punctuation mark that can separate two independent clauses, that is, clauses that could each stand alone as a sentence. The semicolon can also separate items in a series or list, especially if the items contain commas within them. Keep these areas of your life in balance: your career, with its many after-hours obligations; your family and friends, who are your emotional support; and your health, which requires that you rest and exercise. *See also* colon.)

Glossary

Actualities Ambient sound; any sound other than that of the primary speaker in a radio or television broadcast.

Annual Report An annual summary of a company's financial condition, prepared for stockholders, and required by the Securities and Exchange Commission for publicly held companies.

The Associated Press Stylebook and Briefing on Media Law Standard style guide for journalists. Its rules on punctuation, word choice, and new word uses are frequently updated. Also available as a yearly online subscription that allows personal notations (http://www.apstylebook.com).

Audiovisuals (AV) Graphic presentations that use sight and sound to enhance the understanding of a topic.

Backgrounder Gives a company's or client's vital facts and history. Another term for *biography/bio*.

Bio/Biography *See* backgrounder.

Blog A Web page that logs the personal opinions of one person or a group of people, often with response features and links to numerous other Web sites and blogs. Derived from *Web-log*.

Blogosphere Refers in general to the numerous sites on the Internet devoted to personal commentary.

Boilerplate The client's approved company or product description that is included at the end of each press release above the contact information, so that journalists can use it correctly. Boilerplate includes the trademark, copyright, or registered designations where appropriate.

Branding Creating a unique, memorable image for a product or company by coordinating and controlling language, style, and visual elements throughout the marketing, public relations, advertising, selection of a spokesperson or celebrity endorsement, ad placement, partnership selection, event participation, and even charitable giving.

B-roll Secondary video clips that news outlets can use to fill out their breaking news reports or feature stories. Material provided can include footage of the company headquarters, sign, and products (unless a specific product has triggered a crisis or product recall).

Budget Meetings A publication's internal editors' meetings to determine which stories are candidates for the front page that day. On a daily newspaper, these meetings are typically at 10:00 A.M. (to look at which stories reporters are working on) and 4:00 P.M. (to look at which stories are complete), with final decisions on front-page placement made at 6:00 P.M. Public relations writers providing press releases, follow-up information, and access to interviews and articulate sources should be familiar with each publication's internal deadlines, if prominent article placement is desired. *See also* deadline.

Business Wire A fee-based service that distributes media releases through specialized news feeds and provides other services for public relations, investor relations, and journalism. *See also* PR Newswire.

Byline Piece   A piece of writing such as an op-ed piece or a white paper that will appear under an executive or celebrity's byline but that is often researched and drafted by a public relations writer. *See also* ghostwriting.

©   A symbol that designates copyrighted material and may be used in company boilerplate or on first use within a press release or brochure.

Callback   A telephone follow-up to a printed invitation or advisory.

Collateral Advertising   Product or promotional publications meant to be used with a particular product or service.

Comp   Short for *complimentary*; used as a noun, verb, or adjective. A free ticket, sample, meal, or travel accommodation offered to a journalist to facilitate coverage of a story. A journalist can accept only to the extent that the comp is customary in the industry and when explicitly allowed by the publication's code of ethics. *See also* press junket.

Confidential Information   Everything learned while researching and writing public relations materials is confidential until the company releases it publicly. So is private information about any client. *See also* ethics; insider trading; Regulation Full Disclosure.

Consumer Publication   Printed matter intended for general readers.

Convergence   The ways the digital age is bringing together formerly separate media such as print, radio, television, recorded music, and the Internet. Convergence makes content available to consumers in various ways, such as Podcasts, on-demand cable programming, downloadable files, or RSS feeds; makes interactivity possible with instant messaging and online sales or gaming; and allows for repetition, access to archives, and reuse on a Web site of material originally created for other purposes.

Copy   Written text.

Corporate Brochure   A presentation of a company's distinctive capabilities often used as a key item in sales, promotions, and media kits.

Daybooks   Daily local schedules of upcoming news events, published by the Associated Press or other news organizations.

Deadline   The date and time by which the journalist's story must be complete, including all interviews, quotes, and facts double-checked. *See also* budget meetings.

Delayed Lead   A writing style wherein the specific subject of a story doesn't come into clear focus until some time after the first paragraph. The usual intent is to set the background and tone before getting to the main point. *Compare* inverted pyramid.

Demographics   (Demo)   Objective, measurable traits of an audience or target market such as age, gender, and income. *Compare* psychographics.

Digital File Format   Computer files may be written, scanned, or saved in various formats, depending on their intended uses and on preferences. For example, text may be saved as a Word document or as a Rich Text Format. A JPEG file is one option for scanned images such as digital photographs. *See also* JPEG file.

E-mail Pitch   A short version of a pitch letter or a concise e-mail with a complete pitch attached. *See also* pitch letter.

Embargo   Any restriction placed on when specific information may be used, often stating the desired date and time of release. Use with caution and only with trusted journalists.

Emoticon   An informal e-mail convention that combines standard punctuation marks such as :) that can be read sideways as a picture expressing emotion, in this case, a smiling face. Emoticons are not appropriate in professional e-mail, including queries, cover letters, or pitches.

EPK   Electronic press kit. *See* media kit.

Ethics, Code of Professional A code established by the Public Relations Society of America that can be accessed at http://www.prsa.org. The Word of Mouth Marketing Association (WOMMA), which seeks to self-regulate the way companies use online postings for promotional and viral marketing purposes, posts its code at http://www.womma.org.

Experiential Marketing Creating an environment or situation that allows customers to experience the attributes of a brand. The best-known prototype of this is Disneyland, "The Happiest Place on Earth." Also called *experiential branding*.

External Newsletter Printed, e-mailed, downloadable, or Web site material meant to inform those outside the company of news and trends happening within it.

FAQs Frequently asked questions and their answers posted on a Web site or included in a media kit, often on technical topics or product related. Pronounced "facts." *See also* Q&A.

Five W's Who, what, where, when, and why. To be complete, every story—and therefore every press release, every pitch, every news alert, and every photo caption—must answer these five key journalistic questions.

Ghostwriting Writing generated without published credit to its author and often credited to another. *See also* byline piece.

Gift Bag A nicely presented giveaway serving as a thank-you to guests, especially at award ceremonies or charity events. *See also* promotional item.

Gorilla Marketing Usually a short-term tactic to reach consumers directly with the further goal of being so innovative or eye-catching or unusual that the tactic itself gains media coverage. *See also* PR stunt.

In-House Publications Materials generated for perusal within a company—for employees, managers, distributors, or members of an organization. Information in these publications applies directly and exclusively to company matters and is not of particular interest to outsiders. *See also* internal newsletter.

Insider Trading Any use for profit by you or anyone connected to you, even indirectly through third parties, of confidential information that a public company has not already disseminated widely. A public relations person often has access to such information but should never buy or sell stock or gossip about it to anyone, until it becomes public knowledge. *See also* confidential information.

Internal Newsletter Printed, e-mailed, downloadable, or Web site material meant for those who work within a single company's structure. *See also* in-house publication.

Inverted Pyramid A style of news writing in which the most comprehensive information is put in the lead, followed by details, supporting information, and background; constructed so an editor can cut after any paragraph and have a complete story that meets his or her space limitations.

JPEG File The digital file format for photographs preferred by the Associated Press. *See also* digital file format.

Keyword Search Optimization Using the most popular search terms for your category when writing copy to ensure that Internet search engines will rank your content highly in all the categories that are most important to your client or company.

Lead The introductory sentence or paragraph that summarizes information to follow.

Links/Linking *See* Web link.

Media Alert A brief summary of the basic facts surrounding an event, often used when time is too short or the occasion does not warrant a printed invitation.

Media Kit An organized package of information that includes background information on general topics or special events. Traditionally, press kits have included written material and perhaps an eight- by ten-inch black-and-white photograph or a reproduction-quality color slide, both with prepared captions and proper photo copyright credit. In recent years, electronic press kits and video news releases include broadcast-quality video. Now visual material is generally expected to be in digital format on a CD, DVD, or cited as available to be downloaded from a Web site.

Media List   *See* press list.

Media Release   *See* press release.

Narrowcasting   Television and radio that targets audiences with specific demographics or interests.

News Advisory   *See* media alert.

News Conference   Gathering together print and broadcast media representatives to announce and explain a significant and newsworthy subject or event.

News Hole   The proportionate amount of space a publication has available for news and features, as opposed to paid advertising, in any particular issue. The more advertising, the bigger the news hole.

News Release   *See* press release.

News Tip   *See* media alert.

Official Statement   A written comment prepared for the purpose of responding consistently to any question from the media regarding a particular controversial issue. Also referred to as a *position paper*. *See also* talking points.

Op-Ed   Short for *opposite editorial*; a newspaper page, usually facing the editorial page, that prints opinions and points of view.

Opinion-Maker Media   The publications and media most used by leaders in the arenas of politics, the arts, or within an industry, including the *New York Times*, *Washington Post*, *Los Angeles Times*, *Time*, and *Newsweek*; in business, the *Wall Street Journal* and *Business Week*; in entertainment, *Daily Variety* and the *Hollywood Reporter*; and on television, the Sunday morning interview shows, the

main news magazine shows such as *60 Minutes*, morning shows such as *Good Morning, America* and the *Today Show*, and the cable business and news channels.

Paparazzo, paparazzi (plural)   Freelance photographer, usually specializing in images of celebrities.

Photo Alert   An advisory or invitation that stresses the possibilities for photo coverage. Also referred to as *photo-op*.

Pitch Letter   A letter or e-mail to a journalist or editor that introduces a client and story idea or other salient information.

Plagiarism   The unethical use of written expression or photo or video images created by another. Ethical exceptions include the use of short quotations with proper attribution; use of longer excerpts with attribution and written permission; use of material for which your company owns the copyright, such as adapting a company's previously purchased copy for a new purpose or when an executive publishes a byline article written by a staff PR writer or freelance ghostwriter who has been paid under a work-for-hire contract.

Podcast   A digital video or audio file available on the Internet for downloading to a playback device.

P-O-P   Point-of-purchase advertising materials, such as a counter display in a retail store.

Position Paper   *See* official statement.

PR Newswire   A fee-based service that distributes public relations and business announcements. *See also* Business Wire.

PR Proposal   *See* public relations program.

PR Stunt   A one-time event or incident created by a public relations person solely to gain media attention; often referred to as *gorilla marketing*.

Press Junket   A special tour for news media representatives, in which transportation and accommodations are provided by the company that desires publicity. Journalists' ability to accept expense-paid travel depends on the rules of their particular publications, with larger media outlets often explicitly forbid junketeering. *See also* comp.

Press Kit *See* media kit.

Press List A list of targeted press outlets, used for distributing announcements to the press. Contains detailed information, including names of journalists and editors, direct telephone numbers, e-mail addresses, and deadlines, for example. Also referred to as a *media list*.

Press Release The most common written form of public relations, used to announce a client's news and information.

Product Placement Arranging for a fee or as a loan to have a branded product appear in a movie, television program, music video, or video game; a marketing technique that replaces or supplements traditional advertising.

Promotional Item A giveaway or memento, often printed with a company logo, to remind the receiver of the client. These can range from key chains, baseball caps, tee-shirts, and mugs to elegant leather portfolios and totes large enough to carry items and brochures at trade shows. *See also* gift bags.

Psychographics Characteristic psychological traits of a target audience, such as innovator, early adapter, or traditionalist. *Compare* demographics.

Public Relations Program A written proposal for a prospective client or project that details the elements, costs, time line, hoped-for outcomes, and method of assessment for the proposed activity. When officially signed by the client and countersigned by the PR person, it can function as a contract. Also called a *PR proposal*.

Publicity Tour Scheduled publicity appearances in a series of locations or cities, usually developed to publicize books, concerts, or new products or services. *See also* satellite press tour.

Q&A A written series of expected questions and answers drafted by public relations for press or executive use or posted on a Web site (as FAQs) to answer the most commonly asked questions about an issue, company, product, or service.

® A symbol that designates a registered trademark; may be used in company boilerplate or on first use within a press release or article.

Radio Promotion A radio campaign often offering prizes of travel and coveted consumer goods given in exchange for airtime and used to promote entertainment from another medium such as film, television, or the Internet.

Reg FD/Regulation FD/Regulation Full Disclosure The Securities and Exchange Commission rule that requires publicly traded companies to disclose market-moving information broadly through a release to a newswire and not leak it selectively to a favored stock analyst or broker. In a case of unintentional disclosure, the company must make a broad release quickly.

Repro/Reproduction Quality Material A publication-quality image, such as a corporate logotype, photograph, or corporate ad. Standards vary among publications.

Responsive Writing The act of correcting or capitalizing on a situation by writing an editorial response to a publication or preparing a video or audio response to a broadcast to fill in omitted details or otherwise add information that better explains a subject, points out an error, or promotes a client.

RSS/Real(ly) Simple Syndication/Rich Site Summary (RSS) A digital technology that allows news, headlines, or summaries to be sent frequently from Web sites to recipients with links to access the full-length versions.

Satellite Press Tour Live television interviews taking place from a satellite facility. Interviews are scheduled in sequence so the person can be questioned live on-air, usually starting with a national network morning show and working westward by time zone. Media kits, video clips, or copies of books, as appropriate, should be supplied in advance to each outlet to facilitate the interview. The goal is to have the client interviewed by one local morning show or newscast in each major television market within a few hours' time without having to travel from city to city.

Securities and Exchange Commission (SEC) The federal regulatory body governing publicly traded companies and determining rules and punishments for infractions in such areas as full disclosure (Reg FD), insider trading, and financial reporting. *See also* Reg FD and insider trading.

Sound-Bite A short, pithy statement that makes the interviewee quotable in television and radio coverage.

Special Event An activity arranged for the purpose of generating publicity.

Spin A positive story angle that may not be immediately obvious to the journalist or public. The technique has been so extravagantly misapplied that the terms *spin* and *spin doctor* are used disparagingly.

Street Teams Product representatives who go where the potential customers are (malls, parks, beaches, city sidewalks) to pass out tickets, samples, and promotional items and brochures or to demonstrate a new product.

Style Guide An organization's printed guide to matters of grammar and style. In its absence, refer to *The Associated Press Stylebook and Briefing on Media Law*, the industry standard for journalists and editors.

Swag *See* gift bags; promotional items.

Talking Points A short list of key phrases or bullet points to prepare those speaking to the media on an issue, to ensure a united front, and to increase the chance of media coverage by offering short quotable assertions. *See also* official statement; sound-bite.

Target Audience A selected group of people who share similar characteristics and conditions, such as sex, age, income, geographical location, or education and who best represent the most likely potential users of a product or service. *See also* demographics; psychographics.

Tease An enticing lead to a story that tells just enough about the story to urge the reader or listener to continue.

Tip Sheet *See also* media alert.

™ A symbol that designates a trademark and may be used in company boilerplate or on first use within a press release or article.

Trade Publication A publication that focuses on a specific profession or industry.

Trade Show An industry-specific event at which company displays and representatives promote and explain products, usually to wholesalers and the press. Associated PR writing may include product announcements, media kits, media alerts, point-of-purchase materials, signage, brochures, executive speeches, multimedia scripts, and invitations. Events may include press conferences, parties, and entertainments, complete with promotional items and gifts. *See also* gift bags.

Tracking Report A periodic report to the client or company detailing concrete results of public relations efforts by compiling print clippings, CDs or DVDs of audio/video coverage, and breakdowns of media coverage by type. May also include an analysis of the comparative value of print space or airtime based on the various outlets' advertising rates.

User-Generated Content (UGC) Online materials including brand-related and fan-related writing and videos that are created by members of the public and posted to share with others.

Viral Marketing Harnessing the power of positive word-of-mouth and the ability of an idea to spread like an epidemic by using transmission powers ranging from well-connected, talkative individuals and fun items for e-mail forwarding to keyword search functions, blogs, and links on the Internet.

VNR   Video news release; also called an electronic press kit. *See also* media kit.

Web Link   A Web address within Internet content that can be clicked to access another Web site.

White Paper   An analytical byline piece of substantial length (twenty or so pages) that presents an in-depth analysis of a product, issue, trend, or company-generated survey. White papers strive to close the divide between the specialist and the generalist. They are often researched and drafted by a technical writer or public relations writer but appear under the byline of a lead product designer, project manager, or senior executive, depending of the industry.

Wire Services   Companies that supply news to various media on a subscription basis.

References

AOL. "Barack Obama, Russell Simmons, B. B. King, Harry Belafonte and Isaac Hayes Lend Their Voice to AOL Black Voices Celebration of Black History Month," January 30, 2006.

Associated Press. *The Associated Press Stylebook and Briefing on Media Law,* Norm Goldstein, ed. New York: Basic Books, 2004. Also http:/apstyle book.com/.

Byrum, R. B. "Presidential Address." Public Relations Society of America Western District Conference, Honolulu, Mar. 21, 2003.

Charron, C., and others. "Social Computing: How Networks Erode Institutional Power, and What to Do About It." Cambridge, Mass.: Forrester Research, 2006. Retrieved Feb. 13, 2006, from http://www.forrester.com/Research/Document/Excerpt/0,7211,38772,00.html.

Cox, C. "Improving Financial Disclosure for Individual Investors." Testimony before the U.S. House Committee on Financial Services, May 3, 2006. Retrieved July 29, 2006, from http://www.sec.gov/news/testimony/ts050306cc.htm.

Curtain, P. A. "Better Than Drinking Poison: Editors' Perception of the Utility of Public Relations Information Subsidies in a Constrained Economic Climate." Association for Education in Journalism and Mass Communication (ed)., *AEJMC Conference Papers.* Columbia, S.C.: Sept. 27, 1997. Retrieved Jan. 14, 2007, from http://list.msu.edu/cgi-bin/wa?A1=ind9709d&L=aejmc.

"Dame Edna Actor Hits Photog." *Los Angeles Times,* May 4, 2006, p. E5.

Dell Blog. "Direct2Dell: One-2-One Communications with Dell." July 10, 2006. Retrieved Aug, 17, 2006, from http://www.direct2dell.com/one2one/archive/2006/07/07/61.aspx.

Francis, D. "Public Relations Reaches Blogosphere." *New York Sun,* July 18, 2006. Retrieved July 18, 2006, from http://nysun.com/article/36215.

Funk, A. "Getting Stories on Local TV News." Committee of Concerned Journalists. Retrieved July 13, 2006, from http://ccj.p2technology.com/node/70.

Gahran, A. "Ghostwritten Executive Blogs Are Popular, But Are They Good?" Jan. 17, 2006. Retrieved Apr. 6, 2006, from http://contentious.com/archives/2006/01/17.

Goodman Media International. "A Q&A with Author Walter Dean Myers on *Shooter*." New York: Goodman Media International, n.d.

Harris, R. "Humble Depot?" *CFO.com*. June 5, 2006. Retrieved July 17, 2006, from http://www.cfo.com/article.cfm/7025006?f=related.

Heyward, A. "Yes, They *Do* Call This Educational." *Broadcasting & Cable*, Sept. 20, 2004, p. 46.

Howell, S. E., and Vinturella, J. B. "Forgotten in New Orleans." *New York Times*, Apr. 20, 2006, p. A27.

International Association of Business Communicators. "Management Failing to Connect with Employees at Almost Half of Companies, Says Survey." Oct. 11, 2005. Retrieved Nov. 9, 2006, from http://news.iabc.com/index.php?s=press_releases&item=17.

Jobs, S. Commencement address at Stanford University, June 12, 2005.

Kennedy, P. "Letters: First American Has Excellent 401(k) Plan." *Los Angeles Times*, Dec. 5, 2005, p. C2.

Ketchum Public Relations. "Cutting the Cord—Kodak Leads the Wireless Photography Revolution." Internal document, 2006.

Korn/Ferry International. "Executive Women in Finance: Unique Challenges and Opportunities." Los Angeles: Korn/Ferry International, 2006.

Lacy, S., and Coulson, D. C. "Comparative Case Study: Newspaper Source Use on the Environmental Beat." *Newspaper Research Journal*, 2000, *21*(1), 13–25.

Lohr, S. "This Boring Headline Is Written for Google." *New York Times*, Apr. 9, 2006, WK:14.

Lord, M. "Letter: The Few, the Proud, Anyone." *Vanity Fair*, Nov. 2005, p. 122.

McConnell, C. "Letters: Airbus Says Its Design Cuts Room for Error." *Los Angeles Times*, Nov. 11, 2005, p. C2.

"National Briefing Southwest: Texas: Company Revises Statement on Explosion." *New York Times*, May 26, 2005.

National Meningitis Association. "Sample Radio PSA Script." N.d. Retrieved Nov. 5, 2006, from http://www.nmaus.org/programs/pta/index/htm.

Newman, C. "Shall We Dance?" *National Geographic*, July 2006. Retrieved from http://www7.nationalgeographic.com/ngm/0607/feature4/index.html.

NewsLab. "The Shrinking Audience for Local TV News." Retrieved Nov. 5, 2006, from http://www.newslab.org/research/shrinkingaudience.htm.

NewsLab. "TV: The 800-Pound Gorilla; New Research Sheds New Light on TV News Usage." N.d. Retrieved Nov. 5, 2006, from http://www.newslab.org/research/mediause.htm.

Ontario Office of the Fire Marshall and the Ontario Ministry of Natural Resources. "Wildfire Prevention Week: Campfire Safety 2005." Retrieved Nov. 5, 2006, from http://www.ofm.gov.o.ca.english/default.asp.

Public Relations Global Network. "A 'Wild West' in Media Makes Public Relations More Important," Nov. 28, 2005. Retrieved from http://www.prgn.org/pdf/PRGN_Survey_11-28-05.pdf.

Public Relations Society of America. "Statement of the Public Relations Society of America (PRSA) on Video News Releases (VNRs)." N.d. Retrieved June 17, 2006, from http://www.prsa.org/_News/leaders/vnrs0404.asp.

Quality Insights of Pennsylvania. Script. "Memories... Control Your Diabetes." N.d. Retrieved Nov. 5, 2006, from http://qipa.org/pa/media_center/press_psa.aspx.

Reilly, P. C. "Building Global Leaders: The Human Capital Challenge for China." Address to M.B.A. students, Beijing University, Dec. 10, 2003.

Rosenberg, A. "Groaners!" 2006. Retrieved Nov. 9, 2006. http://www.newswriting.com/groaners.htm.

Rubel, S. "Blogging's Impact on Public Relations." CooperKatz & Co. from the Client Advisory Committee meeting of the Chicago Council of Public Relations Firms, Mar. 17, 2005. Retrieved Jan. 14, 2007, from http://www.prfirms.org/resources/publications/default.asp.

Shipley, D. "And Now a Word from Op-Ed." *New York Times*, Feb. 1, 2004. Retrieved Apr. 26, 2006, from http://www.nytimes.com/2004/02/01/opinion/01SHIP.html?ex=1146196800&en=00c213f.

Siegal, A. M., and Connolly, W. G. *The New York Times Manual of Style and Usage*. (Rev. ed.) New York: Times Books, 1999.

Sigal, L. V. *Reporters and Officials: The Organization and Politics of Newsmaking*. Lanham, Md.: Lexington Books, 1973.

Song, Y. "Sourcing Patterns of National and Local Newspapers." Paper presented to the Association for Education in Journalism and Mass Communications, Miami Beach, Fla., Sept. 16, 2002. Retrieved Jan. 14, 2007, from http://list.msu.edu/cgi-bin/wa?A1=ind0209c&L=aejmc.

SourceWatch. "Jim Gibbons." N.d. Retrieved June 27, 2006, from http://sourcewatch.org/index.php?title=Jim_Gibbons.

Stern, J. and Stern, M. "Dying to Appear" (review of *The Dead Beat* by Marilyn Johnson), *New York Times Book Review*, Mar. 12, 2006. Retrieved June 15, 2006, from http://www.nytimes.com/2006/03/12/books/review/12stern.html.

Stross, W. "All the Internet's a Stage: Why Don't C.E.O.'s Use It?" *New York Times*, July 30, 2006, p. BU4.

Strunk, W. Jr., and White, E. B. *Elements of Style*. (4th ed. Needham Heights, Mass.: Allyn & Bacon, 1999.

"UMKC Dean Admits Plagiarism of Speech: Official Says He Failed to Attribute Quotes to Princeton Professor." *Columbia Daily Tribune*, June 15, 2005. Retrieved June 27, 2006, from http://www.showmenews.com/Jun20050615News032.asp.

U.S. Centers for Disease Control and Prevention. "Sample Community Pitch Letter: CDC, Fight the Bite." Apr. 12, 2006. Retrieved Jan. 13, 2007, from http://www.cdc.gov/ncidod/dvbid/westnile/resources/FightTheBite_FactSheet/CommunityEdcationTools/FightTheBite_PrintFiles/SampleCommunityPitchLetter.doc.

U.S. Department of Labor. Occupational Safety and Health Administration. "Lesson A: Understanding the Hazard Communication Standard (HCS), Draft Model Training Program for Hazard Communication." 2003. Retrieved Nov. 5, 2006, from http://www.osha.gov/dsg/hazcom/MTP101703.html.

U.S. Federal Communications Commission. "Broadcast Station Totals as of March 31, 2006." Retrieved May 26, 2006, from http://www.fcc.gov/mb/audio/totals/index.htm.

U.S. Securities and Exchange Commission. *A Plain English Handbook: How to Create Clear SEC Disclosure Documents*. Washington, D.C.: U.S. Government Printing Office, 1998. Retrieved Nov. 9, 2006, from http://www.sec.gov/pdf/handbook.pdf.

U.S. Securities and Exchange Commission. Office of Investor Education and Assistance. "Final Rule: Selective Disclosure and Insider Trading." Aug. 15, 2000. Retrieved Jan. 13, 2007, from http://sec.gov/rules/final/33-7881.htm.

U.S. Securities and Exchange Commission. "Trump Hotels and Casino Resorts, Inc.: Admin. Pro. Rel. No. 45287." Jan. 16, 2002. Retrieved Nov. 9, 2006, from http://www.sec.gov/litigation/admin/34-45287.htm.

VandeHei, J., and Barker, P. "Cheney's Response a Concern in GOP." *Washington Post*, Feb. 15, 2006, p. A1.

van der Pool, L. "PR Firms Riding Economy with Double-Digit Growth." *Boston Business Journal*, June 18, 2006. http://msnbc.msn.com/id/13411568/print/1/displaymode/1098/.

Word of Mouth Marketing Association. "Word of Mouth Marketing Code of Ethics." Feb 9, 2005. Retrieved Nov. 10, 2005, from http://www.womma.org/ethicscode.htm.

Wright, B. "Enron and the Inflexible Obligations of the Legal Profession." Commencement Address, School of Law, University of Virginia, May 9, 2002a.

Wright, B. "Restoring Trust: The Work of America." Address to the Legatus Tri-State Chapter, New York, Oct. 29, 2002b.

Youngman, B. "TV PSA's: Making Them Effective." *Journal of Extension*, 1986, 24(2). http://www.joe.org/joe/1986summer/iw1.html.

Index

D

Q

truth
   accuracy of bloggers, 4
   advocating, 7–8
   deadlines vs., 6–7

U

UGC (user-generated content) sites,
   286, 287
undercover marketing, 234
"Understanding the Hazard
   Communication Standard (HCS)"
   (OSHA), 112
U.S. Federal Communications
   Commission, 124, 135
U.S. Food and Drug Administration,
   53–54, 60
U.S. Securities and Exchange
   Commission. *See* Securities and
   Exchange Commission
Usatine, Richard, 141, 142, 145

V

Vanity Fair, 252
verbs
   active vs. passive, 9, 195
   keeping together with subject in
      speeches, 105
   maintaining tense of, 78
Veronis Suhler Stevenson, 2
victims
   company support of, 277
   don't blame, 271–272
   expressing compassion for, 272
   offering assistance to, 272, 274, 277
video footage
   product placement in, 287
   supplying for crisis communications,
      266–267, 276–277
video news releases (VNRs), 139–147
   about, 139
   ethical standards for, 139
   script for, 140–145

uses of, 140
Videography, 50, 51, 58
Vinturella, John, 258–259
viral e-mail, 235–236
viral marketing, 286
visual imagery of speeches, 98
VNRs. *See* video news releases (VNRs)

W

Web service providers, 227
Web sites, 227–233. *See also* blogs
   corporate brochures on, 217
   corporate time lines on, 81–83
   customer materials on, 230–231
   customer relations with, 232–233
   financial communications on,
      193–194, 231–232
   in-house publications on, 212
   live Webcasting of annual meetings,
      207
   management biographies on, 66
   media information on, 228–229
   monitoring blogger postings, 5–6
   news releases on, 23, 193–194
   producing digital publications for, 222,
      223
   Regulation FD and, 228
   research techniques using, 305–306
   responding to postings on, 252–253,
      261, 278
   reviewing during crisis, 277
   scoops for, 3–4
   services provided for, 227
   subscriptions for future news releases,
      232
   UGC, 286, 287
   Webcasting quarterly conference calls,
      200, 231
White, E.B., 195, 311
Whittington, Harry, 279, 280
who, what, where, when, and why. *See*
   five W's